The Empress Matilda

D1570923

B

FOR VIVIEN IN MEMORY OF ALLEN
who was as indomitable as the empress

The Empress Matilda

Queen Consort, Queen Mother and
Lady of the English

Marjorie Chibnall

BLACKWELL
Oxford UK & Cambridge USA

First published 1991
First published in USA 1992
Reprinted 1993
First published in paperback 1993
Reprinted 1994

Blackwell Publishers
108 Cowley Road, Oxford, OX4 1JF, UK

238 Main Street
Cambridge, Massachusetts 02142, USA

British Library Cataloguing in Publication Data

A CIP catalogue record for this book is available from the British Library.

Library of Congress Cataloging-in-Publication Data
Chibnall, Marjorie.
The Empress Matilda : queen consort, queen mother, and lady of the
English / Marjorie Chibnall.
p.   cm.
Includes bibliographical references (p.   ) and index.
ISBN 0-631-19028-7 (pbk.)
1. Matilda, Empress, consort of Henry V, Holy Roman Emperor,
1102–1167.   2. Great Britain – Princes and princesses – Biography.
3. Great Britain – History – Henry I, 1100–1135.   4. Great Britain –
History – Stephen, 1135–1154.   5. Great Britain – History – Henry II,
1154–1189.   I. Title.
DA198 6 C48 1991
942.04′5′092–dc20
[B]   91–12692
                                                      CIP

Typeset in 10 on 12 pt Sabon
by Graphicraft Typesetters Ltd., Hong Kong
Printed in Great Britain by Athenaeum Press Ltd, Newcastle upon Tyne.

This book is printed on acid-free paper.

Contents

Illustrations

(Between pages 116 and 117)

Maps

Foreword

The Empress Matilda, daughter of Henry I and wife, first of the Emperor Henry V and then of Count Geoffrey of Anjou, led an eventful and active life in both the empire and the Anglo-Norman realm. In the course of my work on this book I have needed to consult many scholars, and I gratefully acknowledge the help received from them.

In particular, John Gillingham kindly read a first draft of the book and suggested many improvements; and the late Ralph Davis has responded patiently and helpfully to my constant queries about the dates of charters. For advice on particular points and for help in obtaining photographs I am very grateful to Martin Brett, David Crouch, Brian Dearden, Alfred Gawlik, Lindy Grant, Maria Hillebrandt, Thomas Keefe, Edmund King, Karl Leyser, Richard Mortimer, Arthur Owen, Oliver Padel and Arnold Taylor.

Over the years I have enjoyed the constant help and support of my colleagues in Clare Hall, Cambridge, and of all my friends in the Battle Conference. To them, and to John Davey and the highly skilled editorial staff of Basil Blackwell, I offer my warmest thanks.

Marjorie Chibnall
Clare Hall, Cambridge

TABLE 1   The English succession

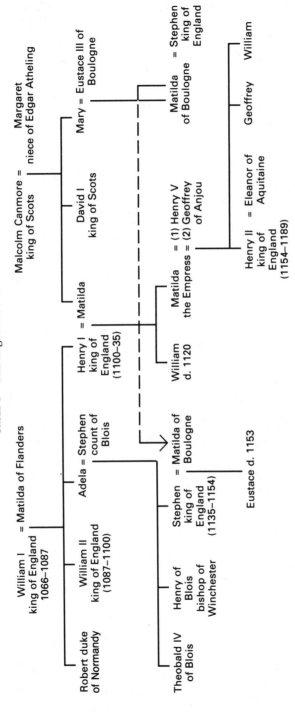

TABLE 2   The Salian emperors

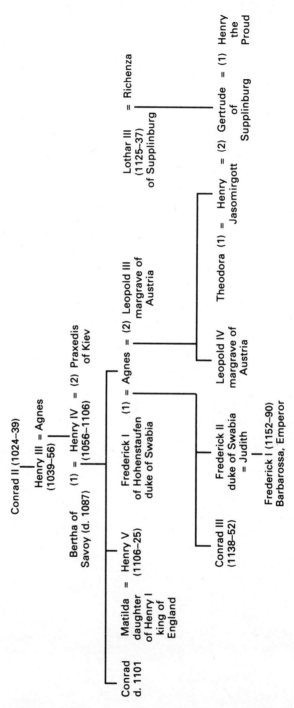

TABLE 3   The counts of Flanders

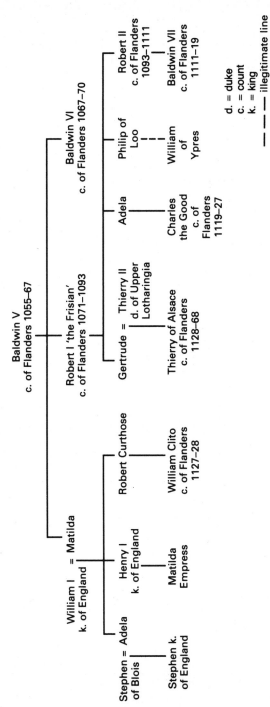

Introduction

There was almost no place for reigning queens in twelfth century Western society. The queens of that age were the wives of kings, or kings' daughters transmitting an inheritance. If, after the death of a ruler, a female heir wielded the sceptre, it was normally for a very brief period, until a suitable husband could be found to wear the crown in his wife's right, or a young son reached an age to be associated with his mother in government. Long before strict rules of primogeniture were established, it was usual for the inheritor of any crown to be male, since military leadership was one of the first duties of his office, and Europe never produced a race of Amazons. The emergence of legal feudalism further weighted the scales against queens; although there were conditions in which women could and did receive homage, even this was restricted, and it was still unprecedented in most regions for them to perform it. Yet many monarchs were involved in feudal obligations, whether or not these were acknowledged. The kings of England in principle owed homage for Normandy and their territories in France; the emperor at Constantinople demanded with intermittent success homage from the Christian rulers of Jerusalem.

In spite of these problems the early twelfth century was a time when rules of succession in most Western kingdoms were still sufficiently fluid for the possibility of female succession to be a live issue if direct male heirs failed. Three daughters of kings, all near contemporaries, who stood in the direct line of succession, forced the problem into the open. Were they merely to transmit the right to rule, or might they exercise it at least until a male heir was of age? The three were Urraca, daughter of Alfonso VI of Castile and León, Melisende, daughter of Baldwin II of Jerusalem, and Matilda, daughter of Henry I of England.

Urraca, a young widow with a two-year-old son, actually exercised full authority immediately after her father's death. Although occasionally at the beginning of her short-lived second marriage to King Alfonso 'the Battler' of Aragon he was associated with her in some acts of government, and within three years she had prudently added her young son's name formally to her own, she was undoubtedly for a time a crowned ruler in her own right.[1] Melisende, married to Count Fulk of Anjou in her father's lifetime, never stood entirely alone, though at first he was not formally associated with her.[2] Matilda's lot was more difficult; supplanted by Stephen she almost, but never quite, grasped the English sceptre. She was queen consort of Germany and empress by association with her husband's title, though she never received an imperial crown from the hands of a legitimate pope. In England she was never effectively more than 'Lady of the English'. Nevertheless when her epitaph called her 'great by birth, greater by marriage, greatest in her offspring' it did not exaggerate the importance of her career. Quite apart from the years of struggle for the English crown, she played her part in government, as the wife first of the king of Germany, then of the count of Anjou, as 'Lady of the English' in the provinces that accepted her, and as regent for her son in Normandy. She needed to exercise all her skills in negotiating and her knowledge of papal business to ensure that, though Stephen had beaten her in the rush to the throne, the succession should ultimately pass, not to his son, but to hers.

It is surprising that her career has attracted so little scholarly attention in England. The fullest assessments have come from Germany, and have never been translated. Moreover Oskar Rössler's biography was written at the end of the nineteenth century, and paid no attention to the last twenty years of her life in Normandy.[3] Karl Schnith's recent, very valuable, articles are scattered in various journals and volumes of essays that are not easily available even to those who can read German.[4] Two popular biographies in English are wholly devoid of

1 Bernard F. Reilly, *The Kingdom of León-Castilla under Queen Urraca 1109–1126* (Princeton, 1982).

2 Bernard Hamilton, 'Women in the crusader states: the queens of Jerusalem (1100–1190)', *Medieval Women*, ed. Derek Baker, Studies in Church History, Subsidia 1 (Oxford, 1978), pp. 143–74; H. E. Mayer, 'Studies in the history of Queen Melisende of Jerusalem', *Dumbarton Oaks Papers* 26 (1972), pp. 93–183; Jane Martindale, 'Succession and politics in the Romance-speaking world *c.* 1000–1140', *England and her Neighbours 1066–1453*, ed. Michael Jones and Malcolm Vale (London and Ronceverte, 1989), pp. 19–41.

3 Oskar Rössler, *Kaiserin Mathilde und der Zeitalter der Anarchie in England*, Historische Studien 7 (Berlin, 1897).

4 Karl Schnith, '*Regni et pacis inquietatrix*', *Journal of Medieval History* 2 (1976), pp. 135–57; idem, '*Domina Anglorum*, Zur Bedeutungsstreite eines hochmittelalterlichen Herrscherinentitels', *Festschrift für Peter Acht*, Münchener Historische Studien 15 (1972), pp. 101–11; idem, 'Zur Vorgeschichte der "Anarchie" in England, 1135–54', *Historische Jahrbuch* 95 (1975), pp. 68–87.

scholarly apparatus.[5] Biographers of King Stephen have tended, as
Bernard F. Reilly put it, to go with the winner; H. A. Cronne's chapter
on the king and the empress allows her only three pages to Stephen's
fifty-three.[6] Yet her role in the struggle for the crown needs to be
assessed more fully if the period is to be understood; and the whole
sixty-five-year span of her life in Germany, Anjou and Normandy no
less than in England deserves to be seen as a whole. For in spite of her
faults, on which recent British historiography has turned a blinding
spotlight, she was a remarkable woman, and her achievements were
lasting.

Unfortunately no contemporary biography of her survives. A *Life*,
said to have been written by Arnulf, bishop of Lisieux, has not yet come
to light.[7] The life of her first husband by David the Scot has also been
lost.[8] But there are many references in chronicles, which range from the
panegyric of Stephen of Rouen in the *Draco Normannicus* and the
laudatory comments of Robert of Torigny, monk of Bec and from 1154
abbot of Mont-Saint-Michel, to the hostile passages in the *Gesta
Stephani* and the gossip of Walter Map. John of Salisbury contributed
information about her relations with the papal court.[9] She had her place
too, though a lesser one, in the German, Italian and Angevin chronicles.
Archival sources are the richest; over a hundred charters or notices of
her charters survive, most of which have been published in the *Regesta
Regum Anglo-Normannorum*, and she was associated with the foundation and endowment of monasteries which remembered her in their
foundation histories, cartularies and necrologies. Letter collections yield
sparse but precious details, notably the letters of Hildebert of Lavardin
and Gilbert Foliot, and the collections in the *Materials for the History
of Thomas Becket*. Several books were dedicated to her. If no biography
in the modern sense could be written from such sources, there is ample
material, particularly if we look at her from the European angle, for
reconstructing the outline of her life, examining her place in the society
and politics of her age, and even attempting to form a balanced assessment of her character.

5 The Earl of Onslow, *The Empress Maud* (London, 1939); Nesta Pain, *Empress Matilda* (London, 1978).
6 H. A. Cronne, *King Stephen 1135–1154* (London, 1970).
7 Thomas Stapleton, *Magni Rotuli Scaccarii Normanniae sub Regibus Angliae*, 2 vols (London, 1840), i, p. xc.
8 M. Manitius, *Geschichte der lateinischen Literatur des Mittelalters* 3 vols (Munich, 1911–31), iii, pp. 356–7.
9 For a detailed description of the chronicle sources for the reign of Stephen see R. H. C. Davis, *King Stephen*, 3rd edn (London and New York, 1990), Appendix III, pp. 144–8.

This book is not another history of Stephen's reign. It attempts, by looking at Matilda's part in the struggle for the throne and in the governance of Normandy and England during his reign, to contribute to a more rounded picture of two troubled decades of Anglo-Norman history. It is also concerned with the part that a female heir to the throne could play in feudal society.

1

Great by Birth

No one could have challenged the claim of Matilda, the future empress, to have been born in the purple. Her father Henry I was crowned by the bishop of London and acclaimed king of England before his marriage to Matilda, daughter of Queen Margaret of Scotland and King Malcolm Canmore. Anselm, archbishop of Canterbury, himself performed the marriage ceremony and crowned the new queen. So the claim of any child of the marriage to succeed to the inheritance seemed securely based; and indeed a legitimate son could have anticipated a secure passage to the throne. There were, however, uncertainties both in Henry's title to the throne and in the validity of his marriage that rebels and critics might attempt to raise in times of adversity. It was all too likely that the uncertainty would be exploited if the designated heir happened to be a woman.

Throughout the eleventh century succession to the English throne was disturbed by wars and conquests.[1] The line of Cerdic had barely been restored after the interlude of Danish rule when Edward the Confessor died childless and the way was opened for a disputed succession and conquest by his distant Norman kinsman, William, duke of Normandy. William's claim was endorsed by the English church in the coronation ceremony after his victory in battle, and he was able to establish a new power base, the Anglo-Norman realm, which comprised both his inherited duchy and his new kingdom. Inheritance customs in Normandy were still fluid; a strong custom favoured the allocation of some

---

1 Among the many books on the background to the Norman Conquest and the lives of the early Norman kings the following will be found useful: John Le Patourel, *The Norman Empire* (Oxford, 1976); Pauline Stafford, *Unification and Conquest* (London and New York, 1989); Frank Barlow, *Edward the Confessor*, 2nd edn (London, 1979); D. C. Douglas, *William the Conqueror* (London, 1964); David Bates, *William the Conqueror* (London 1989); Frank Barlow, *William Rufus* (London, 1983); Marjorie Chibnall, *Anglo-Norman England 1066–1166* (Oxford, 1986); M. T. Clanchy, *England and its Rulers 1066–1272* (Glasgow, 1983).

share in the inheritance to several children, and the eldest son did not
invariably succeed to the ancestral patrimony, particularly if lands acquired more recently were very much more extensive. But a kingdom
was not regarded as subject to the normal rules; its integrity was likely
to be preserved. One major question in 1087, the year that William
died, was whether Normandy should remain indissolubly bound to the
kingdom. By that date William's hands were already tied, since he had
invested his eldest son, Robert, with the duchy over twenty years
earlier. They had subsequently quarrelled so bitterly that Robert went
into exile and even took up arms against his father. He was not at
William's deathbed. It was there that the king finally recognized,
perhaps reluctantly, that Robert must keep Normandy; but he was
determined to deny him the English succession. If he did not formally
designate his second son, William Rufus, he made his preference clear.
Henry, the third surviving son, had to be content with a substantial sum
of money and perhaps his mother's lands in Normandy. He learned,
during thirteen years as a dispossessed younger brother, to plan for a
more prosperous future and to profit from the mistakes of his siblings.

During the fraternal feuds that followed, Henry sided sometimes with
one brother, sometimes with another, and sometimes stood alone. After
Robert's departure on crusade in 1096 the situation became less
fraught. William Rufus administered the duchy of Normandy; Henry
had some lands in the Cotentin, was frequently at his brother's court,
and sometimes fought at his side. But in so far as there was any family
agreement about the succession, Henry had no prospect of any part
in it, unless both his brothers died without legitimate heirs. Henry's
position was further compromised because he had done homage to
Robert at some date, possibly for the Cotentin. His prospects changed
dramatically in 1100.

Robert left Jerusalem to return home by way of southern Italy and
there married Sibyl of Conversano, so raising the possibility of con-
tinuing the senior line of heirs. Then, before Robert had reached Normandy, William Rufus was killed, probably accidentally, while hunting
in the New Forest on 2 August.[2] Henry, who was in the hunting party,
saw his opportunity and lost no time in establishing a strong position.
He galloped straight to Winchester, secured the keys of the treasure
store, and claimed the crown in the interests of peace and order. The
handful of magnates and bishops who were on the spot, after a half-

2 The most critical account of the circumstances of William's death is given by
C. Warren Hollister, 'The strange death of William Rufus', *Speculum*, 48 (1973), pp. 637–
53; reprinted, *Monarchy, Magnates and Institutions in the Anglo-Norman World*
(London and Ronceverte, 1986), pp. 59–76.

hearted protest from William of Warenne, were persuaded to accept
him as king. On 5 August he was crowned at Westminster by Maurice,
bishop of London. Robert reached Normandy to find himself supplanted. Later events were to prove that swift action to seize the
treasure and to persuade the leading prelates to add their blessing by
coronation was the surest way to settle any doubts about the royal
succession. Ability in managing men and leading armies would be
needed to hold a crown won in this way. Henry had that ability; the
career of his brother Robert Curthose suggests that he had not. Within
six years Robert had lost Normandy to his younger brother. From 1106
until his death in 1135 Henry effectively ruled both kingdom and
duchy.

One of Henry's first actions after his coronation in 1100 was to recall
Anselm, archbishop of Canterbury, who had been driven into exile by
Rufus;[3] another was to seek a wife. Matilda, daughter of the late Scots
king, Malcolm Canmore, was his choice. This was partly, perhaps,
because an alliance with the Scots royal house might protect his northern frontier, but most of all because her mother, Margaret, was the
great-granddaughter of Edmund Ironside. Chroniclers were quick to
note the significance of this; she was 'a kinswoman of King Edward, of
the true royal family of England',[4] 'descended from the stock of King
Alfred.'[5] Henry himself was only the third king in the Norman line,
whereas Margaret's ancestry stretched back to the West Saxon Cerdic.
The children of such a union would have a particularly strong hereditary claim to the English throne.

There was one possible impediment to the marriage. As a child she
had been sent to England to be brought up under the care of her aunt
Christina, abbess of Wilton. At times she had been seen wearing a veil,
and it was rumoured that she was a nun. Henry turned to his archbishop, Anselm, for help. The situation was a difficult one, for Anselm
arrived back in England only on 23 September, and the question of
reconciling church reform with the royal demands that bishops should
do homage, which had been the chief cause of his exile, was still
unsettled. Anselm was a man of peace, but he was also a man of
conscience. His personal preference was that all women who had worn
the veil at any time, even without making a formal profession or being

---

3 The best account of Anselm's life and thought is given by R. W. Southern, *St Anselm
and his Biographer* (Cambridge, 1963).

4 *A-SC*, s.a. 1100.

5 *The Ecclesiastical History of Orderic Vitalis*, ed. Marjorie Chibnall (6 vols, Oxford,
1969–1980), v, pp. 298–9. See also *Eadmeri Historia Novorum in Anglia*, ed. M. Rule
(RS, 1884), p. 121.

offered at the altar, should remain in the cloister; but he undertook to investigate the case.

The findings are known principally from the *Historia Novorum* of Eadmer, Anselm's devoted biographer, who was sometimes swayed by his partiality,[6] and from an account written more than forty years later by Hermann of Tournai, who depended on hearsay.[7] According to Eadmer, Matilda denied that she had ever been placed in the monastery as an oblate; instead she claimed that her aunt Christina, a severe disciplinarian who did not spare the rod when disobeyed, had forced her to wear the veil as a protection against the lusts of the Normans, but that when out of her aunt's sight she herself had torn it off and trampled on it. She added that her father had once seen her wearing a veil and had snatched it away, saying that he would rather have seen her wedded to Count Alan than a cloistered nun. Hermann of Tournai added the picturesque story that the particular Norman against whom her aunt wished to protect her was William Rufus. The king had come to the abbey professing a wish to pray there and had visited the cloister; but when he saw Matilda veiled among the other nuns he left abruptly, so proving that his interest was in her and not in prayers or in the roses the abbess had taken him to admire. Whatever the truth about her father's intentions, witnesses from the convent swore that Matilda had never been a professed nun. Anselm left a final decision to the bishops; they pointed out that Anselm's predecessor, Archbishop Lanfranc, had recognized that women who had fled to monasteries 'not for the love of the religious life, but for fear of the Normans', and had never taken any vows, might return to the world and marry.[8] Anselm was prepared to accept the ruling of a man he admired. He stated publicly, according to Eadmer, that the case had been thoroughly investigated and settled; adding that if anyone knew of a lawful impediment to the marriage he should declare it openly. No one raised any objection, and Anselm himself blessed the marriage. Shortly afterwards he crowned Matilda as queen.

Queen Matilda's children were born within three years of the marriage. Although English and Norman chroniclers occasionally mentioned the births of royal and ducal children, it was still exceptional for

6 Eadmer, *Historia Novorum*, pp. 121–6. See also *Councils and Synods*, i, pp. 661–7; Anselm, *Opera Omnia*, ed. F. S. Schmitt (6 vols, Edinburgh, 1946–1961), iv, pp. 60–1, ep. 177.

7 Hermann of Tournai, *Liber de restauratione monasterii S. Martini Tornacensis*, *MGH SS*, xiv, pp. 278–81. Hermann may have depended on a report from Baldwin, the former advocate of Tournai, who became a monk of Bec.

8 *The Letters of Lanfranc*, ed. H. Clover and M. Gibson (OMT, 1979), pp. 166–7, ep. 53.

them to do so. The date of Matilda's birth can be calculated only from the most reliable statements of her age at the time of her betrothal to the emperor.[9] According to the Winchester chronicler she was eight years and fifteen days old when she set out for her new home at the beginning of Lent in 1110. This indicates a birthday about 7 February 1102. The date fits neatly into a few months when the queen does not figure as a witness to charters issued in her husband's travelling court, and appears to have been residing near to Abingdon, at Sutton Courtenay.[10] From there she issued two writs in favour of Faritius, abbot of Abingdon, who was a royal physician; one was witnessed by Grimbald, another royal physician.[11] The statement by some historians that an earlier child had been stillborn about July 1101 rests on later, unreliable, evidence,[12] and seems implausible, as it allows no time for a normal second pregnancy. Matilda's brother William is believed to have been about a year younger; though Rössler argued that he and Matilda were twins the evidence is against this. The expression *geminam pro-lem*, which Rössler took to refer to twins could equally well be applied to two children. William of Malmesbury stated positively that they were born at different times;[13] and on 23 November 1103 Pope Paschal II wrote to King Henry congratulating him on the birth of his son.[14] It is unlikely he would have waited nearly two years to send the message.

Nothing is known of Matilda's childhood and early education. It was usual for royal children at this date to be taught their letters and prepared for the practical duties that lay ahead. Boys were placed under a tutor who was responsible for arranging their training in martial skills no less than in letters and manners; sometimes they were sent to other courts for training until they were old enough for knighthood. Investment with the sword still meant more than a token of status; the custom of requiring any new ruler to be knighted before he was

9 The evidence is discussed in Rössler, App. I, pp. 417–20.

10 The Manor House at Sutton Courtenay includes a barrel-vaulted undercroft which the late J. M. Fletcher suggested may have dated from the late eleventh or early twelfth century. It seems therefore to mark the site of the chamber block in the royal manor house, where Queen Matilda stayed for her confinement. I owe this information to Dr C. R. J. Currie.

11 *Regesta* iii, nos 565, 567.

12 The story probably arose from the statement of Wace in the *Roman de Rou*, ed. A. J. Holden (3 vols, Société des anciens textes français, Paris, 1970–1972), ii, p. 268, vv. 10335–10340, that when Robert Curthose invaded England in July 1101 he chivalrously refrained from attacking Winchester because the queen was lying in childbed there. This statement is uncorroborated.

13 Malmesbury, *GR*, ii, 494: 'Haec igitur duobus partubus, altero alterius sexus, contenta, in posterum et parere et parturire destitit.'

14 Anselm, *Opera*, iv, pp. 226–8. ep. 305.

crowned, even if he happened to be a minor, still lay in the future.[15] Girls were either placed in a nunnery or kept in their mother's court. Queen Matilda's own experiences at Wilton may have deterred her from choosing a nunnery for the education of her daughter, and young Matilda probably remained with her mother. The queen still sometimes travelled round the country with her husband; she witnessed charters at Exeter, Canterbury, Norwich, Aylesbury, Rockingham, Cannock and Cirencester as well as Windsor and Westminster where great courts were regularly held. In 1106–7 she paid her only visit to Normandy in the king's company.[16] The sources do not indicate whether she took her young children with her in her travels, as Queen Eleanor of Aquitaine did only occasionally;[17] it cannot be taken for granted.

The queen's circle was cultured and religious. William of Malmesbury praised her hospitality and the company she kept. He said that after giving birth to two children she forsook the court and lived for many years at Westminster; there she kept great state, as her rank required, but herself followed a pious and ascetic way of life. She loved the music of the church and attracted to her court musicians and learned poets, who were liberally rewarded.[18] This account may belong to the years after young Matilda left England, but the queen's wish to have learned clerks and cultured men around her must have influenced conditions in her household from the early part of the reign. Her clerks included Bernard, her chancellor, who in 1115 became the first Norman bishop of St Davids. During her husband's absences in Normandy she frequently acted as regent in England[19] and she had at all times responsibility for the administration of her own household and estates.

Some time between 1104 and 1107 a certain cleric, probably Turgot, bishop of St Andrews, wrote at her request a life of her saintly mother Margaret, and dedicated it to her.[20] The tone is frankly hagiographical:

15 The knighting of minors in the thirteenth century is discussed by M. D. Legge, 'The inauguration of Alexander III', *Proceedings of the Society of Antiquaries of Scotland*, 80 (1945–6), pp. 77–80.

16 *Regesta*, iii, nos 808, 809; C. H. Haskins, *Norman Institutions* (Harvard Historical Studies, Cambridge, Mass., 1925), p. 310.

17 Ralph V. Turner, 'Eleanor of Aquitaine and her children', *Journal of Medieval History*, 14 (1988), pp. 321–33.

18 Malmesbury, *GR*, ii, 494–5.

19 C. Warren Hollister and J. W. Baldwin, 'The rise of administrative kingship', *American Historical Review*, 83 (1978), pp. 874–5, reprinted *Monarchy, Magnates and Institutions*, pp. 229–30; Antonia Gransden, *Historical Writing in England c.550–1307*, p. 116, n. 71.

20 Lois L. Huneycutt, 'The idea of the perfect princess: the *Life of St Margaret* in the reign of Matilda II (1100–1118)', *Anglo-Norman Studies*, 12 (1990), 81–97, discusses the date and context of the work, and corrects the hypothesis of Derek Baker in *Medieval Women*, pp. 119–41. The longer version of the *Life* is edited by Hodgson Hinde, *Symeonis Dunelmensis opera et collectanea* (2 vols, London, 1868), i, pp. 234–54.

the queen of Scotland, he wrote, always aspired to the kingdom of the angels, and he left no doubt that her holy life must have earned her a place in it. His biography shows the ideal queen that Matilda had before her, and gives a few indications of her own upbringing, which may have influenced her care of her children. Margaret was literate and devoted to the study of scripture from her early years; she taught Christian doctrine and morals to her children. Her husband never learned to read, but loved the books she loved for her sake. Her children were brought up strictly for their own good: the tutor in charge of her sons' education was told not to spare the rod if they were guilty of the moral peccadilloes to which children are prone. It is not clear whether the same regime was imposed on her daughters in the nursery; certainly her sister Christina, abbess of Wilton, proved just as strict a disciplinarian to the young nuns in her charge, as Queen Matilda had somewhat ruefully experienced. 'I went in fear of the rod of my aunt Christina,' she said later, 'and she would often make me smart with a good slapping and the most horrible scolding.'[21]

Much of the *Life* is given over to describing Queen Margaret's fasts, almsgiving and devotions, her mercy to prisoners and compassion to orphans. These are the good works prescribed in the Gospels, and so the natural subject matter of hagiographers. Nevertheless the picture shows incidentally a queen actively concerned in the good government of the kingdom, hearing lawsuits, presumably on behalf of her husband, busying herself with affairs of state. She established in the palace a 'workshop of sacred arts', in which women 'of noble birth and approved gravity of manners' were employed in making and embroidering copes, chasubles, stoles, altar cloths and all manner of priestly vestments; but she herself was not so employed. She merely supervised conduct and paid the women an occasional visit. Her daughters grew up to be literate and experienced enough in practical business to help their husbands in the work of government: the elder, Matilda, as queen of England, the younger, Mary, as countess of Boulogne. The presumption is that Matilda's daughter, the future empress, was educated strictly, with a view to active participation in government when she reached marriageable age. We know that she was literate; and it is unlikely that she was expected to know more about embroidery than how to provide a distant and benevolent supervision for the activities of the ladies of the court.[22]

Young children and unmarried girls did not appear in the hall; even if brought up in the queen's household rather than in a nunnery, young

21 Eadmer, *HN*, p. 127.

22 George Lyttelton's attribution (in 1769) of the making of the Bayeux Tapestry to the orders of the Empress Matilda, quite apart from the misdating, is totally unwarranted (Shirley Ann Brown, *The Bayeux Tapestry* (Woodbridge and Wolfeboro, 1988), p. 10).

Matilda would not have mixed with the young knights being trained by her father. She may, however, have met in her mother's inner circle some of those who were later to play an important part in her life. One was her uncle David, the youngest son of Malcolm Canmore. He witnessed a number of the queen's charters, and was likely, from the similarity of some of his tastes and ambitions, to have been a favourite kinsman.[23] He was born about 1085, a sixth son with only modest expectations. By the time of his sister's marriage to King Henry three of his brothers had died, but two still stood between him and the throne of Scotland, to which he can scarcely have aspired at that date. Henry took him into the royal household and brought him up among the young nobles who frequented his court and fought in his household troops. They already included two of the king's bastard sons, Robert of Caen and Richard; and all lived in hope of earning escheated lands and wealthy marriages. David unexpectedly inherited an estate in southern Scotland when his unmarried brother Edgar died and was succeeded by another brother, Alexander, as king of Scotland in 1107. He remained, however, at the English court; and in 1113 or 1114 King Henry gave him as his wife the wealthy heiress, Countess Matilda of Senlis, who brought him estates in the south-east Midlands and also the honour of Huntingdon. He shared his mother's high moral standards, and like his sister was a generous patron of religious houses, especially those of the newer, more ascetic orders. It was natural that he should feel goodwill towards his young niece and wish to help her in later life, though circumstances limited what he could do. During young Matilda's childhood he was only a landless aspirant; by the time of her return to England as a widow in 1126, his unexpected succession to the kingdom of the Scots eighteen months earlier meant that his gratitude to King Henry and affection for his sister were bound to be tempered by a prudent regard for the interests of his own kingdom. Matilda might have fared better if he had been no more than earl of Huntingdon when she made her bid for the English throne.

The young knights in her father's court included both her future rival for the throne and her two staunchest supporters. Stephen of Blois, the third son of King Henry's sister Adela, was already a favourite with the king, and received wide estates by stages after 1106. He was first given Mortain, then Lancaster; finally his marriage about 1124 to the queen's niece Matilda, only child of Eustace of Boulogne, brought him the honour of Boulogne. Robert, the king's favourite bastard, and Brian fitz Count, a younger, possibly illegitimate son of Alan Fergant, count of Brittany, were both married to wealthy heiresses. Robert was given the

23 See G. W. S. Barrow, *The Kingdom of the Scots* (London, 1973), pp. 172–87.

hand of Robert fitz Hamon's daughter Mabel and the honour of Gloucester; Brian was married to Matilda, Miles Crispin's heir, who brought
him the honour of Wallingford. Both men owed everything to the king
and never forgot the debt. Among the other young scions of the nobility
the twin sons of Robert of Beaumont, Robert and Waleran, were in a
different position; they were younger men, born in 1104, who stood to
inherit great estates and did not come into the king's guardianship until
their father died in 1118.[24] Matilda can scarcely have known them
during her childhood; although they received their earliest education
from Faritius, abbot of Abingdon, who was the king's doctor, they were
little more than five years old when she left England for Germany.

Of the churchmen active in the king's court, only one survived to play
a part in Matilda's later career: Roger, bishop of Salisbury, was already
one of King Henry's most active administrators in the kingdom, though
not yet described as 'first after the king'.[25] But Anselm, the ageing
archbishop of Canterbury, who had already (perhaps reluctantly) made
possible the marriage of her parents, was to remain a strong influence in
the life of the child he scarcely saw. Queen Matilda continued to regard
him with gratitude and affection. A handful of letters that she wrote to
him between 1100 and 1106 were couched in the terms of a humble
and respectful daughter to her revered spiritual father;[26] she witnessed
one charter as 'Matilda, daughter of Anselm'. If the language seems
at times formal and the style pedantic, overweighted with classical
allusions to Cicero, Quintilian, Pythagoras and Socrates as well as to
Scripture and the fathers of the church, this may have been the fruit of
her convent education. Her first letter, urging him not to fast too much,
expressed the gratitude she undoubtedly felt as she remembered that he
had blessed her marriage and crowned her queen. Later letters were
addressed to him in exile, for the fragile truce between king and
archbishop broke down in 1103, and Anselm left for Rome. He went in
the hope that, by appeal to Pope Paschal II, he might find some way of
reconciliation with the king that did not involve disobedience to the
recent papal decrees forbidding prelates to perform homage or receive
investiture from lay hands. By this time Matilda's duties as queen were
weighing upon her; affection and gratitude towards the archbishop

24 David Crouch, *The Beaumont Twins* (Cambridge, 1987), pp. 3–7.
25 Edward J. Kealey, *Roger of Salisbury* (Berkeley, Los Angeles and London, 1972),
chs 1,2.
26 Anselm, *Opera*, iv, pp. 150–2; v, pp. 244–6, 248–9, 326–7, 339, 344 (epp. 242,
317, 320, 384, 395, 400). She addresses him as *dominus* and *pater*; some letters begin,
'pie colendo patri et digne reverende domino'; 'dilectissimo domino suo et patri'; 'domino
suo et patri carissimo.' She calls herself his handmaiden (ancilla): 'humillima eius ancilla';
'minima sanctitatis eius ancilla'; 'devota sanctitatis eius ancilla.'

were tempered by loyalty to her husband, and reluctance to act in any way against his wishes.

Anselm was well aware that the wife of a secular ruler must have secular no less than spiritual duties, just as an archbishop had; but for him the spiritual always came first, and he would have preferred her to have the same priorities. This may account for the slight coldness that has been detected in his letters to her.[27] He still addressed her as his dear daughter; but she was also the respected and glorious queen of England, the lady to whom the archbishop of Canterbury owed loyalty. His letters urged her to use her influence to persuade her husband not to listen to evil counsellors. When she pleaded with him not to be provocative or show ill will towards her husband, he replied that he had never been provocative in his letters, but that he could not do anything that he himself had heard condemned as unlawful when he was in Rome; to do so would violate the law of God. When he heard that she was not treating the churches that were in her own hands well, he admonished her firmly to mend her ways: 'I plead with you as my lady, counsel you as my queen, admonish you as my daughter, that the churches of God which are in your power should be able to recognize you as a mother, as a nurse, as a kind queen and lady.' He was pleased when she accepted his correction humbly, but to her request that he should return to England he repeated that he could not do so until the king was prepared to obey the laws of God voiced by the church. When she tried to please him by securing the appointment of a monk of Winchester as abbot of Malmesbury, saving the rights of the archbishop, he replied that she had done well, but he could not accept the man as abbot because he had foolishly attempted to send a cup as a present, and so laid himself open to the charge of simony. The correspondence suggests that however genuine Matilda's religious devotion, and however much she wished to be a loving spiritual daughter, her duties as queen came first with her, just as she had preferred a royal marriage to a life in the cloister. In this her daughter was to take after her.

From 1104 Anselm's letters to the queen sometimes commended both her and her children to the protection of God. At the time that Matilda's son William was born, about August 1103, the rift with the king was too deep for his return. Anselm's friend and fellow monk from Bec, Gundulf, bishop of Rochester, who was also loved and revered by

27 Southern, *St Anselm*, pp. 191–3. The letters are: Anselm, *Opera*, iv, pp. 153–4, 156, 207–10, 216–17; v, pp. 250–1, 261–2, 184–6, 328–9, 351 (epp. 243, 246, 288, 290, 321, 329, 346, 347, 385, 406). He addresses her as 'gloriosae reginae Anglorum, reverendae dominae, filiae carissimae,' or 'dominae et filiae in deo dilectae, reginae Anglorum.'

the queen, baptized and stood godfather to the boy.[28] By 1106 King Henry's need for church approval in order to complete the conquest of Normandy from his brother Robert forced him to modify his attitude to church reform. A compromise was reached by which the king renounced investiture and Anselm agreed that prelates might perform homage and receive their temporalities from the king before consecration; both sides surrendered something, and Anselm was able to return to England.[29] Old and frail, he took up once more the duties of his office. When Henry was in Normandy in the autumn of 1108 he wrote asking Anselm to act on his behalf in England, and committing his son and daughter to his care. Anselm replied protesting his insufficiency but agreeing to undertake the tasks laid on him.[30] Although he died the following May, he could have seen something of the children entrusted to his spiritual care. Young Matilda was seven at the time; memories of Anselm may have been at the root of the special love of the abbey of Bec that she showed in later life.[31]

While Henry was in Normandy envoys from the Emperor Henry V came to him with a proposal that brought his young daughter into the clearer light of history. He wrote to Anselm from Rouen in late 1108 or early 1109, telling him that he had brought to a successful conclusion negotiations with the emperor of the Romans 'by the grace of God, to the honour of God and ourselves and holy church and the Christian people.'[32] There may have been discussion about the recent compromise

28 *The Life of Gundulf Bishop of Rochester*, ed. Rodney Thomson (Toronto, 1977), p. 61.

29 Eadmer, *HN*, pp. 182–3; *Councils and Synods*, i, pp. 689–90. In the late eleventh and early twelfth centuries the recurrent conflicts between kings and bishops, which on the surface were about ceremonies and symbols were in reality concerned with the source and nature of a bishop's authority. Prelates had spiritual authority and spiritual wealth, such as tithes and the oblations of the altar, but they were also great magnates who held great estates and sometimes owed military service to the king. To many at the time a bishopric was 'a single indivisible whole, comprising lands and authority, sacramental power and territorial rights' (Southern, *St Anselm*, pp. 166–7). Even when it became clear that a prelate could receive his spiritual rights from a bishop by investiture with his pastoral staff there were difficulties about the ceremony conferring temporal authority. To strict reformers homage, the most solemn bond between lord and vassal, was unacceptable because in the course of the ceremony, hands which consecrated the Host in the Mass would be placed between hands that had shed blood and killed men (Canon of Urban II's 1096 council of Clermont, cited Orderic, v, p. 23 n. 5). Fealty, which simply involved an oath of loyalty, was more acceptable, particularly if it was sworn before consecration.

30. Anselm, *Opera*, v, pp. 410–12 (epp. 461–2).

31 M. Chibnall, 'The Empress Matilda and Bec-Helluoin', *Anglo-Norman Studies*, 10 (1988), pp. 35–48.

32 Anselm, *Opera*, v, p. 410 (ep. 461).

over investitures, a problem not yet settled in Germany. But the outstanding issue was to arrange a marriage for the king's daughter. The
initiative seems to have come from the emperor; this is implied by the
accounts of the mission given by both Henry of Huntingdon and
the *Anglo-Saxon Chronicle*, as well as by later sources. A letter from
the emperor to Queen Matilda, asking for her support in a matter he
had communicated to her husband, must surely refer to the same
negotiations.[33]

The prospect of an alliance with the most powerful prince in western
Europe came at a moment when Henry I was still only recently established in his kingdom, and the conquest of Normandy from his brother
Robert Curthose had not yet been accepted by Louis VI, the young king
of France. Strategically his position would become much stronger once
he had a son-in-law on the eastern frontier of France. Moreover the
prestige of the alliance would enhance his own very recent regal status
at least as much as his own marriage to the descendant of kings. He was
willing to pay handsomely for the advantages: Matilda's dowry was
estimated at 10,000 marks in silver, which he raised by levying an aid
for the marriage. To the emperor the advantage lay in the wealth of
England; he urgently needed the money for a great expedition to Rome
to secure imperial coronation at the hands of the pope. So the negotiations in Normandy went smoothly. After King Henry's return to England, imperial envoys joined him at his Whitsun court at Westminster
(13 June 1109) and the contracts were confirmed with the necessary
oaths. The Whitsun court, wrote Henry of Huntingdon, was the most
splendid the king had ever held.

On 17 October his young daughter made her first appearance in a
royal council at Nottingham. She was one of the witnesses to a royal
charter creating the see of Ely, and added her cross as Matilda 'sponsa
regis Romanorum' – the betrothed wife of the king of the Romans.[34] In
February 1110 imperial envoys arrived to escort her to her future
husband. Among them was Burchard, a clerk of Henry V's chapel, later
to become bishop of Cambrai, who had probably been an envoy during
the earlier negotiations. She left with a retinue of nobles and clergy,
including Roger, son of Richard of Clare, and Henry, archdeacon of
Winchester. According to Orderic Vitalis her escort hoped to make
fortunes in Germany, as other Normans had done in Apulia, but the

33 *A-SC* s.a. 1109; Henry of Huntingdon, p. 237. For a detailed account of the
negotiations see Karl Leyser, 'England and the empire in the twelfth century', *TRHS*, 5th
ser., 10 (1960), pp. 61–83, reprinted, *Medieval Germany and its Neighbours 900–1250*
(London, 1982), pp. 191–213, esp. pp. 192–5; Rössler, p. 64.

34 *Regesta*, ii, no. 919. The original charter is in the British Library, Cart. Harl. 43
C11.

wily emperor soon sent them all home. Orderic, who never lost a chance to decry Norman aggressiveness and greed, exaggerated here, for archdeacon Henry either remained or returned to become bishop of Verdun, and Matilda may have been allowed to keep some of her household knights: Drogo, her knight who later became a Premonstratensian canon, certainly had a Norman name.[35] The break with the past may have been softened by a few familiar faces; but when she landed at Boulogne in February 1110 and travelled to Liège to meet her future husband for the first time she entered a new world. She was just eight years old, and the next sixteen years of her life were spent in the empire.

35 Orderic, vi, pp. 166–9; see below, p. 180.

2

Greater by Marriage

Henry V became king of Germany in 1106 in a period of bitter civil strife, after he himself had been, with papal backing, in open rebellion against his father Henry IV.[1] His initial alliance with Pope Paschal II did nothing to lessen the underlying causes of friction between pope and king, or to ease the social and political tensions in the realm. Although the prestige he enjoyed as heir to Charlemagne, and the extent of his authority over Burgundy and northern Italy no less than Germany made him the greatest monarch in western Europe, in practice his rule involved a constant struggle to maintain traditional revenues, raise levies, and recover estates alienated during the civil wars. There were no such steady and regular sources of revenue as the English gelds (nation-wide taxes assessed on property, originally imposed to buy off the Danish invaders), and a considerable part of the regular armies was made up of household troops, who had to be paid in cash. The heads of the leading ducal families were far less closely bound by obligations of service than were the greatest English vassals. And the reliance of the German king on the support of the church was very much greater.

To speak of an 'Ottonian–Salian imperial state–church system', as some historians have done is, as Uta-Renate Blumenthal has pointed out, an exaggeration: it implies an institutionalized system which did not exist.[2] But cooperation with the church was particularly important

1 A detailed, fully documented account of the reigns of Henry IV and Henry V is in G. Meyer von Knonau, *Jahrbücher des deutschen Reiches unter Heinrich IV und Heinrich V* (Leipzig, 1890–1909). Karl Leyser's papers on the history of the period are invaluable: Karl Leyser, *Medieval Germany and its Neighbours 900–1250*. especially chs 7, 8, 9. There are two useful general surveys translated into English: Horst Fuhrmann, *Germany in the High Middle Ages c.1050–1200* (Cambridge, 1986), and Alfred Haverkamp, *Medieval Germany 1056–1273* (Oxford, 1988).

2 Uta-Renate Blumenthal, *The Investiture Controversy* (Philadelphia, 1988), p. 34; Timothy Reuter, 'The Imperial church system of the Ottonians and Salians: a reconsideration', *Journal of Ecclesiastical History*, 33 (1982), pp. 347–74.

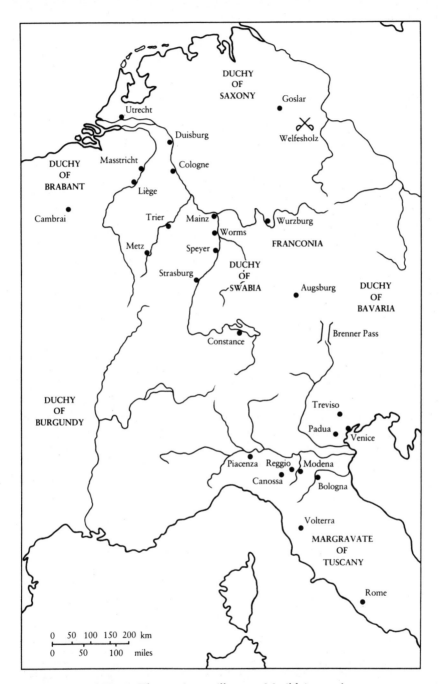

MAP 1   The empire, to illustrate Matilda's travels

to the German monarchs of the tenth and eleventh centuries; the bishops were endowed with extensive lands and served as the chief agents of imperial authority. Many of them were trained in the royal chapel; service as royal clerk or chancellor was a step towards promotion to a bishopric.[3] Consequently control of episcopal elections was vitally important to the king. The church gained protection from this dependence; abbeys in particular were sheltered from the depredations of the nobility, and episcopal sees secured privileges. Even when the elections of prelates were nominally free the successful candidate needed royal confirmation; this was followed by a ceremonial handing over of the abbey or bishopric by means of some symbol. In the tenth century the symbol was a crozier; the handing over was known as the ceremony of investiture. The new bishop or abbot swore an oath of fealty, and consecration by the metropolitan or his representative followed. Originally a ring was given at the time of episcopal consecration, as a symbol of the marriage of the bishop to his church. Henry III (1039–56) adopted the custom of himself giving the ring with the crozier at the time of investiture.

During the eleventh century a movement for reform of every aspect of church life steadily gained strength. Lay influence had resulted in many churches becoming the property of wealthy laymen who regarded the bishoprics and abbeys under their control as family preserves. Many prelates and other clergy married and passed on church preferment to their children: frequently money changed hands to secure a benefice. The early reform movement which insisted on clerical celibacy and condemned the purchase of benefices as simony found favour with many kings. Henry III himself was a convinced reformer; he even supported free elections provided 'free' meant freedom from family pressure or contamination by simony. He still expected candidates of his choice to be elected provided they were men of good character. He never questioned investiture; as heir of the Merovingians and Carolingians he considered that the duty of protecting and supervising the church had been laid upon him by God. Trouble began when the demand of some reformers that investiture by laymen be forbidden coincided with the increasing centralization of the church and the attempts of reforming popes to enforce the laws being refined by canon lawyers. Henry III's son, Henry IV, who was determined not to surrender any of his traditional rights and duties, clashed with reforming popes striving to free the church from the cruder forms of lay control. The situation was made worse by discontent among his leading vassals,

3 Josef Fleckenstein, 'Hofkapelle und Reichsepiskopat unter Heinrich IV', *Investiturstreit und Reichsverfassung*, ed. Joseph Fleckenstein (Sigmaringen, 1973), pp. 117–40.

especially the nobility of Saxony. Recently Karl Leyser has stressed that the crisis of Germany in the late eleventh century was due as much to the disturbances in Saxony, beginning with the great uprising of 1073, as with the better-known conflict of church and state (*regnum* and *sacerdotium*).[4] At the heart of the grievances were royal seizures of land, by force or by legal process, and the extortions necessary for building and manning frontier fortresses. The Saxons were ready to fight for redress and to provide a refuge for Henry's enemies; papal excommunication of the king found not merely moral support among some of the bishops, but military support with its heart in Saxony. The last straw came with the defection of the king's young son, Henry, who joined the rebels with papal support and was even chosen as king before his father's death. The old king fought to the end, holding out in Lotharingia and the lower Rhine valley where the family lands of the Salians lay, and many cities and even churchmen remained loyal. On 7 August 1106 he died in Liège, still excommunicate. It was five years before the pope consented under duress to grant absolution, so that his body could be removed from the unconsecrated chapel where it had lain, for burial in the cathedral of Speyer, which he had helped to rebuild.

At the time of his accession Henry V was about twenty years old; he had been knighted by his father in 1101 at the age of fifteen, an age that was becoming normal for the knighting of kings' sons in Germany.[5] Initially he was at peace with both the pope and the Saxon nobles who had been his allies in the struggle against his father. The honeymoon lasted only a short time; but at least in the early years of his reign Germany remained quiet, and Paschal II went out of his way to avoid open conflict even over investitures. According to the author of the 'Deeds of the archbishops of Trier' (*Gesta Treverorum*), the princes chose Bruno, a learned and public-spirited man who was archbishop of Trier, as the young king's representative and counsellor in government and external affairs, known as *vicedominus regiae curiae*.[6] Henry already had some practice in conducting warfare and negotiating with the princes of the empire, but Bruno's more mature experience was needed to help him in the arduous tasks of government which confronted

4 Karl Leyser,'The crisis of medieval Germany', *Proceedings of the British Academy*, 69 (1983), pp. 409–43.

5 On the date of Henry's birth and knighting see the important paper by R. Gaettens, 'Das Geburtsjahr Heinrich V, 1081 oder 1086?', *Zeitschrift des Savigny-Stiftung für Rechtsgeschichte, Germ. Abteilung*, 79 (1962), pp. 52–71. The 'knighting' or conferment of arms on a German king or duke, which perpetuated a Carolingian tradition, is discussed by J. Flori, *L'Essor de la Chevalerie* (Geneva, 1986), pp. 57–8.

6 *Gesta Treverorum*, ed. G. Waitz, *MGH SS* viii, p. 193; Gaettens, op. cit. supra n. 5, pp. 52–71.

him. Bruno was one of the envoys he sent to the pope to urge that he should be allowed to keep his traditional rights of investiture; and though Paschal would not give way in principle he was prepared to be flexible.[7] He was engaged in negotiations with the kings of both France and England at the time, and was willing to tolerate much in the hope of gradually achieving a general settlement.[8] Henry's immediate task was to restore the royal fortunes after years of civil strife and to recover lost estates; his next was to organize a great expedition to Rome to receive imperial coronation from the pope, and establish his authority in the kingdom of Italy. His father had never been crowned emperor; as a result some chroniclers described Henry himself as the fifth Henry in the kingdom and the fourth in the empire. Money was needed for an expedition of sufficient strength and magnificence; the resources of the kingdom were severely strained, and the obligations of the princes were limited by custom. The wealth of England was tempting; Matilda's dowry of 10,000 marks in silver made it possible for him to plan an expedition on a magnificent scale. Early marriage was important for him in order to secure an heir; as the fourth Salian king he had reason to hope that a son of his would have a strong claim to the succession, but there was a danger that a predominantly hereditary monarchy might become more elective if he died childless.[9] A child wife would force him to wait for a few years, but he was young enough not to regard this as an impediment in view of the wealth she would bring with her.

Matilda arrived in Liège in February 1110, and her future husband met her and received her 'as befitted a king'.[10] The city of Liège was the greatest in Lotharingia after Cologne; the imperial city of Aachen with the royal palace of Charlemagne was in the diocese of the bishop of Liège.[11] The bishop himself was a prince of the empire, 'wielding a double sword, as a great king and a great priest.'[12] Up to that time the bishop had been fanatically loyal to the king; the cathedral schools provided some of the pamphleteers who defended his rights against the

7 Fuhrmann, p. 87; Blumenthal, p. 157.

8 For the English settlement see above, pp. 15–16.

9 On the question of the movement from a mainly hereditary to a formally elective monarchy see Ulrich Schmidt, *Königswahl und Thronfolge im 12 Jahrhundert* (Cologne, Vienna, 1987); *Königswahl und Thronfolge in ottonisch-salischen Zeit*, ed. E. Hlawitschka (Darmstadt, 1971).

10 Matilda's movements in 1110 are traced by Rössler, pp. 12–14; Meyer von Knonau, vi, pp. 116–21.

11 For Liège see L. F. Genicot, *Les Eglises mosanes du xie siècle* (Louvain, 1972), pp. xxv–xxxv; John van Engen, *Rupert of Deutz* (Berkeley, Los Angeles and London, 1983), pp. 14–18.

12 *De fundacione et lapsu monasterii Lobiensis*, *MGH SS* xiv, p. 552.

pope. Sigebert, monk of Gembloux, who was an adviser of the higher clergy of Liège, was amongst the ablest of the royal partisans up to the time of his death in 1112.[13] The schools of Liège drew students from all over north-west Europe, and the city buzzed with canons: some 270 were attached to the cathedral and six other collegiate churches. Henry V was knighted there in 1101, and at Christmas 1107 he was made a canon of the cathedral. From the time of Otto III in the late tenth century, German kings were accustomed to hold the office of canon in some of the greater churches of the empire; this canonical office added another element to the spiritual, priestly functions of the successor of Charlemagne, a ruler already sanctified by anointing and coronation.[14] It was an aspect that the defenders of the royal right to investitures built into their arguments.

Liège in many ways exemplified the complexities of imperial government and church reform. The bishop from 1091 to 1119 was Otbert, who had sworn fidelity and performed homage to the excommunicated King Henry IV, and had supported two intruded and possibly simoniacal abbots until Duke Godfrey of Bouillon, the later crusader, and some of his own vassals forced him to remove them and bring back stricter prelates. Yet monastic reform, which owed much to Richard of Saint Vanne, was fermenting in the diocese; among the monks of St Lawrence, just outside the city, Rupert of Deutz was devoting his theological knowledge and literary ability to an attack on the evils in the church, and in the abbeys of St Lawrence and St Hubert 'the reformed abbots continued, in spite of irregularities, to work with the condemned prelate.'[15]

In the emperor's court at Liège Matilda performed the first of her new duties; she was asked to intercede for Godfrey, duke of Lotharingia, who had been disgraced.[16] Intercession was an age-old duty

13 Gesta abbatum Gemblacensium, MGH SS viii, p. 550; Jutta Bauman, Sigebert von Gembloux und der Tractat 'De investitura episcoporum' (Sigmaringen, 1976), p. 135.

14 Joseph Fleckenstein, 'Rex canonicus, Uber Entstehung und Bedeutung des mittelalterlichen Königskanonikates', Festschrift Peter Ernst Schramm, ed. P. Classen, P. Scheibert (Wiesbaden, 1964), pp. 57–71.

15 Van Engen, Rupert of Deutz, pp. 27–38.

16 Annales Patherbrunnenses, ed. Paul Scheffer-Boichorst (Innsbruck, 1870), p. 120: 'Ibi apud Leodium domnus rex Anglici regis filiam, honorifice ut regem decet, sponsam suscepit. Godefridus dux Lotharingiae gratiam regis ob novae interventum reginae promeruit.' The same entry, copied from the Annales Patherbrunnenses, occurs in the Chronica Regia Coloniensis, ed. G. Waitz (Scriptores Rerum Germanicarum in Usum Scholarum, Hanover, 1880), p. 49. Twelve years later Godfrey's daughter Adeliza became the second wife of Henry I and so Matilda's stepmother. I am indebted to Professor Karl Leyser for the information that Scheffer-Boichorst's suggestion that 'Godfrey' was a mistake for Henry of Limburg was based on inadequate evidence.

and privilege of queens in many different societies. It was embodied in ancient legends. Homer told how, when the shipwrecked Ulysses was befriended by the princess Nausicaa she knew how he should best seek help from her father, King Alcinous: 'Walk quickly through the great hall until you reach my mother,' she said, 'and clasp her knees; once you have secured her sympathy you may confidently expect help.'[17] In Germany the right of the queen consort to intervene in response to petitions and in support of royal grants was firmly established. Matilda's name appears in charters and chronicles from time to time during her years in Germany as the petitioner who obtained mercies or favours from the king, and she was remembered afterwards as 'the good Matilda'.[18]

The royal cortège then moved on to Utrecht, a wealthy trading city and favourite royal residence,[19] for the Easter festivities on 10 April. Here the formal betrothal took place, and the emperor provided rich countergifts for Matilda's dower. Probably these included lands in the region of Utrecht, from which she later made gifts to the church of St Lawrence in Oostbroek.[20] Henry's court was attended by princes from the western part of the empire, including Robert of Flanders; it was an occasion for making preparations for the expedition to Rome, and receiving promises of support. It was also an occasion for exercising justice after a long period of disorder; a man found guilty of conspiring to murder archbishop Conrad of Utrecht in 1099 was executed.[21] Pacification of a troubled region, recovery of alienated property, and preparations for the Roman expedition continued to be the emperor's main preoccupations as the imperial cortège moved down the Rhine to Cologne, Speyer and Worms. Finally, at Mainz on 25 July, all was ready for the coronation of the young queen. The day chosen was the feast of St James; a day peculiarly appropriate, since among the treasures of the royal chapel was a very precious relic, the hand of St James.[22] Was it, one may ask, because of the very special place of St James in Matilda's memories that she later considered herself to have a particular right to dispose of the relic, in spite of all attempts to annex it

17 Homer, *Odyssey*, Book vi.

18 Rössler, pp. 2, 12, 28. At first her interventions are described by the emperor as those of 'dilecta conjunx Mathildis consors' (Meyer von Knonau, vi, p. 283); after their marriage in 1114 she is called *regina* (ibid., vi, pp. 290–1).

19 For Utrecht see Ferdinand Oppl, *Stadt und Reich im 12 Jahrhundert (1125–1190)* (Vienna, Cologne and Graz, 1986), pp. 165–70.

20 *Oorkondenboek van het Sticht Utrecht tot 1302*, ed. S. Muller and A. C. Bouman (Utrecht, 1920), i, no. 302.

21 *Annales Patherbrunnenses*, p. 122.

22 Karl Leyser, 'Frederick Barbarossa, Henry II and the hand of St James', *EHR* 90 (1975), pp. 481–506, reprinted, *Medieval Germany and its Neighbours*, ch. 9.

permanently to the coronation treasures? The details of the ceremony were later given, no doubt by Matilda herself, to Robert of Torigny.[23] The archbishopric of Mainz was vacant at the time, so Archbishop Frederick of Cologne, one of the most loyal of Henry's prelates, anointed her queen, while Bruno, archbishop of Trier, held her reverently in his arms. If the crown was one of those which she later gave to the abbey of Bec, it must have been several sizes too large. She was then sent away to be prepared for her future life in Germany under the guardianship of the faithful Bruno of Trier, so that she could learn the German language and German customs and be ready to undertake the duties of a queen as soon as she was old enough for marriage.

Information about her German education comes from Norman sources, and was probably derived from Matilda herself or members of her household after her return as a widow in 1125. There is a brief statement in the *Interpolations* of Robert of Torigny. Benoît of Sainte-Maure, in his verse *Chronique des ducs de Normandie*, wrote more expansively that it was the emperor's wish 'that she should be nobly brought up and honourably served, and should learn the language and customs and laws of the country, and all that an empress ought to know, now, in the time of her youth.'[24] Trier, on the Moselle, where German and French cultures mingled and there were excellent schools in the cathedral was a good place for her education in the serious business of government that lay ahead of her. Archbishop Bruno, the chosen counsellor of the king, was well qualified to be her mentor during Henry's absence in Italy. The years 1111 to 1113 were some of the most decisive in the reign. On reaching Rome Henry found Paschal II unwilling to crown him unless he renounced investitures.[25] When negotiations broke down he seized pope and cardinals by force of arms, and kept them prisoners until he had extorted the privilege of Ponte Mammolo – thereafter called, in a Latin pun, not a *privilegium* but a *pravilegium*. This granted Henry imperial coronation and the right to invest prelates with ring and crozier before consecration. The concessions were almost immediately revoked by the pope, but at least Henry could now boast the title of Emperor. After his return to Germany the first open stirrings of discontent among the princes were crushed by a successful campaign in Lotharingia, and the dissidents in Saxony had not yet emerged in open rebellion in alliance with reformers and papal sympathizers in the church. Matilda had no part in the events of these

23 Robert of Torigny, *Interpolations*, pp. 280–1.

24 Ibid., p. 281; *Chronique des ducs de Normandie par Benoît*, ed. Carin Fahlin (Lund, 1951–67), ii, pp. 604–6, esp. vv. 43255–43263.

25 Blumenthal, pp. 168–70; Friedrich Hausmann, *Reichskanzlei und Hofkapelle unter Heinrich V und Konrad III*, Schriften der MGH (14, Stuttgart, 1956), pp. 18–25.

years. She began to share the emperor's throne and public life only
in January 1114, shortly before her twelfth birthday, when she was
formally married to Henry at Worms, in the most magnificent court in
living memory.

Many German chroniclers noted the pomp of the occasion. The
fullest description is in an anonymous imperial chronicle, now MS 373
in the library of Corpus Christi College, Cambridge.[26] It was dedicated
to the emperor, and was probably brought to England by Matilda. The
author described how the emperor celebrated Christmas at Bamberg,
and made arrangements for his marriage, which was planned to take
place at Epiphany, at Worms, and continued:

> He had been betrothed three years before to Matilda, the daughter of
> Henry king of the English, a girl of noble character, distinguished and
> beautiful, who was held to bring glory and honour to both the Roman
> empire and the English realm. She was born of ancient lineage, most
> noble and royal on both sides, and gave promise of abundant future
> virtue in everything she said and did, so that all hoped she might be the
> mother of an heir to the Roman empire. The nuptials were attended by
> such a great concourse of archbishops and bishops, dukes and counts,
> abbots and provosts and learned clergy, that not even the oldest man
> present could remember ever having seen or even heard of such a huge
> assembly of such great persons. For the marriage was attended by five
> archbishops, thirty bishops and five dukes, one of whom, the duke of
> Bohemia, acted as chief butler. As for the counts and abbots and pro-
> vosts, no one present could tell their numbers, though many observant
> men were there. So numerous were the wedding gifts which various kings
> and primates sent to the emperor, and the gifts which the emperor from
> his own store gave to the innumerable throngs of jesters and jongleurs
> and people of all kinds, that not one of his chamberlains who received or
> distributed them could count them.

As far as worldly pomp and ceremony went, the remainder of Matilda's
long life must have been something of an anticlimax.

Otto of Freising, who wrote his chronicle about thirty years later,
with the benefit of hindsight, took a more cynical view of the great
court:

> Because almost all the princes of the realm met together there, conspira-
> cies were hatched, and it was possible to plot openly as well as in secret.
> As a result the wretched empire, which had enjoyed only a few years of
> peace, was torn apart and disturbed by internal conflicts both north and
> south of the Alps.[27]

26 *Anonymi Chronica Imperatorum Heinrico V dedicata*, ed. F. J. Schmale and
I. Schmale-Ott (Ausgewahlte Quellen zur Deutschen Geschichte des Mittelalters, 15,
Darmstadt, 1972), p. 262.

27 Meyer von Knonau, vi, p. 288; Otto of Freising, *The Two Cities*, trans. C. C.
Mierow (New York, 1928), p. 421.

Anselm of Gembloux, the continuator of Sigebert's universal chronicle, suggested one cause of uneasiness and insecurity: the emperor had deceitfully seized his chancellor, Adalbert, and other princes of the realm, and without trial or judgement had thrown them into prison, so that all stood in fear of similar treatment. This was not a complete explanation of the troubles of the realm, though it indicated the events that had brought rebellion to a head.

Adalbert played a leading part in the reign of the emperor and, though the young empress was at first only a bystander, the events in which he was involved must have been an unforgettable part of her education in the harsh realities of government. As German chancellor and later archchancellor he was a powerful influence on the king when he was planning his journey to Rome.[28] The *Gesta Treverorum* hinted strongly that it was because of Adalbert's hostility that Bruno of Trier withdrew from his position as chief counsellor to the king.[29] Adalbert restored the chancery, which had become completely disorganized in the years of civil war, and developed it further. He accompanied the emperor to Italy, and took a leading part in preparing the negotiations with the pope. Henry rewarded him with the archbishopric of Mainz, the greatest in the kingdom. As one of the ecclesiastical princes of the empire, he now had the dual responsibilities of a great territorial lord and the holder of a spiritual office. Added to this were his own personal dynastic ambitions; he used his power for the territorial aggrandizement of his family, and in this most of all he forfeited the confidence of the emperor. At the same time, however, he recognized his spiritual obligations and began to move towards the reform party in the church. In 1112 Henry seized the archbishop without warning and imprisoned him, probably in the grim fortress of Trifels, where he languished for three years. He accused Adalbert of usurping power, refusing to hand over castles he had unjustly occupied, stirring up rebellion in Saxony, persuading his nephew, Frederick duke of Swabia, to take up arms against his uncle, inciting uprisings in Italy and plotting against his life.[30] Adalbert was released partly through the intercession of other churchmen, among whom archbishop Bruno of Trier magnanimously played a leading part, and the pleas of the citizens of Mainz. In 1115 he was formally reconciled to the emperor; he continued to hold the office of chancellor. But the imprisonment had been brutal; Henry was a hard man, and Adalbert said later that he emerged more dead than alive, and that some of the hostages who had offered themselves in return for his

28 His career in the chancery and his quarrel with Henry V are described by Haus-mann, *Reichskanzlei und Hofkapelle*, pp. 3–4, 8–33.

29 *Gesta Treverorum*, MGH SS, viii, p. 193.

30 *Mainzer Urkundenbuch*, ed. Manfred Stimmung (Arbeiten der Historischen Kommission für den Volkstaat Hessen, Darmstadt, 1932), pp. 358–9, no. 451.

release had been mutilated and starved. He also claimed that he had been punished for no reason except his loyalty to the church.[31] This was no more the whole truth than were the statements in Henry's manifesto, but the emperor had made an enemy for life. Matilda must have remembered long afterwards how a loyal chancellor may change when he becomes an archbishop.

Before the emperor agreed to release Adalbert his position had been weakened by rebellion in both the Rhineland and Saxony, leading to military defeat, and by the growing strength of the reform party among the bishops. In the autumn of 1114 his forces were defeated at Andersnach near Cologne. A worse disaster followed when the army he had sent into Saxony suffered a crushing defeat at Welfesholz on 11 February 1115.[32] At the same time opposition in the church was becoming formidable. Frederick, archbishop of Cologne, had hitherto been one of the most loyal of the prince bishops, but his genuine interest in the new intellectual and religious movements, added to his territorial ambitions, finally led him to join the papal party in 1114. Up to that time, although Henry had been declared excommunicate by Guy, bishop of Vienne, with the approval of the pope, the sentence had never been pronounced on German soil and so the German church was able to ignore it. In April 1115 Archbishop Frederick pronounced the sentence in Cologne; and for seven years a strong party in the German church was implacably hostile to the emperor.[33]

In the face of such opposition Henry had little choice but to plan a new approach to Paschal II in the hope of securing a lasting reconciliation with the church. He had another compelling reason to return to Italy, where the great Matilda of Tuscany, countess of Canossa, had died on 24 July 1115, after making him the heir of all her imperial fiefs and allodial lands in Tuscany, Emilia and Lombardy.[34] As for much of her life she had been a friend of successive popes, and had previously willed her lands to the papacy, quick action was necessary. If he could make good his claim he might hope to establish a really effective power base in the Italian kingdom, from which to advance to Rome. So after celebrating Christmas at Speyer he moved in mid-January 1116 to Augsburg, where he prepared to cross the Brenner Pass into Italy.

Matilda frequently appeared at her husband's side during the two years following her marriage. German queens and empresses traditionally played an important part in the ceremonial and often in the

31 *Mainzer Urkundenbuch*, pp. 517–20, no. 600; *Gesta Treverorum*, p. 193.
32 Meyer von Knonau, vi, pp. 323–5
33 Van Engen, *Rupert of Deutz*, pp. 228–9.
34 Fuhrmann, pp. 75, 90–1.

actual work of government. When the anonymous imperial chronicler wrote that the emperor took Matilda as his wife and made her his consort in the kingdom,[35] it should not be supposed that the term had the somewhat neutral meaning of 'queen consort' in a modern constitutional monarchy. The wives of emperors had played a prominent part in government by their husband's side since the time of the tenth-century Saxon rulers; Richenza, the masterful wife of Henry V's successor, Lothar III, has been described as co-ruler.[36] Matilda was no exception. The multifarious duties of a German emperor demanded his constant vigilance in all parts of Germany and in northern Italy; he, even more than the German princes, whose female kinsfolk were prepared to support them even in military enterprises, needed a wife to accompany him to the other end of his empire. Matilda frequently intervened to sponsor royal grants, though her name normally stood at the head of a group of prelates and lay princes, never alone; she also petitioned from time to time on behalf of those seeking reconciliation with her husband.[37] The language of chroniclers reinforces the evidence of charters to show that her presence was not merely formal; she shared the emperor's regality. Besides this, she was gaining the practical experience she would need should she outlive her husband and be left (like the mothers of Otto III and Henry IV) as regent for a young son.

In December 1115 Matilda was with her husband at Speyer, and added her approval to a privilege for the Cluniac house of Rüggisberg, in company with the faithful Bruno, archbishop of Trier, and the newly released and reconciled Adalbert, archbishop of Mainz.[38] Early in 1116 she travelled with the emperor to Augsburg, where he assembled forces

35 *Anonymi Chronica Imperatorum*, p. 262.

36 Wolfgang Petke, *Kanzlei, Kapelle und Königliche Kurie unter Lothar III (1125– 1137)* (Forschungen zur Kaiser und Papstgeschichte des Mittelalters, Cologne, Vienna, 1985), pp. 407–13, at p. 413: 'In der Reihe des deutschen Königinnen des Hoch-und Spätmittelalters gilt Richenza als die letze Mitherrscherin von Rang.' See also Th. Vogelsang, 'Die Frau als Herrscherin im hohen Mittelalter' (Göttingen Bausteine zur Geschichtswissenschaft, 7, 1954), pp. 58–9. Among the nobility also women often supported their kinsfolk. See Karl Leyser, 'The German aristocracy from the ninth to the early twelfth century', *Past and Present*, 41 (1968), pp. 25–53, reprinted *Medieval Germany and its Neighbours*, pp. 161–89, esp. p. 187; he mentions among others Sophia, the widow of Berthold of Zähringen, who brought 800 knights to help her brother Henry the Proud at the siege of Falkenstein in 1129, and was left by him in charge of the operations there.

37 See Karl Leyser, 'The Anglo-Norman succession 1120–1125', *Anglo-Norman Studies*, 13 (1991), pp. 233–9, esp. n. 15. Her name occurs as sponsor in eighteen known charters: once in 1111, twice in 1114, once in 1115, three times in 1116, once in 1117 and in 1119, twice in 1120, once in 1122 and 1124, three times in 1125, once in an undated document and in addition once in a plea (*placitum*) of 1125.

38 Meyer von Knonau, vi, pp. 340–1.

in preparation for crossing the Alps into Italy. On this occasion he took only a relatively small force with him, consisting mainly of his own household troops. He was accompanied by a few spiritual princes who were prepared to ignore the papal anathema, including Burchard of Münster, Gebhard of Trento, Hermann of Augsburg, Hugo of Brixen and Udalrich of Constance, and some secular magnates, among whom were Duke Henry of Carinthia and Count Henry, the brother of Duke Welf.[39] His nephew Frederick, duke of Swabia, and Godfrey, count palatine, were left as regents in Germany. Although the expedition was not on the scale of the great Roman expedition of 1111 it was large and impressive enough to show his intention of reinforcing imperial authority in Italy as well as claiming the Matildine lands. The crossing was made in early March by the Brenner Pass, a route often favoured by the German armies. The royal party reached Treviso and, after a brief stay in the palace of the doge of Venice on 11 and 12 March, they moved on into the Po valley, visiting the cities of Padua and Mantua as well as the castles of Governolo and Canossa, where Henry IV had performed penance and achieved his dramatic if short-lived reconciliation with Pope Gregory VII forty years earlier.[40] The autocratic rule of Countess Matilda had left rebellion simmering in the cities, and Henry arrived determined to conciliate the citizens and win their support for his claims to be the heir of the counts of Canossa as well as king of Italy. He was remarkably successful in establishing his authority both in the March of Verona, where the citizens of Verona, Padua, Vicenza and Treviso had been loyal to his father, and in Emilia and Tuscany, where he appeared as heir to the Matildine lands, ready to mitigate the harshness of the old countess.[41] He was generous in his grants of privileges, which in the long run helped to weaken the imperial power, but had the immediate result of placating the whole region and keeping the routes open for his forces to move freely. In Bologna, where the citizens had revolted and destroyed a palace in the city, he granted that it should be rebuilt in a suburb, and won the loyalty of the citizens. Rights granted to them helped to secure the prosperity of the schools, where Irnerius and other jurists brought their knowledge of Roman law to reinforce the secular claims of the emperor. At Canossa he was welcomed by the feudal vassals, and a laudatory poem *On the coming of the Emperor and Queen* greeted him and welcomed the new young Matilda who, with her husband, might take

39 Meyer von Knonau, vi, pp. 356–7.
40 Meyer von Knonau, vi, p. 358; vii, pp. 2–4.
41 See Luigi Simeoni, 'Bologna e la politica italiana di Enrico V', *Atti e Memorie delle R. deputazione di Storia Patria per l'Emilia e la Romagna*, ser. v, 2 (1936–7), 147–66; Oppl, *Stadt und Reich*, pp. 342–51, 358–62, 410–17, 445–8, 526.

the place of the old.[42] At the same time he turned a conciliatory face towards the pope; and Abbot Pontius of Cluny, who joined him at Governolo, went ahead to attempt to mediate and prepare the way for a meeting in Rome and a relaxation of the sentence of anathema which had undermined his authority in Germany.

A year after his arrival in Italy he was ready to move south towards Rome. His army had been considerably augmented by contingents from northern Italy, and he could count on strong support from some of the feuding factions in the Papal States and Rome itself. Ptolemy, count of Tusculum, whose domains extended from the Apennines to the sea on the line of communication between Rome and Capua, favoured him; and he was joined by John Frangipani, whose deadly rivals, the Pierleoni, supported Pope Paschal. In spite of the efforts of Abbot Pontius and the other envoys, the approach of the army appeared rather as a hostile invasion than a peaceful escort, and Paschal could not easily forget Ponte Mammolo. He withdrew south and took refuge at Monte Cassino, leaving his supporters in control of the great fortress of Castel San Angelo, and the rest of the city open to the imperial army.[43] Henry decreed a triumph to celebrate some successful skirmishes on the way south, but if the bitter narrative in the *Liber Pontificalis* is to be believed, it was an empty triumph. The cheering in the streets was, the writer claimed, all purchased: 'great show, little glory'.[44] When he entered Rome in March 1117 the clergy had withdrawn; he was told that his warlike acts belied his soft words and that he had in his company excommunicates (Count Ptolemy and the abbot of Farfa), with whom all intercourse was forbidden. He did, however, receive a visit from three cardinals, with an offer of final peace if he would renounce investiture with the ring and crozier. To this he replied that it was an ancient right of the crown that he could not renounce.

Easter in 1117 fell on 25 March. It was customary, if the emperor was in Rome for a great feast, for him to have the crown placed on his head in one church and go in procession to another, and Henry was determined to celebrate his presence in Rome with all the pomp and ceremonial he regarded as his due. Deadlock had been reached in negotiations with the cardinals, and not one of them was prepared to participate. In order to give a show of legality to the proceedings, he turned to the man who had come to him as an envoy from the pope, the archbishop of Braga, Maurice Bourdin.

42 *MGH SS*, xii, p. 409, *De adventu imperatoris et reginae*.
43 Meyer von Knonau, vii, pp. 7–8; *Chronica monasterii Casinensis, MGH SS*, vii, pp. 523–4.
44 *Liber Pontificalis*, ed. L. Duchesne (3 vols, Paris, 1886–1957), ii, pp. 303–4: *magnus apparatus, parva gloria*.

As a result of political and ecclesiastical rivalries in the Spanish kingdoms, the archbishop had come to Rome two years earlier to appeal against a sentence of suspension.[45] An able and ambitious man, he had gained Paschal's favour and been reinstated, but instead of returning to his troubled see he had remained in Rome at the papal Curia. Ambition or the emperor's powers of persuasion induced him to betray the trust the pope had placed in him, and he agreed to perform a ceremonial crowning. Although the bridge across the Tiber was controlled by papal supporters in the Castel San Angelo, the imperial party was able to cross by boat and reach the basilica of St Peter.[46] There is some vagueness in the sources about the dates of the crown-wearings, particularly what may have happened at Easter; but the emperor remained in Rome until Pentecost (13 May), and on that day Matilda was crowned with him in St Peter's in the chapel of St Gregory by the archbishop of Braga. Since she later claimed to have been crowned twice, there may have been a ceremony at Easter as well. These were at best crown-wearings, comparable to those of the Norman kings of England on great church festivals.[47] Henry had already been solemnly crowned and anointed emperor in 1111 and, though Pope Paschal then acted under duress, there was no doubt of his imperial status. Matilda's position was more dubious. Even if she and her husband regarded Archbishop Bourdin as virtually a papal legate, the pope declared him excommunicate in a papal synod at Benevento in April – after Easter but before Pentecost.[48] Her imperial status could only be justified as legitimate by virtue of her husband's office, because she had been his anointed queen and betrothed wife at the time of his coronation in Rome. Official records continued to call her *regina Romanorum*, the title she used on her seal and in her charters.[49] After the death of Paschal in January 1118 and the election of John of Gaeta as Pope Gelasius II on 24 January, Henry managed to secure the election of the archbishop of Braga in opposition as Gregory VIII; but the antipope's

45 Reilly, *Urraca*, pp. 237–40.
46 Meyer von Knonau, vii, pp. 31–3.
47 Martin Biddle, 'Seasonal festivals and residence: Winchester, Westminster and Gloucester in the tenth to twelfth centuries', *Anglo-Norman Studies*, 8 (1986), pp. 51–72.
48 See Falco of Benevento, *Chronicon*, ed. G. del Re (Cronisti e scrittori sincroni napoletani, 1, Naples, 1845), s.a. 1117. Possibly this was only locally known; his excommunication was repeated by Calixtus II in the Council of Reims, in November 1119 (Orderic, vi, pp. 274–5).
49 P. Scheffer-Boichorst, *Neues Archiv der Gesselschaft für ältere deutsche Geschichtskunde*, xxvii, pp. 109–13, called attention to a charter of Henry V for Piacenza dated in the reign of Henry VII, which contains a clause, *excepto imperatore et regina*. See also *Origines Guelficae*, i, pp. 657–8, no. 122, for a case heard *Coram Domina nostra Mathilde regina ... tempore Henrici serenissimi Imperatoris*.

reign was a dismal fiasco. He never commanded any real following, and three years later he was captured at Sutri and imprisoned for life in the abbey of Cava.[50] Matilda at least enjoyed the pomp of crown-wearing and riding through Rome to joyful acclamations, whether or not they were purchased by gifts and favours. She clung to her imperial title after leaving Germany up to the day of her death and, whatever her official status, it became widely recognized, at least as a courtesy title. She allowed the Norman chroniclers to believe that the crown had been placed on her head by the pope himself. A similar ambiguity of usage had hung over her husband's father, Henry IV, who was never crowned emperor; the records are inconsistent in giving or denying him the imperial title.[51]

Among the steps taken by Henry to strengthen his following in Rome was his arrangement of the marriage of his natural daughter, Bertha, to Count Ptolemy of Tusculum.[52] Immediately after Pentecost he and his wife left the city to escape the summer heat and returned to north Italy. Here for a year he continued to strengthen his position in the Matildine lands and to conciliate the cities.[53] But as the difficulties of his regents in Germany increased he resolved to return and deal with the rebels north of the Alps, leaving his young wife with the army to act as his regent in Italy.[54] His unexpected return was a blow to the rebels. Meanwhile Matilda undertook the formal duties of government and gained political experience. She had already assisted her husband in the government of the Matildine lands; on 11 September 1117 she presided at a court at Rocca Carpineta near Reggio in a property case brought by Hugh, provost of the church of Reggio, on behalf of his bishop, and pronounced judgement in his favour. Iubaldus, judge and advocate, who was present with her, no doubt advised on the law of the region and the practice of the courts. Hartmann, one of the emperor's chaplains, witnessed after her own chaplain Altmann.[55] The records of her work when left alone as regent are sparse, but one document describes a case at Castrocaro, where she presided and gave a judgement in favour of the abbot and convent of S Maria outside the gate of Faenza,

50 *Liber Pontificalis*, ii, pp. 326, 347; Orderic, vi, p. 184.

51 Some chroniclers numbered his son Henry as the fourth among the emperors and fifth among the kings of Germany, but this was by no means universal.

52 *Chronica Monasterii Casinensis*, MGH SS, vii, p. 524.

53 Meyer von Knonau, vii, pp. 37–77.

54 Meyer von Knonau, vii, p. 77 n. 39: 'Imperator ... efferatus animo Italiae suis copiis cum regina relictis, Germanicis regionibus nimis insperatus exhibuit.'

55 Archivio Capitolare Reggio Emilia n. 265 (inaccurately published by Ughelli, *Italia Sacra*, ii (1717), pp. 287–8, where Altmann is wrongly called *regius capellanus*). I am grateful to Dr Alfred Gawlik, who sent me photocopies of Matilda's Italian *acta*.

pronouncing the ban on anyone who attempted to contravene it. On this occasion Philip, the imperial chancellor for Italy, was present, and the record was written by her own clerk, Burchard.[56] There is also some evidence that her activity continued into 1119, before she rejoined her husband in Lotharingia.[57] She was with him in November when she witnessed a charter on behalf of St Michael's church there.[58]

By that time Henry was urgently seeking a way out of his protracted struggle with the pope. Because of his excommunication his authority was questioned in many parts of Germany: his weakness is shown by the very small number of charters he issued in the years 1118–21.[59] Adalbert, archbishop of Mainz, remained his relentless enemy. He had no chance of restoring order permanently in face of the opposition of the reformers, who included former supporters like Frederick of Cologne, and all parties were anxious for a settlement. The death of Gelasius II and the election of Henry's enemy, Guy of Vienne (who had first pronounced him excommunicate), as Calixtus II was a blow to the emperor's hopes of winning over any of the reforming party. Calixtus, however, was a practical man and a distant relative of the Salian kings; he was determined to look for a reasonable compromise. New negotiations, conducted with the aid once again of Abbot Pontius of Cluny, were helped by the subtle reasoning of William of Champeaux, a founder of the school of Saint-Victor.[60] He argued that Henry as German king would not necessarily lose the services of his church if he renounced investiture as a spiritual office – a compromise that had already been reached in England. Although conditions there were different, it might be adapted to apply to the special status of the German church.

When in October 1119 Calixtus held a council at Reims, he was near enough to German territory for a meeting between pope and emperor to be arranged at Mouzon. It broke down in disarray during the preliminary negotiations, with one side complaining that the papal party had been intransigent and the other that the emperor had come with a huge

56 Archivio di Stato Faenza, archivio delle corporationi religiose soppresse, A 1. 1–11 (formerly m. II n. xix). It is inaccurately printed by Ughelli, ii, pp. 364–5, who misread Burchardus as Burebundus. For the chancellor Philip see Hausmann, *Reichskanzlei und Hofkapelle*, pp. 49–50.

57 P. Scheffer-Boichorst, 'Urkunden und Forschungen zu der Regesten der staufischen Periode', *Neues Archiv*, 27 (1902), pp. 109–13.

58 Meyer von Knonau, vii, pp. 142–3.

59 Heinrich Büttner, 'Erzbischof Adalbert von Mainz, die Kurie und das Reich in den Jahren 1118 bis 1122', *Investiturstreit und Reichsverfassung*, ed. J. Fleckenstein (Sigmaringen, 1973), pp. 395–410, esp. p. 399, gives the number of known charters as thirteen altogether, of which three are forgeries; only in 1122 was the normal level of ten annually reached.

60 Fuhrmann, pp. 91–2.

army determined to take the pope prisoner.[61] Henry's excommunication was renewed and Archbishop Adalbert was appointed papal legate. The pope's pragmatism at that moment extended only to granting exemption to Bruno of Trier, Henry's faithful ally, from the new legate's authority. But he was anxious not to close the door on new negotiations; and the emperor acted with some caution. When he and his wife visited Constance at Easter 1121 and found the bishop away and the clergy unwilling to communicate with him, he carefully avoided giving any provocation. Instead he confirmed a grant made in his presence to the nearby abbey of St Peter, without attempting to visit it since, as an excommunicate, he would have been unwelcome.[62] There were a few disputed episcopal elections, notably at Wurzburg where Henry and the majority of the clergy elected an underage candidate,[63] but there were no local schisms on the scale that had existed under Henry IV. By such moderation the emperor ensured that some at least of the bishops would stand by him, and the existence of a group of moderate reformers acted as a brake on the extreme animosity of Adalbert. The final settlement was achieved on 23 September 1122 outside the walls of Worms with the assistance of three papal legates: Lambert, cardinal bishop of Ostia (later Honorius II), Saxo, cardinal priest (a later supporter of Anacletus), and Gregory, cardinal deacon (later Innocent II).[64] If Matilda, whose presence with her husband is attested in several charters about this time, was with him at Worms she would have made the acquaintance of some personalities involved in the struggle for power and reform that beset the papal Curia at that time.

Much has been written about the concordat of Worms: different interpretations began almost as soon as the ink was dry on the two documents that recorded it. It was one of those notable compromises where both sides could claim to have maintained their essential position, which cut away the dead wood of ancient controversies and allowed the parties to concentrate their attention on a vigorous young crop of new problems. It also established some clear principles on the nature of spiritualities and temporalities.

The terms of the compromise were recorded in two separate documents. Henry V's charter was addressed generally to the Roman church.[65] In it he renounced investiture with the ring and crozier and

61 Orderic, vi, pp. 264–7.
62 *Casus monasterii Petrishusensis*, MGH SS, xx, pp. 662–3.
63 Büttner, *Erzbischof Adalbert*, pp. 403–5.
64 Büttner, *Erzbischof Adalbert*, p. 406; Blumenthal, p. 172.
65 The two documents are printed in *MGH Constitutiones*, i, nos 107–8, pp. 159–61. For some assessments see Peter Classen, 'Das Wormser Konkordat in der deutschen Verfassungsgeschichte', *Investiturstreit und Reichsverfassung*, ed. Fleckenstein, pp. 411–60; R. L. Benson, *The Bishop-Elect* (Princeton, 1968), pp. 228–37: Leyser, 'England and the empire'.

promised that elections should be free. In principle, therefore, it was binding on his successors. The letter of Calixtus II, on the other hand, was addressed personally to Henry; it granted that bishops and abbots in the kingdom of Germany might be elected in his presence, provided that elections took place without simony or violence. The elect should receive the temporalities from the emperor by means of the sceptre, before consecration; in the other parts of the empire this investment should follow within six months of consecration. The concessions, being personal, were not necessarily binding on future popes; but pre-existing customs were strong enough for individual emperors to regard them as virtually binding. The most important advance towards a solution was the clear distinction drawn between spiritual and temporal investiture. This had existed in practice in England and Normandy since the late eleventh century; it was more difficult to draw a clear line in Germany because of the much stronger claim of Charlemagne's successors to spiritual no less than temporal power. At least practice in the empire would in future recognize that the ceremony of investiture contained both lay and ecclesiastical elements that were separable. The earlier compromise reached in England in 1106 may have helped to point the way. Reciprocally, the clear concession at Worms that election might take place in the presence of the emperor, which had not been explicit in the English settlement, may have strengthened the claims of future English kings to the same right. There were close contacts between the courts of England and Germany at this time, and no doubt the kings learnt from each other.

In November 1122 the procedure agreed in the concordat of Worms was followed for the first time, when the emperor invested the new abbot of Fulda with the regalia.[66] There was still room for fresh conflict. Like King Henry I of England he had lingering regrets over the surrender of some symbolic rights, and his successor, Lothar, did not finally renounce his claim to investitures until 1133.[67] The substance of power, however, would depend on how freedom of election was interpreted in the future. Elections in the king's presence could be influenced considerably without violence; at all times theoretical rights and claims had to be tempered by political realism. One problem that was to trouble Matilda in her future career in England and Normandy even more than in Germany was how in practice to preserve the royal influence that was necessary for firm rule without violating the spiritual freedom of the church.

66 Ekkehard, *Chronicon*, ed. G. Waitz *MGH SS*, vi, p. 260.
67 Lothar Speer, *Kaiser Lothar III und Erzbischof Adalbert I von Mainz* (Cologne and Vienna, 1983), pp. 59–66.

There is evidence before 1122 of contacts between the courts of England and Germany where common problems could have been discussed and views exchanged. While the imperial army was encamped around Rome in the spring of 1117 Ralph d'Escures, archbishop of Canterbury, arrived on a mission to the pope from the English king, and with papal permission spent a week in the emperor's company.[68] The papal Curia, the focal point for so many appeals, was at all times a likely meeting place for envoys from the courts of Europe. There were contacts too at the personal level. Among the young nobles who were drowned when the *White Ship* sank in 1120 was a kinsman of the emperor, who had been attending King Henry's court.[69] It is even possible that Matilda herself may have met her father in 1119. The evidence is tenuous, but worth investigating; it is contained in a Westminster charter of doubtful authenticity, which the editors of *Regesta Regum Anglo-Normannorum* misleadingly dated between 1114 and 1116, on the assumption that it was issued by the king in England.[70] However, the authentication '*per* Othver fitz Earl', who was castellan of the Tower of London, implies that the king was not in England, since his representative was to authenticate it. The date, therefore, could be any time before Othver was drowned in 1120, and the statement that it was witnessed by Matilda the empress becomes plausible. In November 1119 she was with her husband at Liège, only two hundred miles from Gisors, where her father met the pope after the council of Reims.[71] This was a time when she might conceivably have paid a brief visit to her father without any chronicler noting the fact. Even if they did not meet, envoys might have hurried to and fro exchanging messages. There was much to discuss; arrangements had to be made after the death of Matilda's mother the year before, and possibly Henry was already negotiating for the hand of Adeliza of Louvain, the daughter of an imperial vassal, whom he married about a year later. The breakdown of the attempted reconciliation of pope and emperor at Mouzon must have made an exchange of views between the courts on election and investiture desirable.[72] Matilda certainly had time to see or communicate with her father before she moved eastward towards Goslar with her husband.

In December 1120 the future of the English crown was changed in a way that must have drawn the English and German courts still closer

68 Eadmer, *HN*, p. 243.
69 Orderic, vi, pp. 304–7.
70 *Regesta*, ii, no. 1174.
71 Orderic, vi, p. 282; Malmesbury, *GR*, ii, p. 482; Eadmer, *HN*, pp. 258–9.
72 Meyer von Knonau, vii, p. 142 n. 29.

together. Henry I's only legitimate son, William, who had been recognized as heir to England and Normandy, and had just married the young daughter of the count of Anjou, was drowned in the *White Ship*. The nearest male heir in blood was now William Clito, son of Robert Curthose. He already commanded some sympathy among the Norman nobles and was favoured by the king of France. Henry's thoughts turned to securing allies on the frontiers of the French dominions: Germany at least was closely bound to him, though even if he began to contemplate ways of ultimately making his daughter his heir, it must still have seemed a remote possibility. He hurried on the negotiations for his own remarriage, and in January 1121 he married Adeliza, daughter of Godfrey, duke of Lotharingia and count of Louvain: a man who enjoyed the favour of the emperor.[73] His chief hope was that a son would be born of the marriage, but as hopes of an heir receded year by year the situation remained critical up to the time of Clito's death in 1128. Louis VI, Clito's most powerful ally, was only too ready to recover the ground he had lost by his defeat in the battle of Brémule in 1119, and he fomented revolt against the English king.

In Germany the settlement of the investiture controversy at Worms in September 1122, which brought a measure of peace to the church, still left many social and political problems unresolved. Saxony was in ferment and required the emperor's constant vigilance. Disputed elections at Liège and Worms sparked off local revolts in the great cities, already divided by endemic hostility between the forces of bishops, townsmen and emperor.[74] From the time of her political apprenticeship in Italy Matilda had to be ready to shoulder responsibility and to play her part in diplomacy and royal government. As the succession crisis in England deepened, her participation in negotiations with her father became more necessary than ever. If Henry, though always anxious to keep his options open while he could still hope for a child by his second marriage, was already considering the possibility of somehow making her his heir, he must have wished to discuss the options personally and secretly.[75] In May 1122, when his position in Normandy was being seriously threatened because of the number of leading magnates attracted to William Clito's cause, she planned to visit England and meet her father. He travelled into Kent to prepare to meet her. Unfortunately Charles, count of Flanders, who as a vassal of the king of France was anxious not to offend him, refused to allow her a safe passage

73 Orderic, vi, pp. 308–9; *A-SC* s.a. 1121.
74 Meyer von Knonau, vii, pp. 120–36.
75 The succession problem at this date is fully discussed by Karl Leyser in an important paper, 'The Anglo-Norman succession'.

through his territory, and the visit had to be abandoned.[76] The refusal did not prevent an alliance being made, and in 1124 an imperial army advanced as far as Metz in order to distract King Louis's attention from affairs in Normandy. In this it succeeded, as the victory of a small body of Henry's household knights at Bourgthéroulde put an end to the Norman rebellion at a time when the French king was unable to lend support to the rebels. The size of the French army may, as the French chroniclers believed, have restrained the emperor from engaging in battle,[77] if his intention had ever been to attack rather than to divert. In any case an uprising in the normally loyal city of Worms forced him to withdraw from Metz. During the rising the citizens of Worms destroyed the royal palace outside the walls, and he acted sternly, for Worms had been granted renewed privileges only ten years previously. The rebels were heavily fined.[78]

The imperial court celebrated Christmas at Strasburg, and then moved to Mainz and on down the Rhine to Liège, Duisberg and Utrecht in the spring. Until 1122 Henry's only previous visit to Utrecht had been in 1110; this was his third visit in three years. This interest, and his determined effort to break the power of the bishop of Utrecht and bring the city directly under imperial rule, indicates the importance he now attached to keeping communications with England open by a route not controlled by the count of Flanders. Whatever the implications of Otto of Freising's note that he was proposing on the advice of the English king to impose a general tax on his whole kingdom, he must have been in close consultation with his father-in-law.[79] But by May his health was failing; he was suffering from cancer, and the most crucial question to be decided was the succession to the empire. Although he was the fourth member of his line to rule, there was a danger that rivals would seek to make an election more than merely formal. His attempts to strengthen the central power of the monarchy had aroused resentment among the princes, to add to the opposition that had begun to build up in Saxony in the 1070s.[80] They were ready to seize any

76 Waverley Annals, *Annales Monastici*, ii, p. 218; Rössler, pp. 60–2; William Farrer, *An Outline Itinerary of King Henry the First* (Oxford, 1919), p. 100.

77 Suger, *Vita Ludovici grossi regis*, ed. H. Waquet (Paris, 1929), pp. 262–3; Meyer von Knonau, vii, pp. 274–9; Walter Map, *De Nugis Curialium*, p. 459, says that the emperor threatened to besiege Paris and King Louis replied with a contemptuous insult, 'Twprut Aleman', demonstrating his confidence in his strength.

78 Heinrich Büttner, 'Die Bischofstädte Basel bis Mainz in der Zeit des Investiturstreits', *Investiturstreit und Reichsverfassung*, ed. J. Fleckenstein, pp. 356–7; Oppl, *Stadt und Reich*, p. 174.

79 On this see Karl Leyser, 'The Anglo-Norman succession 1120–1125'.

80 See Karl Leyser, 'The crisis of medieval Germany'.

opportunity of strengthening the elective element in the succession; and Henry's marriage had remained childless. One near contemporary, Hermann of Tournai, said that the empress had had a child who lived only a short while; the statement is uncorroborated and Hermann is an unreliable source, who was determined to prove that because Matilda's mother had worn the veil of a nun her marriage was doomed to bring nothing but misfortune and sorrow.[81] Nevertheless there may have been some foundation for the story, since Matilda's father could scarcely have pinned his hopes for the English succession on her if she had been thought to be sterile. Other church chroniclers attributed the lack of an heir to the emperor's sins. He too was not sterile; he had had at least one natural daughter before his marriage.[82] But the marriage itself for some unknown reason was as unsuccessful in leaving an heir to a troubled kingdom as the marriage of Henry I and Adeliza of Louvain. There was no obvious male heir to offer to the electors when Henry V died at Utrecht on 23 May 1125.[83]

The situation was in some ways similar to that of 1024, when the emperor Henry II had died childless, and the archbishops, bishops and princes of the stemlands had met at Kamba to elect a successor.[84] On that occasion the emperor's two closest kinsmen were two Salian cousins. Conrad the elder persuaded his rival, Conrad the younger, to renounce his claim, and was himself elected as Conrad II. The dying emperor had given the imperial insignia to his wife Kunigunde, and she in turn gave them to his successor after the election. A hundred years later the empire had been severely shaken by the wars of the investiture contest and the Saxon rebellions, and the electoral principle had gained in strength, but a case could still be made out for some kind of blood right. There was, however, no obvious claimant among the various nephews of Henry V. His sister Agnes had been twice married, first to Frederick, duke of Swabia, who died in 1105, and then to Leopold, margrave of Austria. The two sons of her first marriage, Frederick and Conrad, had at times been active at their uncle's court; Frederick had been left as regent in Germany in 1117–18 and, though he had later been involved in rebellion, he was at Utrecht when Henry died. Conrad, however, had left on a pilgrimage to Jerusalem the year before and did not return for many months. Leopold and Henry Jasomirgott, the sons of the second marriage, were as near in blood and, though younger,

---

81 Hermann, *Liber de restauratione*, MGH SS, xiv, p. 282.
82 See above, p. 33.
83 Ekkehard, ed. Schmale, p. 374; Meyer von Knonau, vii, pp. 322–3.
84 K. Leyser, *Medieval Germany and its Neighbours*, pp. 175–6; Ferdinand Geldner, 'Kaiserin Mathilde, die deutsche Königswahl von 1125 und das Gegenkönigtum Konrads III', *Zeitschrift für bayerische Landesgeschichte*, 40 (1977), pp. 3–22, esp. pp. 13–14.

could have been considered if hereditary right had been regarded as of prime importance. Henry V appears to have made no clear designation of a successor. He entrusted the imperial insignia to his wife Matilda and placed her in the care of his nephew, Frederick of Swabia, as his heir. This, however, implied only that Frederick was to inherit the family lands. Certainly they had for a long period been closely bound up with the imperial estates; but had Henry V wished to influence the election in Frederick's favour he could have handed the insignia to him, and he chose not to do so.

Exactly what he envisaged, and how much responsibility rested on his young wife, are questions which continue to be disputed by historians.[85] The view that he wished Conrad to succeed him and to marry Matilda cannot be sustained, as Henry would never in that case have agreed to him going away to Jerusalem when his own health was so precarious, and there is some evidence that Conrad was already married.[86] As for Frederick, his allegiance had been far from constant and, though reconciled, he may not yet have been fully trusted. We can only speculate on what instructions Henry may have given to Matilda when he handed over the insignia for safe keeping in the castle of Trifels. Imperial widows had in the past played a part, sometimes little more than purely formal, in the transmission of the empire. In 1024 Kunigunde, the widow of Henry II, had given the insignia to Conrad II after the election.[87] Agnes, the powerful widow of Henry III, who had acted as regent during the minority of her son Henry IV, was in an exceptionally strong position, as an oath had been taken to her by the magnates of the realm recognizing her rights if her son died while still a minor; and even in 1076 Pope Gregory VII suggested to the German princes that she should be consulted if they wished to elect a king.[88] No oath had been taken to Matilda, but it seems to have been customary for the consent of a widowed empress to be requested at least formally when a successor was elected. After the death of the next emperor, Lothar III in 1138, his widow Richenza was invited to approve the election of his successor;[89] and Matilda would surely not have had less right in 1125.

85 There is a good, critical summing-up of the debate by Ulrich Schmidt, *Königswahl*, pp. 34–58.

86 Schmidt, *Königswahl*, p. 42, correcting Geldner, 'Kaiserin Mathilde'.

87 'Imperatrix Chunegunda regalia insignia, quae sibi imperator Heinricus reliquerat, gratanter obtulit et ad [imperan]dum quantum huius sexus auctoritatis est, illum corroboravit.' *Gesta Chuonradi Imperatoris*, ch. 2, *Wiponis Opera*, 3rd edn, ed. Harry Bresslau (Scriptores Rerum Germanicarum in usum Scholarum, Hanover and Leipzig, 1977 reprint of 1915 edn), p. 15.

88 Geldner, 'Kaiserin Mathilde', pp. 39–40.

89 Geldner, 'Kaiserin Mathilde', pp. 40–1.

It still remains an open question, however, whether her consent could have been any more than formal in the conditions prevailing when her husband died. Could she, a young widow of only twenty-three, have helped to tip the scales against a free election and towards hereditary right in spite of opposition from powerful princes and prelates? It is scarcely credible that she could, though the question is an intriguing one. We do not know what considerations induced her to hand over the insignia to Adalbert, archbishop of Mainz, before the election; if her husband had given her no clear instructions she may simply have done what Adalbert told her was expected of her. Having the insignia may have strengthened his hand; nevertheless she could scarcely have had any choice but to surrender them after the election, no matter what choice had been made.

After Henry V's death his body was carried up the Rhine and buried beside his father in the cathedral of Speyer. Arrangements for the election of a successor were then undertaken by Adalbert, archbishop of Mainz, as the leading prelate of the realm. [90] He had never forgotten his imprisonment by the emperor and had no wish to see any of the Salian kindred on the imperial throne, though there is no reason to suppose that he had any particular animosity towards Frederick of Swabia. His first action was to obtain the insignia from the empress; Otto of Freising later spoke of deceit,[91] and Adalbert may have persuaded her that this was the customary procedure. On the other hand, Orderic Vitalis, writing about ten years later, approved his conduct of the election, describing him as an outstandingly powerful and energetic man who providently averted the danger of schism or unlawful usurpation of the empire.[92] Orderic's most likely source of information was someone in the entourage of the empress, who returned shortly afterwards to Normandy. It seems likely therefore that, whatever may have happened, Adalbert did not forfeit Matilda's good opinion. She may have respected his very real ability, and regarded him with less suspicion than her husband had done. Certainly she had been persuaded a little earlier to sponsor a request made by him for a privilege in favour of the church

---

90 The most impartial account of the election comes from the pen of an anonymous eyewitness, who wrote shortly afterwards: *Narratio de electione Lotharii in regem Romanorum* (ed. W. Wattenbach, *MGH SS* xii, pp. 509–12). Otto of Freising later recorded the interpretation favoured in the Hohenstaufen party: *Ottonis Episcopi Frisingensis et Rahewini Gesta Frederici*, ed. F. J. Schmale, (Ausgewählte Quellen zur deutschen Geschichte des Mittelalters, 17, Darmstadt, 1965), p. 168; trans. C. C. Mierow, *The Deeds of Frederick Barbarossa* (New York, 1953), pp. 47–8.

91 Otto of Freising, loc. cit. supra n. 90.

92 Orderic, vi, pp. 360–7.

of Mainz. If Orderic's opinion owed anything to her views, she did not
bear him a grudge afterwards, though the election defeated the hopes of
her husband's family and crucially affected her own future.

When the magnates, accompanied by their armies, met for the election they accepted the procedure proposed by Adalbert. The Bavarians,
Swabians, Franconians and Saxons each chose ten of their number, who
in turn chose a further three or four electors. They agreed on Leopold,
margrave of Austria, Lothar of Supplinburg, duke of Saxony, and
Frederick of Swabia. Otto of Freising also names Charles the Good
of Flanders, but the better sources omit him; probably if he was
approached he refused to participate. Leopold, though married to the
late emperor's sister, favoured Lothar, so isolating Frederick, who was
forced to accept the election of one of his uncle's most turbulent
subjects.[93] It was not long before he was in open rebellion against
Lothar, and his brother Conrad was elected anti-king; but by that time
Matilda had ceased to be personally involved in German affairs.

If she had borne a son she might, as an emperor's widow, have
expected to enjoy a position of power and influence comparable to that
of Agnes, the widow of Henry III, during her son's minority. As it was
she depended on her husband's kinsfolk, who might have arranged
a second marriage for her among the princes of the empire, some of
whom sought her hand. The alternative to marriage was entry into a
religious house. This had been the choice of the empress Kunigunde in
1024. It was also the choice of Matilda's own sister-in-law, Matilda of
Anjou: when her husband was drowned in the *White Ship* only a few
months after her marriage she took the veil at Fontevraud, and in due
course became its abbess. The Empress Matilda, though she had at least
the normal piety of Anglo-Norman aristocratic ladies, never showed
any sign of a vocation for the cloister. She chose to return to her father.
King Henry can have left her in no doubt where her duty lay. She was
his one legitimate child, a young woman of twenty-three, with many
years of potential child-bearing ahead, and on her hung all his hopes
of leaving his realm to his direct descendants. Possibly, although some
contemporaries believed she was reluctant to leave Germany,[94] her own
inclinations tended that way; her future there with an enemy on the
throne offered only bleak prospects. Shortly after the election she returned to her father in Normandy, bringing with her magnificent jewels

93 Lothar Speer, *Kaiser Lothar III*, pp. 57–9 is critical of the view that Adalbert
engineered the election of 1125 to exclude Frederick of Swabia.

94 Malmesbury, *HN*, pp. 2–3. Geldner, 'Kaiserin Mathilde' thought that she remained
in Germany until 1126; but the evidence of William of Malmesbury and Robert of
Torigny is against this.

and personal regalia, and one precious relic, the hand of St James, which she had not surrendered to Archbishop Adalbert with the other treasures of the imperial chapel. In September 1126 she crossed the Channel with her father and once again entered England, which she had not seen for over sixteen years.

3

Political Inheritance

German Experience

How far was Matilda fitted for the role her father intended her to play when she returned from Germany as a young widow? The scarcity of sources for the first twenty-three years of her life makes this a difficult question to answer. Some things are clear: certainly she successfully carried out the duties of her august station with complete competence, and she was kindly remembered in the empire. She was 'the good Matilda'. Discordant notes in the chronicles are very rare. Theoderic, sacristan of Deutz, began his brief summing-up of Henry V's reign by saying that he did much harm to the country with the counsel of his wife, but Theoderic was hostile to the emperor and careless of his facts.[1] On the other hand, the joy of the poet of Canossa welcoming the coming of the new young Matilda to take the place of the old is equally unreliable, as he had never seen her.[2] But most of the brief references in chronicles and charters to her acts as intercessor or initiator are quietly approving in a way that suggests more than formal courtesy.[3] Her husband certainly trusted and relied on her from the time she was sixteen. Perhaps this is not surprising, since there were few among his kinsmen and bishops on whom he could depend absolutely. His nephew Frederic allowed himself to become entangled in the rebellion of Worms in 1124.[4] Frederick, archbishop of Cologne, turned against him and joined the reforming party after many years of devoted loyalty; and

---

1 *Theoderici aeditui Tuitiensis opuscula*, ed. O. Holder-Egger, *MGH SS*, xiv, p. 572: 'Hic, cum consilio suae coniugis, multa mala huic patriae irrogare vellet.' Theoderic wrote *c*.1164, and his inaccuracy is illustrated by his statement that the emperor was put to flight in an engagement at Andernach, when in fact he had not been with the army.

2 See above, p. 40.

3 See for example Meyer von Knonau, vi, pp. 208, 282; vii, pp. 44, 143, 146; Rössler, p. 22.

4 Meyer von Knonau, vii, pp. 280–1; Büttner, 'Die Bischofsstädte', pp. 356–7.

even Bruno, archbishop of Trier, was sufficiently ambivalent to secure personal privileges from Calixtus II in the same council of Reims in which the emperor was excommunicated.[5] Matilda acted as regent in Italy in 1118 and 1119, and a few years later acted on Henry's behalf in Lotharingia when rebellion called him to Saxony. She was personally involved in negotiating an alliance with her father; and her husband left the imperial regalia in her keeping when he died.[6]

As patron and intercessor, another queenly role, she was much in demand. Suitors for privileges and pardons applied to her to approach the emperor. Historians in search of patronage dedicated their works to her, as their predecessors had done to other queens and royal ladies.[7] Hugh of Fleury liked to find his patrons among the children of William the Conqueror. His treatise on the royal power and priestly dignity, defending royal rights in episcopal elections, was dedicated to Henry I. 'I follow in the footsteps of the men of old,' he wrote, 'who used to offer their studies to learned kings.'[8] The letter of dedication in his *Chronicle* was addressed to Henry's sister Adela, countess of Blois, whom he described as not only nobly born but deeply learned.[9] By the time he had completed his chronicle of the more recent acts of the Frankish kings, young Matilda was the wife of an emperor. Hugh offered his book to her; this time he stressed her very high birth and lofty station, and described the descent and acts of the rulers of Normandy from Rollo to her father King Henry, to flatter her ear.[10] He ended with a hope that she would honour the work with her approval, and that God would bless her marriage with children. She was clearly still a very young bride; if Hugh stressed her nobility rather than her learning this was perhaps less an indication that pride was already a dominant characteristic than a recognition that she was still too young to be called learned with any plausibility.

Another dedication, offered shortly after her return to England, was also due more to her birth and status than to any known personal interests or qualities. William of Malmesbury had undertaken to write his *History of the Kings of England (Gesta Regum Anglorum)* at the request of Queen Matilda shortly before her death in 1118. By the time the work was completed the monks of Malmesbury were looking round desperately for a new patron and protector. The abbey had been vacant

5 Van Engen, *Rupert of Deutz*, pp. 228–9; Büttner, *Erzbishof Adalbert*, pp. 401–2: *Gesta Treverorum*, pp. 196–7.

6 See above, pp. 37–41.

7 K. Leyser, *Rule and Conflict in an Early Medieval Society* (London, 1979), pp. 50–1.

8 *Hugonis Monachi Floriacensis tractatus de regia potestate et sacerdotali dignitate*, ed. E. Sackur, *MGH Libelli de Lite*, ii, pp. 466–7.

9 Hugh of Fleury, *Historia Ecclesiastica*, *MGH SS*, ix, pp. 349–51.

10 *Liber qui modernorum regum Francorum continet actus*, *MGH SS*, ix, p. 376.

since 1118, and was administered by the bishop of the diocese, Henry I's favourite, Roger of Salisbury. The monks hoped to find a patron who could persuade the king to allow the election of a new abbot. In 1126–7 the empress, newly returned from Germany, was spending her first winter in England, and the late queen's brother, King David of Scotland, was also present at the royal court. The monks addressed an appeal to King David, a known patron of monks, begging him to commend their messenger and the book he brought to his niece, the empress. Their letter to Matilda herself spoke of the hopes they pinned on her as the legitimate heir of the king and the fount of mercy and pity, and dwelt on the virtues of her mother and the interest she had shown in the deeds of her ancestors: an interest that must surely be shared by her daughter. Once again the emphasis in the dedication was on the distinction of her royal birth, and the value history had always had for kings and queens in the past, because it taught them to imitate the triumphs and avoid the mistakes of their predecessors.[11] The dedication was conventional, addressed to a patron as yet unknown; it tells us nothing of her personal qualities.

When Philippe de Thaon later sent one of his works to her he too was thinking more of her status, though he may have believed the book would interest her. Philippe, who considered that he had been cheated of lands in England that were rightly his, sought favours from all the queens of England in turn – Matilda II, Adeliza of Louvain, the empress herself when she seemed to have the crown within her grasp, and finally Eleanor of Aquitaine.[12] The book offered to Matilda was the *Livre de Sybille*.[13] Prophecies, whether of Merlin or the Sibyls, were fashionable in courtly circles in the mid twelfth century, and the empress probably shared the tastes of the cultured lay circles in which she moved. These, however, were works of relaxation. A safer guide to her character comes in a short poem addressed to her by Hildebert of Lavardin, archbishop of Tours, who knew her; he implied that learning was among her virtues.[14]

Indeed, it is unlikely that the schooling for which Bruno of Trier was

11 E. Könsgen, 'Zwei unbekannte Briefe zu den *Gesta Regum Anglorum* des Wilhelm von Malmesbury', *Deutsches Archiv*, 31 (1975), pp. 202–14; Rodney M. Thomson, *William of Malmesbury* (Woodbridge, 1987), pp. 34–5.

12 M. Dominica Legge, 'L'influence littéraire de la cour d'Henri Beauclerc', *Mélanges offerts à Rita Lejeune* (Gembloux, 1969), i, pp. 679–87.

13 *Le Livre de Sibylle by Philippe de Thaon*, ed. Hugh Shields (Anglo-Norman Text Society 37, 1979), pp. 17–23, 89–90.

14 *Hildeberti Cenomannensis episcopi carmina minora*, ed. A. B. Scott (Leipzig, 1969), no. 35. The editor thought that this poem was dedicated to Queen Matilda II; but it has been shown by Therese Latzke, 'Die Fürstinnenpreis', *Mittellateinisches Jahrbuch*, ed. Karl Langosch and Fritz Wagner, 14 (1979), pp. 50–3, that the recipient must have been the Empress Matilda.

responsible stopped at German language and manners; she received an education that fitted her for public life. On the other hand, she was never required to take a personal decision in any crisis during her husband's lifetime. When Henry left Italy he had pacified the kingdom by granting generous privileges to the great cities. The feudal lords of Tuscany were accustomed to the rule of a woman and readily accepted the young empress in place of the old countess when she presided in court. She was backed by a well-organized chancery with her husband's Italian chancellor, Philip, bishop-elect of Ravenna, in command; and had skilled lawyers, some of them trained at Bologna, to advise her on the technicalities of law and procedure. Her role was to uphold the dignity and authority of the emperor, and she filled it worthily. Her ability to act in an emergency was not tested until 1125; and even then her freedom of action was so circumscribed that she may have believed she had no right to withold the regalia from Adalbert before the imperial election. So she never gained at first hand the experience that might later have stood her in good stead.

Naturally she had her own household, though its composition is shadowy. Unlike her English mother she appears not to have had a queen's chancellor; her few surviving deeds were authenticated by the imperial chancellor. Philip, who supported her in Italy, was later brought to Germany as German chancellor, and in that capacity he witnessed Matilda's charter for the abbey of St Lawrence, Oostbroek, on 14 March 1122 and her last charter for St Martin's church in Utrecht on 26 May 1125.[15] The names of two or three of her chaplains are known. Altmann, who was present at her judgement in Rocca Carpineta in September 1117, is described as queen's chaplain.[16] The record of the plea heard by her at Castrocaro in 1118 was written by her chaplain, Burchard.[17] One chaplain, Henry archdeacon of Winchester, who came to Germany with her, was given the bishopric of Verdun in 1114 or 1115.[18] Her household knights, apart from Drogo, who later entered monastic life,[19] are unknown, and so are the ladies of her household.

Drogo's conversion and later career as a Premonstratensian canon in

15 Hausmann, *Reichskanzlei und Hofkapelle*, pp. 49–50; *Oorkondenboek van het Sticht Utrecht*, i, pp. 277–8, 291 (nos 302, 318).

16 'Ego Altemannus regine capellanus interfui et subscripsi'; for reference see above, ch. 2, n. 55.

17 'nos quidem, Burchardus clericus et capellanus clarissimae dominae reginae Matildis ... iussu et consensu dominae nostrae reginae Matildis scripsimus.' See above, ch. 2, n. 56. As a result of incorrect transcription in early editions, the clerk's name appears wrongly as 'Burebundus' in Hausmann, *Reichskanzlei und Hofkapelle*, p. 89.

18 Greenway, *Fasti*, ii, p. 91; see above, p. 17.

19 See below, p. 180.

France exemplify the influence of movements of church reform in Germany. These penetrated the court of the emperor himself, as well as many of the monasteries and episcopal chapters, particularly in Lotharingia and the Rhineland. One of the aristocratic courtiers who followed Henry V to Rome in 1111 was Norbert, a son of the lord of Gennep and possibly a kinsman of the emperor, who had been brought up in the household of Frederick, archbishop of Cologne, and presented to a canonry at Xanten. He was among those who were shocked by the treatment of the pope at Ponte Mammolo, though his conversion to the monastic life did not take place for three more years. In 1114 he withdrew for a period of retirement in the abbey of Siegberg near Cologne, where the abbot, Cuno, was a friend and patron of the Benedictine theologian and reformer, Rupert of Deutz. Norbert himself was cast in a different mould from Rupert, who later became a Benedictine abbot. A fervent preacher with a strong evangelical interest, he became the founder of the Premonstratensian canons.[20] According to an unpublished account of the abbey of Notre-Dame de Silly (in Gouffern), the empress had a great feeling of devotion to St Norbert, whom she had seen at her husband's court. Drogo knew both Norbert and Hugh, who had been a chaplain in the suite of Burchard, bishop of Cambrai, when he went to negotiate Matilda's betrothal to the emperor. Hugh later joined the Premonstratensians, and followed Norbert as the second abbot of Prémontré.[21] One of Norbert's patrons was Frederick, archbishop of Cologne, who more perfectly than any other prelate exemplified the fine balance between the interests of an aristocratic prince bishop keenly alive to the territorial ambitions of his see and an ardent supporter of monastic reform. St Norbert was able to found a house at Cappenberg near Cologne in 1122; Archbishop Frederick himself founded a house of Augustinian canons at Steinfeld, which joined the Premonstratensians later, and in January 1122 he founded the first Cistercian abbey in the German kingdom at Camp and peopled it with monks from Morimond.[22] Before she left Germany the young empress saw church reform in both its active political guise and its encouragement of more austere forms of religious life. The two were not isolated from each other, as Archbishop Frederick's career illustrated. Another aspect of this ambivalence, which can hardly have escaped her notice, was the activity of her husband's kinsfolk, the dukes of Zähringen, who were consolidating their power in the Black Forest by the foundation of

20 *Vita Norberti Archiepiscopi Magdeburgensis*, ed. R. Wilmans, *MGH SS* xii, pp. 663–706; H. M. Colvin, *The White Canons in England* (Oxford, 1951), pp. 1–4; Van Engen, *Rupert of Deutz*, pp. 226–9.
21 Stapleton, *Magni Rotuli Scaccarii*, i, pp. lxxxviii–xc.
22 Van Engen, *Rupert of Deutz*, pp. 314, 324 and sources there cited.

reformed monasteries at this time.[23] She showed her own interest in the austere side of the monastic movement by one of her first endowments; on 14 March 1122 she granted the site and adjacent land to the abbey of Oostbroek, founded in a marshy spot near Utrecht in honour of the Virgin Mary and St Lawrence by a group of knights who had laid down their arms and embraced the monastic life.[24]

As queen consort Matilda witnessed and was sometimes involved in negotiations with great magnates and churchmen and leading citizens. She met papal legates, and so built up connections with the papal Curia, though she never met a canonically elected pope and the cheers at her crown-wearing in Rome must surely have had a hollow ring. She learnt, when the clergy of Constance turned away from the emperor and loyal cities such as Cologne shut their gates, what the practical consequences of resisting papal reform to the point of excommunication might mean. Her training was in a hard school. Enemies were ruthlessly punished; even an archbishop who rebelled had to suffer imprisonment of the harshest kind. In spite of this, it was unwise to bear resentment; if a former enemy of ability could be reconciled and won over with favours he was worth cultivating. Sometimes she herself was the channel through whom reconciliation was sought. So she witnessed the exercise of political judgement, even if her own judgement was not put to the test until 1125. She was well trained to be a queen consort; she was not trained to be anything either more or less.

Anglo-Norman Initiation

To her father, weathering the greatest crisis of his reign, Matilda brought hope of a solution to his problems.[25] His second marriage still

23 Geoffrey Barraclough, *Medieval Germany 911–1250* (2 vols, Oxford, 1938), ii, pp. 182–9, citing Theodore Mayer's inaugural lecture to the University of Freiburg.

24 The early history of the abbey was characteristic of the 'flight from the world' by members of the knightly class. In 1113 a small group of knights led by Theoderic of Algo and Hermann renounced their arms (*cingulum militare*) and retreated to live an austere life of prayer and renunciation in a marshy spot outside Utrecht. With the approval of Bishop Godebold of Utrecht, whose confirmation in 1125 (*Oorkundenboek van het Sticht Utrecht*, no. 313, pp. 286–8) described the foundation, they established a Benedictine abbey which became known for its strict observance. The beginnings of Llanthony Prima in the Black Mountains, where one of the chaplains of Matilda's mother was among the first hermits, was very similar, though Llanthony developed into an Augustinian house. See D. W. van Hetteren, 'L'ordre bénédictin en Hollande, *Revue Bénédictine*, 7 (1890), pp. 511–13; for Llanthony see F. Cowley, *The Monastic Order in South Wales* (Cardiff, 1977), pp. 30–1.

25 For the crisis see C. Warren Hollister, 'The Anglo-Norman succession debate of 1126', *Monarchy, Magnates and Institutions*, pp. 145–69.

remained childless after more than four years. His nephew William Clito declined the role of Edgar Atheling, and refused to renounce his claims to the succession in return for reconciliation. By fighting ineffectively for immediate recognition he forfeited any chance he might have had of being accepted as Henry's heir. In any case Henry probably doubted his capacity for rule, and would never have accepted him. Clito enjoyed the favour of the king of France, and there was much sympathy for him among the barons of eastern Normandy. Henry worked relentlessly to check any possible advances elsewhere; although the marriage alliance he had arranged between his son and the daughter of Fulk of Anjou foundered in the wreck of the *White Ship,* he was able to induce Calixtus II to annul a marriage planned between Clito and Fulk's daughter Sibyl on grounds of consanguinity. He secured the hand of his niece Matilda, the heiress of Boulogne, for his favourite nephew Stephen of Blois. A rebellion of Norman and Norman–French magnates, who supported Clito's claim, came to nothing. It collapsed when a reckless charge led by Waleran of Meulan and Amaury of Montfort against the seasoned royal household troops at Bourgthéroulde ended in disaster. The horses of the rebels were shot down by the king's archers on their flanks, and the men were surrounded and captured. Amaury's captor defected and allowed his prisoner to escape, but the rest were taken into captivity.[26] Waleran spent two years in the king's prison at Rouen; he was carried back to England for a further three years' imprisonment in the boat in which the king brought his daughter home.[27] If Waleran met the empress on the journey it was an inauspicious renewal of a childhood acquaintance.

There has been much speculation about the plans Henry may have had for the succession before the death of Matilda's husband presented him with a solution. He had been watching the situation in Germany closely for some time, but even if he was warned in advance of the seriousness of the emperor's illness it is most likely that he never definitely made up his mind. He played for safety, keeping his options open while hoping that his second wife would bear a son. That possibility, though receding, still remained open; Matilda provided him with an insurance policy. He immediately took steps to secure her acceptance by the magnates; his brother-in-law and former protégé, David king of Scots, came south to lend his support. At the beginning of January 1127, before his Christmas court had dispersed, the king obtained oaths of allegiance to his daughter from all the bishops and magnates present. They swore, according to John of Worcester, to defend her loyally

---

26 Orderic, vi, pp. 348–51; Torigny, *Interpolations,* pp. 294–5.
27 A-SC, s.a. 1126.

against all others if she outlived her father and he left no legitimate
son.[28] They were not asked to do homage. The Anglo-Saxon chronicler
wrote that he held his court at Christmas at Windsor, 'and there he
caused archbishops and bishops and abbots and earls and all the thegns
that were there to swear to give England and Normandy after his death
into the hand of his daughter.'[29] John of Worcester described a second
oath a year later at the Easter court (29 April 1128); William of
Malmesbury, like the Anglo-Saxon chronicler, mentioned only one and
dated it at Christmas.[30] Malmesbury had more to say about motive, the
other two described events more fully; there is enough common to the
three accounts to carry conviction. Certainly the substance of the oaths
was that all who took them agreed to accept Matilda as their lady if
Henry died without a male heir. There was also some debate about
precedence in the order of taking the oath; the archbishop of Canterbury and the bishops swore first, the abbots claimed the right to come
next as spiritual lords, but the secular princes were called before them.
After King David had sworn, Anselm, abbot of Bury St Edmunds,
objected on behalf of the abbots that they had been denied their proper
precedence. To this the king replied that what was done could not be
undone, and that they were to stop talking and take the oath; at which
the abbots fell into line.

Proceedings during the oath-taking were controlled by Roger, bishop
of Salisbury, who, in addition to his ecclesiastical office, was the principal administrative official in the kingdom, high in the king's favour
and 'second only to the king'.[31] From 1118 until his death in 1139 he
held in his own hand the abbey of Malmesbury, where the historian
William's life was spent. So William knew him, and probably spoke the
truth when he wrote:

> I myself have often heard Roger bishop of Salisbury saying that he was
> released from the oath he had taken to the empress because he had sworn
> only on condition that the king should not give his daughter in marriage
> to anyone outside the kingdom without consulting himself and the other
> chief men.[32]

William added, however, that he could not say whether a man like
Roger, who knew how to adapt himself to any occasion, was speaking
the truth or not. Since further oaths were taken in 1131, after Matilda's
marriage, it is difficult to see how the bishop could defend himself

28 John of Worcester, pp. 22–3.
29 A-SC, s.a. 1127; see also SD, ii, p. 281: Eadmer HN, p. 292.
30 John of Worcester, pp. 26–7; Malmesbury, HN, pp. 3–5.
31 Kealey, Roger of Salisbury, ch. 2.
32 Malmesbury, HN, p. 5.

against a charge of perjury; but he was not alone in trying to free himself from the obligations of an oath he had taken reluctantly.

It has been suggested that there were already two parties in a court divided on the difficult question of whether to accept a woman, widowed and still childless, as heir to the throne.[33] Some, undoubtedly, would have preferred William Clito, and Roger of Salisbury may have been one of them. Matilda was shrewd enough to realize he was only a reluctant friend. If she took up the appeal of the monks of Malmesbury to help them to recover their right of free election she met with no success,[34] for Roger continued to hold the abbey until his death in 1139; but he would have resented her intervention. It was, according to the Anglo-Saxon chronicler, at her suggestion, supported by King David, that Henry's brother Robert, for long a prisoner in the great castle of Devizes in the charge of Roger of Salisbury, was transferred to Cardiff, where he could be held more securely by Robert, earl of Gloucester.[35] Robert's loyalty was never in doubt; the king had implicit trust in him and in another of his protégés, Brian fitz Count. Robert could never be a contender for the throne; his illegitimate birth excluded him, and he himself knew that it did. Although some twenty years previously King Alfonso of Castile had proposed to make his illegitimate son Sancho his heir in preference to his daughter Urraca, Sancho's untimely death in battle put an end to the scheme,[36] and the conditions in the Anglo-Norman realm were different. William the Bastard's succession to the duchy of Normandy in 1035 had led to a hard and bitter struggle; and England had a well-established tradition against bastard kings. Earl Robert may at times have favoured the early acceptance of Matilda's son rather than Matilda herself, but he never put himself forward as a rival, and if any approaches were made by others he rejected them. Brian fitz Count came from one of the Breton families who had been King Henry's earliest supporters even before he secured the throne; he owed everything to the king, who had brought him up in his court and given him lands and offices and the hand of Matilda of Wallingford, one of the wealthiest heiresses in the country.[37]

33 Hollister, 'Succession debate', pp. 153–62.

34 Könsgen, 'Zwei unbekannte Briefe', pp. 204–14.

35 A-SC, s.a. 1126.

36 Reilly, Urraca, pp. 25–6. Davis, King Stephen, pp. 13–14 considers Robert of Gloucester to have been a possible candidate, but does not offer any convincing evidence for this assertion.

37 Judith A. Green, The Government of England under Henry I, (Cambridge, 1986), pp. 247–8; A. Morey and C. N. L. Brooke, Gilbert Foliot and his Letters (Cambridge, 1965), pp. 105–23. An article by K. S. B. Keats-Rohan on Brian fitz Count is forthcoming in Oxoniensia.

The king was a good judge of character, and his trust in these two men was not misplaced. Both were employed in preparing the way for a smooth transfer of authority when the time came.

King Henry's immediate task was twofold. He carried out a major financial reorganization, putting Robert of Gloucester and Brian fitz Count in charge of a special audit of the treasury in the financial year 1128 to 1129.[38] He also looked for a suitable husband for his daughter, again making use of both men in the negotiations. Speedy action was needed, for William Clito's fortunes suddenly revived in a way that must have reminded contemporaries of the familiar metaphor of the wheel of fortune. No sooner had the leading English barons been pledged to support Matilda than the king of France provided a bride for Clito: the daughter of Rainer, count of Montferrat, who was a kinswoman of the queen of France.[39] Then, on 2 March 1127, Charles the Good, count of Flanders, was murdered before the altar in the church of St Donatian at Bruges. King Louis took advantage of the dispute that followed to secure the election of William Clito as count of Flanders on 23 March.[40] So Henry, after establishing footholds on the eastern frontier of Normandy through alliances in Lotharingia, his wife's homeland, and Boulogne, held by his nephew Stephen, now found his most hated rival powerfully established in Flanders and allied with the king of France. It was more than ever vital for him to prevent Anjou being drawn into the hostile camp.

Although many historians have written of the Angevins as traditional enemies of the Normans, this is not true of the eleventh and early twelfth centuries.[41] There had been conflicts over Maine, but they were now settled and the counts of Anjou regarded the counts of Blois and Champagne, not the duke of Normandy, as their traditional rivals for power. It was only after the brutalities committed by Angevin troops when they invaded Normandy in the early years of Stephen's reign that Norman chroniclers began to write of them with loathing. Henry, who had already negotiated a marriage between his son and a daughter of the count of Anjou, had no reason to fear that an Angevin husband for his daughter would prove more unacceptable to his vassals than any other husband from outside the kingdom. His thoughts turned to the possibility of another marriage alliance with Anjou, where Count Fulk's eldest son, Geoffrey, was just reaching marriageable age. At the same time he worked relentlessly to undermine Clito's authority in Flanders.

38 Green, *Government*, p. 47.

39 Orderic, vi, pp. 370–1.

40 Galbert of Bruges, *The Murder of Charles the Good*, trans. James Bruce Ross (New York, 1967), pp. 118–19; Orderic, vi, pp. 370–1.

41 John Gillingham, *The Angevin Empire* (London, 1984), pp. 6–7.

Clito's election had not gone unopposed; his hereditary claim as the great-grandson of Count Baldwin V of Flanders through his mother was weaker than that of Thierry of Alsace, the grandson of Baldwin's son, Robert I 'the Frisian'.[42] Henry energetically supported Thierry's candidature, and favoured him in the rebellion that broke out in August of that year. Within a year the issue was settled by the death of William Clito from a wound received in battle, on 27 or 28 July 1128.[43] By that time Matilda was the wife of Geoffrey of Anjou.

The negotiations for her marriage began in the spring of 1127. William of Malmesbury, writing some fifteen years later, believed that the king's mind was made up from the first. 'There is no doubt', he wrote, after describing Matilda's return to England, 'that some princes of Lotharingia and Lombardy came to England more than once ... to ask for her as their lady, but gained nothing from their efforts, the king being minded to establish peace between himself and the Count of Anjou by his daughter's marriage.'[44] It is doubtful that Matilda accepted the proposal without protest. She was an empress proud of her status, and Geoffrey, a mere count's son, was a boy almost ten years her junior. He too may have been reluctant at first.[45] The argument put forward that Geoffrey was descended from Charlemagne may have flattered Angevin pride, but cannot have carried much weight with Matilda. Robert of Torigny, who knew her personally, said that she had been unwilling to acquiesce in the marriage.[46] A letter of Hildebert of Lavardin, a devoted friend of her father, seems to point the same way; he wrote, he claimed, as soon as favourable winds enabled him to send a letter, to beg her to set his mind at rest about a report brought to him from England that she was causing distress to her father through her disobedience.[47] Hildebert's plea may have helped to overcome her reluctance. Whatever her personal wishes she finally acquiesced in her duty. In May 1127 she was escorted to Rouen by her brother Robert of

42 See p. xi for a genealogical table.

43 Orderic, vi, pp. 376–7; Galbert of Bruges, p. 307.

44 Malmesbury, *HN*, p. 2.

45 See John Gillingham, 'Love, marriage and politics in the twelfth century', *Forum for Modern Language Studies*, 25 (1989), pp. 296–7.

46 Torigny, *Interpolations*, p. 230.

47 Migne, *PL*, 171, cols 291–2: 'Ex quo igitur comperi ventos in vestrum obsequium aspirare, statim litteras ad vos dedi, ratus adventum de Anglia, qui voluntatem regis nobis aperiret, quive declarant quam affectam de contumelia filiae patris pectus induerit.' Peter von Moos dates the letter 1129, at a time when Matilda was estranged from her husband, but, as she was then in Normandy on good terms with her father and the letter indicates that she and Hildebert were on different sides of the Channel, 1127 is a more acceptable date (Peter von Moos, *Hildebert von Lavardin 1056–1133* (Pariser Historische Studien 3, Stuttgart, 1965), pp. 365–7).

Gloucester and Brian fitz Count for formal betrothal to Geoffrey of Anjou. Bishop Roger of Salisbury later complained that only they and John, bishop of Lisieux, were consulted about the marriage.[48]

The marriage was delayed for a year. During that time, arrangements for the future of Anjou were completed in order to ensure that Matilda would begin her second marriage at least as the wife of a count. Geoffrey's father, Fulk, had been on a pilgrimage to Jerusalem and knew the kingdom. There, too, succession was to pass through a woman. King Baldwin II had no sons, and was seeking a husband for his daughter, Melisende, to help her in the government and defence of a kingdom perpetually threatened with attack. King Louis VI is said to have suggested Fulk, who was a widower, ambitious, able, and a seasoned warrior. Baldwin seemed prepared to treat him and Melisende as joint heirs to the kingdom of Jerusalem.[49] Fulk's departure would enable his son to succeed him immediately as count of Anjou. On 10 June 1128 young Geoffrey was given his arms as a knight by his future father-in-law, King Henry, at Rouen.[50] On 17 June the marriage was blessed at Le Mans by Bishop Guy of Ploermel assisted by John, bishop of Sées. Fulk left immediately for Jerusalem, with the expectation of becoming king after his marriage, which was celebrated at Whitsuntide in 1129.

In spite of the oaths taken to Matilda much remained vague in her future prospects, and even more so in those of her second husband. How did King Henry envisage Geoffrey's role? and what was Geoffrey himself led to expect? Some Angevin chroniclers believed that the count was destined for joint rule. John of Marmoutier, author of the *Historia Gaufredi ... comitis Andegavorum* wrote after Geoffrey's death in 1151, and depended partly on hearsay stories and a fertile imagination. He described the joyful reception in Angers of the new lord and lady who were to succeed to the rule of Britain. Allowing his imagination a free rein, he even named William Clito, count of Flanders, as one of the participants in a tournament after the wedding, though William, a bitter enemy, was at that time engaged in the fatal campaign that led to his death in Flanders. John of Marmoutier cannot, however, be so lightly dismissed when he took from the more sober history of Henry of Huntingdon the statement that after King Henry's death Geoffrey and Matilda jointly claimed England because of the oaths taken to

---

48 Malmesbury, *HN*, p. 5. For the dates of the betrothal and marriage see J. Chartrou, *L'Anjou de 1109 à 1151* (Paris, 1928), pp. 21–2.

49 Orderic, vi, pp. 390–1; Hamilton, 'Women in the crusader states', pp. 148–50.

50 John of Marmoutier, *Historia Gaufredi ducis Normannorum et comitis Andegavorum*, in *Chroniques des comtes d'Anjou et des seigneurs d'Amboise*, ed. L. Halphen and R. Poupardin (Paris, 1913), pp. 178–80.

Matilda.[51] The Durham chronicler also stated that it was agreed that Geoffrey should succeed to the kingdom if Henry died without a male heir born in lawful marriage.[52] And the chronicler of Le Mans indicated that Geoffrey not unjustly aspired to the crown of the kingdom overseas and the duchy of Normandy.[53] So it is possible that Geoffrey expected his future position to be similar to that of his father. The only indication that his father-in-law had any such positive plans for him is an ambiguous statement by William of Malmesbury about Henry's death-bed wishes.[54] It is an open question whether Geoffrey would have been acceptable to the English baronage who did not know him. Like his own father, King Henry kept his options open to the day of his death. He lived in hope of a grandson, and he did not know when he was to die.

The marriage almost foundered as soon as it began. The Durham chronicler recorded that King Henry was no sooner back in England than he heard that his daughter had returned to Normandy, poorly escorted and repudiated by her husband. His account is impossibly compressed, for he dated the marriage in 1129 and Matilda's precipitate departure from Anjou only a few days later.[55] In fact the marriage was celebrated in 1128, so, if she returned to Rouen after her father had left Normandy in mid-July 1129, the uneasy union must have lasted for a year before the cracks showed. The causes are nowhere openly stated; there must have been temperamental difficulties, and perhaps the fact that after a year no heir had been conceived offered a pretext for attempting to dissolve the union. Both parties were strong-willed and imperious; if Matilda had been schooled in political necessity, Geoffrey, at sixteen, had not. Historians have tended to put the blame on Matilda; even Chartrou, on the whole moderate in his assessment, said that she had a detestable character.[56] This is a hasty judgement based on two or three hostile English chroniclers; such evidence as there is suggests that Geoffrey was at least as much to blame. Moreover the root of the trouble was probably as much political as personal.

Some hints are contained in the letters of Hildebert of Lavardin. Since the one letter to Matilda which shows her at odds with her father was written when she was in England, it must date from before 1128.[57]

51 Henry of Huntingdon, p. 260; John of Marmoutier, *Historia Gaufredi*, pp. 181–2; Chartrou, *L'Anjou*, p. 48.

52 SD, ii, pp. 281–2.

53 *Actus pontificum cenomannis in urbe degentium*, ed. Busson and Ledru (Société des Archives historiques du Maine, 2, 1902), p. 445.

54 See below, p. 65.

55 SD, ii, p. 283.

56 Chartrou, *L'Anjou*, pp. 36–7.

57 See above, n. 47.

After leaving Anjou she remained in Normandy until her brief return with her father in the late summer of 1131. The letter cannot, therefore, date from the years of estrangement. Another letter to Geoffrey, count of Anjou, written probably in 1131, urged him not to go on a pilgrimage to Compostela because his duty as count lay in keeping order in his own lands. Hildebert added that he had heard from the king of England (oddly called *avunculus*, which is more usual for an uncle than a father-in-law) that he was highly displeased at the proposal and condemned it out of hand.[58] A slightly later letter to King Henry expressed pleasure at the news that he was now reconciled to the count, who had fallen in with his wishes in everything concerning him and his daughter.[59] The implication is that Geoffrey, not Matilda, was responsible for the breach.

In 1129 Henry's thoughts seem to have been running on the coronation of his heir. There were as yet no established insignia for use in successive English coronations; each of the Norman kings was crowned hastily, and with a new crown. William I, after the fashion of the French kings who left their crowns to the abbey of Saint-Denis, bequeathed his coronation crown and other insignia to his own abbey of St Stephen at Caen. William II recovered them in 1095 by offering land to the abbey in exchange;[60] by this date his own coronation was long past, and he appears never to have removed the crown from the abbey. Henry I had no time to send to Normandy before his own hasty coronation. In 1129, however, he confirmed the English manors and churches of the abbey, 'in exchange for the crown and other regalia which William I left to St Stephen, and the monks restored to Henry at Caen.'[61]

Charter evidence also shows that he was on good terms with his daughter during this period, and was actively preparing her for her future role in England. In May 1129 he issued a charter for the abbey of Fontevraud, granting an annual payment for the food of the nuns in Lent out of the farms of London and Winchester. A notification of the terms of the grant, addressed generally for England and Normandy, was separately confirmed by the Empress Matilda, with different witnesses.

58 Migne, *PL*, 171, cols 131–3, ep. 15: 'Audivimus autem venerabili regi Anglorum, tuoque avunculo, id quod te facturum significas displicere altius, id ferre graviter, id constanter improbare.'

59 Migne, *PL*, 171, col. 272, ep. 46.

60 L. Musset, *Les actes de Guillaume le Conquérant et de la reine Mathilde pour les abbayes caennaises* (Mémoires de la Société des Antiquaires de Normandie, 37, Caen, 1967), pp. 132–4; M. Chibnall, *The World of Orderic Vitalis* (Oxford, 1986), pp. 186–7.

61 *Regesta*, ii, no. 1575.

It may have been taken to her in Anjou by Richard and Ralph de la Haye, whose father, King Henry's steward, witnessed the royal grant; Hugh de Boceio, another witness of her signature, whose name does not occur in any royal charters, may have been a member of her household.[62] The notification shows that the king was already associating her with grants made out of farms paid into the exchequer in England. An act for Cluny, issued in 1131, when he and his daughter were together in Rouen, points to exactly the same intention. It is a notification that he has granted to St Peter of Cluny 100 marks of revenue yearly in England – 60 marks from the farm of London and 40 marks from that of Lincoln. The charter was written by one of the royal scribes and witnessed by King Henry and his daughter, the Empress Matilda.[63]

While the king was in England in 1130 his brother-in-law, David king of Scots, spent almost a year at the royal court. As earl of Huntingdon he was one of the king's vassals, and duty might have taken him there, but he was also concerned for the future of his sister's child.[64] This must have been under discussion while she remained in Rouen as her husband campaigned actively against rebels in Anjou and impetuously contemplated cutting his losses and going off on a pilgrimage to Compostela. Matilda's future was a matter of vital importance to the whole realm of England. Finally King Henry brought her back from Normandy in late August 1131. At a great council held at Northampton on 8 September it was decided that she should be restored to her husband, who was asking for her and was prepared to receive her back with all the honour due to her station. In the same council Matilda received an oath of fealty from all who had not given one before, and a renewal of the oath from all who had previously sworn.[65]

Since Matilda's return was settled at a great council, whose decision was accompanied by oaths of fealty, the personal difficulties between her and Geoffrey cannot have been too great to be overcome once the political grounds for discontent had been removed. Of the marital

62 *Regesta*, ii, no. 1580, 'Ego Matildis imperatrix concedo donum quod rex Anglorum pater meus dedit et concedit ecclesie de Fonte Ebraldi, videntibus filiis Roberti de Haia, scilicet Richardo et Radulfo, et inde facio crucem istam proprio manu mea, vidente Hugone de Boceio et aliis quampluribus.'

63 *Regesta*, ii, no. 1691; original in Paris, Bibl. Nat., Collection de Bourgogne lxxx, no. 217; T. A. M. Bishop, *Scriptores Regis* (Oxford 1961), p. 67, no. 643. I am grateful to Dr Maria Hillebrandt for providing me with a photocopy of the charter, clearly in the hand of Scribe XIII (ibid., Plate Vb).

64 Orderic, iv, pp. 276–7; Green, *Government*, p. 93.

65 Henry of Huntingdon, p. 252; Malmesbury, *HN*, p. 10. J. H. Round brushed these references aside and asserted (*Geoffrey de Mandeville*, p. 31, nn. 2, 3) that there was no contemporary authority for any oath to Matilda after her marriage.

relations between them we know nothing; in a political union such as theirs affection was something of a bonus, not an essential element. If Matilda, first thrown into marriage as a child bride barely twelve years old, never experienced any real joy in the marriage bed it would not have been surprising. She learnt to live with her husband, as her mother had done, just long enough to bear their children. If Geoffrey found her cold and proud, the conventions of the day allowed him to take mistresses. He learnt to treat his wife as a partner necessary for the maintenance and extension of his inheritance. Up to the time of the reconciliation, he may have felt disillusioned by his prospects. Whatever hopes he may have had of joint rule were belied by the facts; he had not been included in any oaths of fealty, his father-in-law did not involve him in any decisions affecting England, and news from Jerusalem may have suggested that his father was faring rather better there. In fact Fulk had a difficult struggle to secure recognition as joint ruler, but he may have sent home hopeful messages which, if they reached Anjou in the summer of 1129, could have provided the last straw that nearly broke the marriage.[66] The oaths at Northampton at least made clear that the barons were prepared to accept Matilda, even though she had married outside the realm without their knowledge.

There was another problem that certainly became acute later and may already have acted as an irritant: the control of the border castles between Normandy and Anjou. Matilda's dowry included some of the castles confiscated from Robert of Bellême after his rebellion, as well as revenues from the dues of Argentan which he had once held. Both Orderic Vitalis and Robert of Torigny, writing in Normandy and in a position to know the facts, mentioned the castles as a bone of contention between Geoffrey and his father-in-law in 1135, and they may have been a cause of earlier friction.[67] Henry clearly intended his daughter's rights to be expectative and was determined to hold the castles as long as he lived; it was important for Geoffrey that his wife should control them as a foothold for entering Normandy when the king died. That problem, however, remained in abeyance for a time after the reconciliation.

For a few years after 1131 the marriage prospered. A son, Henry, was born at Le Mans in March 1133. On Easter eve he was baptized in the cathedral by Guy of Ploermel, bishop of Le Mans, and placed under the protection of St Julian, the patron of the cathedral church.

66 Orderic's incorrect belief (Orderic, vi, pp. 390–1) that 'Count Fulk effortlessly acquired the kingdom of Jerusalem', and could even, had he wished, have had the crown before the death of his father-in-law, may be an expression of beliefs held in Normandy and Anjou at the time.

67 Orderic, vi, pp. 444–5; Torigny, *Chronicle* (ed. Howlett), p. 128.

Matilda offered a pall to St Julian in gratitude, and her father gave an annual rent in England.[68] He returned to Normandy on 2 August 1133, and before long Matilda joined him in Rouen.[69] There, at Pentecost 1134, her second son, Geoffrey, was born. His birth nearly cost Matilda her life. Robert of Torigny has described how, when she lay critically ill at Rouen, she arranged for the distribution of her wealth to various churches and begged her father to allow her to be buried at Bec-Hellouin. He resisted, arguing that she should lie beside her ancestors, the dukes Rollo and William Longsword, in the cathedral church at Rouen, but in the end gave way to her wishes.[70] She recovered, however, and Henry prolonged his stay in Normandy, dealing with local disturbances and rejoicing in his grandsons.[71] The succession seemed secure. Further oaths may have been taken from his prelates and barons: Roger Howden wrote much later that the king made the archbishops and earls and barons of all his dominions swear fealty to the Empress Matilda and her infant son Henry, and designated Henry to be king after him.[72] This, however, is late testimony, written long after Henry II had become king. In any case, if fealty was sworn at this time it could only have been in Normandy; Matilda is not known to have visited England after 1131.

Trouble erupted over the border castles. William Talvas, son of the former rebel Robert of Bellême (who up to at least 1130 had still been alive in prison in England), asked for the return of some of his father's castles in Maine. Geoffrey of Anjou, his lord and friend, supported this demand; he also pressed to have the castles of Matilda's dowry handed over. Robert of Torigny said that Geoffrey wished Henry to do fealty to him and Matilda for the castles; if any such request was made it would certainly have been unacceptable.[73] Whatever may have been asked, Henry angrily refused. Henry of Huntingdon blamed Matilda for the trouble, but at the worst she can have been only partly to blame.[74] She may have been quick-tempered herself, but she was caught between two obstinate and strong-willed men. A few years previously she had quarrelled with her husband and stood by her father's wishes. She was not prepared to quarrel with him again; she returned to Anjou, and a

68 *Act. pont. cen.*, p. 432; *Chronicae Sancti Albini Andegavensis* in *Chroniques des Eglises d'Anjou*, ed. P. Marchegay and E. Mabille (Paris, 1869), p. 33.

69 She witnessed one of his charters in Rouen in 1134 (*Regesta*, ii, no. 1902).

70 Torigny, *Interpolations*, pp. 304–5; in 1134 Whit Sunday fell on 3 June; Chibnall, 'The Empress Matilda and Bec-Hellouin', pp. 35–6.

71 Henry of Huntingdon, p. 253.

72 Roger of Howden, *Chronica*, ed. W. Stubbs (RS 1868–71), i, pp. 186–7.

73 Torigny, *Interpolations*, pp. 304–5.

74 Henry of Huntingdon, p. 254.

border war broke out. It was still demanding her attention and Geoffrey's when her father died.

During the years between her marriage and her father's death, Matilda spent many months in Rouen. Anjou saw its countess only intermittently. The Angevin charters and chronicles mentioned her only as the wife who brought promise of future power to Count Geoffrey, or as the mother of his sons.[75] The acts of the bishops of Le Mans recorded her gifts to the cathedral. By contrast she came to know Normandy well: better than she knew England. Rouen was the metropolitan city and the chief centre of commerce in the duchy. It has been suggested by Judith Green that a Norman exchequer audit may have been introduced by Henry rather later than was previously believed, at the very end of his reign, and that it formed part of his plans to prepare the way for the smooth succession of his daughter.[76] Such a theory fits the available evidence. Henry had ample time to advise his daughter on statecraft when they met in Rouen during these years. When Walter Map wrote his *Courtiers' Trifles* in Henry II's reign his comments on Matilda were revealing:

> I have heard that his mother's teaching was to this effect, that he should spin out the affairs of everyone, hold long in his own hand all posts that fell in, take the revenues of them, and keep the aspirants to them hanging on in hope; and she supported this advice by an unkind analogy: an unruly hawk, if meat is often offered to it and then snatched away or hid, becomes keener and more inclinably obedient and attentive. He ought also to be much in his own chamber and little in public: he should never confer anything on anyone at the recommendation of any person, unless he had seen and learnt about it.[77]

Map put this forward in criticism of the empress and regarded the advice as vexatious. But it reads like a lesson in practical statecraft that Matilda may have learnt from either the conduct or the precepts of her own pragmatic and powerful father. Such conduct may not have made Henry loved, but it was effective in strong government.

Unfortunately for Matilda some of his methods set examples she would have been wise not to follow. The author of the *Gesta Stephani* justified the failure of some of Stephen's followers to keep the oaths sworn to her on the grounds that they had been extorted. They complained that 'with that loud utterance that nobody could resist she rather

75 Marchegay and Mabille, pp. 34, 144–5; Chartrou, *L'Anjou*, pp. 377–8; *Act. pont. cen.*, p. 445.

76 Judith A. Green, 'Unity and disunity in the Anglo-Norman state', *Historical Research*, 62 (1989), pp. 120–3.

77 Walter Map, *De Nugis Curialium*, p. 479.

compelled than directed the leading men of the whole realm to swear to accept her as his heir.' The same chronicler complained of Matilda that when fortune began to favour her, she 'put on an extremely arrogant demeanour instead of the modest gait and bearing proper to the gentle sex', and sometimes when former adherents of the king submitted to her, she received them ungraciously and 'drove them from her presence in fury after insulting and threatening them.'[78] Conduct acceptable in a powerful king whose barons had reason to fear his anger was not acceptable in a 'Lady of the English' fighting an uphill struggle to establish her authority. Matilda's political apprenticeship was as good as her father knew how to make it; but it left her poorly prepared for the role she was called upon to play for the next decade.

78 *Gesta Stephani*, pp. 10–11, 118–21.

4

Disputed Succession

Preliminary Skirmishes

The death of each of the first three Norman kings of England led to a disputed succession. There was no clear custom of primogeniture, and grave uncertainty prevailed over the rights of female heiresses. Both William Rufus and Henry I had to overcome the claims of their elder brother, Robert Curthose; Matilda was challenged by a cousin who traced his descent through the female line. In 1135, as in 1087 and 1100, the rival claimant was too far away to act quickly, and speed won the day. William Rufus was at least at his father's deathbed, and knew that he was the old king's preferred heir to the kingdom of England. Even if not formally designated, he carried a letter to Lanfranc, archbishop of Canterbury, conveying the king's wishes;[1] and Lanfranc voluntarily did what the king expected of him, by crowning Rufus as the king knew he would. Robert Curthose, unreconciled to his father, was in exile in France. He was absent in August 1100 also, when Rufus died in the New Forest. Henry, with the speed of his brother William, though without any kind of designation as heir, secured the crown and the treasure at Winchester. Both kings had to begin their reigns by fighting off their frustrated elder brother and his adherents; both in time by different means added effective rule in Normandy to the English succession. The situation was not dissimilar when Henry died at Lyons-la-Forêt after a short illness on 1 December 1135; but it was much more perilous.

Henry had been detained in Normandy by border warfare resulting from his quarrel with his son-in-law over the castles that made up Matilda's dowry and those claimed by William Talvas of Bellême. Matilda was with her husband in Anjou, and Stephen, her undeclared rival, was in the county of Boulogne which he governed in his wife's right. Accounts of the king's last moments are contradictory, and reflect

1 Orderic, iv, pp. 96–7.

the wishes and outlook of each writer. Orderic Vitalis concentrated on showing that his admired patron made a Christian end, confessing his sins to Hugh, archbishop of Rouen, pardoning all exiles, revoking sentences of forfeiture, and giving instructions for the burial of his body at Reading.[2] The one concrete detail added by Orderic is that he told his son Robert to pay the members of his household and his stipendiary troops out of the treasure kept at Falaise; but there is no suggestion that he asked Robert to make any use of the treasure in helping the next claimant to the throne. Archbishop Hugh, in a letter to Pope Innocent II, testified that he had spent three days with the king, offering him spiritual comfort, and had given him absolution and extreme unction. 'So he rested in peace,' the letter ends, 'God grant him peace, for peace he loved.'[3] William of Malmesbury, a determined supporter of the Angevins, claimed that, 'when he was asked ... about his successor he assigned all his lands on both sides of the sea to his daughter in lawful and lasting succession, being somewhat angry with her husband because he had vexed the king by not a few threats and insults.'[4] If there is any truth in this, it implies that Henry had previously intended Matilda to rule jointly with her husband, and that his only change of mind on his deathbed was to exclude her husband. A contrary account comes from the hostile *Gesta Stephani*, which reports the claim of Stephen's supporters that the oaths they had taken to Matilda had been extorted by force and were invalid, and that Henry himself had shown repentance at the end for 'the forcible imposition of the oath on his barons.'[5] Hugh Bigod was said by John of Salisbury to have declared that the king had absolved those who had taken the oath from the obligation to keep it.[6]

Such arguments were later justifications of conduct. At the time it was Stephen's quick action that was decisive; he immediately crossed to England, was accepted as king by the citizens of London (whose trading connections with his Boulogne lands helped to win them to his side), and then proceeded to Winchester. There his able brother, Bishop Henry of Winchester, persuaded the initially reluctant archbishop of Canterbury to crown him king, the custodian of the treasure to hand over the keys, and the magnates who were present to accept him. On 22 December he was anointed king.[7]

Not all the magnates were present; those who had been with the king when he died took an oath not to abandon his body except by common

2 Orderic, vi, pp. 448–9.
3 Malmesbury, *HN*, pp. 13–14.
4 Malmesbury, *HN*, p. 13.
5 *Gesta Stephani*, pp. 10–12.
6 *Historia Pontificalis*, p. 85.
7 Davis, *King Stephen*, p. 16.

consent until they had taken it to England for burial. They included Robert of Gloucester, William of Warenne, Rotrou of Mortagne and the Beaumont twins, Robert of Leicester and Waleran of Meulan. The cortège accompanied the king's bier to Rouen, where the entrails were buried in the priory church of Notre-Dame-du-Pré. Thence they proceeded to Caen, where they waited about four weeks for a favourable wind. During the delay they met other Norman magnates either at Neubourg or at Lisieux to discuss the succession, and had decided to offer Normandy to Stephen's older brother, Theobald, when the news reached them of Stephen's coup. 'All the barons', according to Orderic, 'immediately determined, with Theobald's consent, to serve under one lord on account of the honours which they held in both provinces.'[8] Whatever may have been thought about Matilda's claims, it seems that at the moment they were in abeyance. Only the author of the *Gesta Stephani* reported a story that Robert of Gloucester had suggested that the realm should be granted to Matilda's son.[9] Apparently feeling was running against female succession; but young Henry, then in his third year, was scarcely a serious contender.

Matilda, together with Geoffrey of Anjou, acted as quickly as possible to assert her rights where they were most likely to be accepted. In the first week of December she made straight for the border castles which were her dowry.[10] The castellan, Guigan Algason (Wigan the Marshall), received her as his liege lady, and handed over to her the castles of Argentan, Exmes and Domfront.[11] In addition Geoffrey was given possession of Ambrières, Gorron and Châtillon-sur-Colmont in Maine. He entrusted these to Juhel de Mayenne, who laid claim to them, on condition that he would help to recover the inheritance of his wife and sons.[12] Juhel remained true to his undertaking; he later acted as a guarantor of the treaties made between Matilda and Geoffrey de Mandeville and Aubrey de Vere in 1141.[13] William Talvas accompanied the count to press his claims to the confiscated castles that had once belonged to his father, which King Henry had been keeping in his own hand at the time of his death: they included Sées and Alençon.[14]

---

8 Orderic, vi, pp. 448–9, 454–5.

9 *Gesta Stephani*, pp. 12–15.

10 Orderic, vi, pp. 454–5, says that Geoffrey of Anjou sent her ahead; Robert of Torigny that Geoffrey and Matilda obtained possession of certain Norman castles, which he names (Torigny, *Chronicle*, ed. Howlett, p. 128; ed. Delisle, i, pp. 199–200).

11 Orderic's expression is that he received her *ut naturalem dominam*. *Chronicae S. Albini Andegavensis* (ed. Marchegay and Mabille, p. 34) states that Count Geoffrey received Domfront and Argentan in 1135. I owe the identification of Guigan Algason as Wigan the Marshall to Dr K. S. B. Keats-Rohan.

12 Torigny, *Chronicle* (ed. Howlett, p. 128; ed. Delisle, i, pp. 199–200).

13 *Regesta*, iii, nos 275, 634.

14 Torigny, *Chronicle* (ed. Howlett, p. 128; ed. Delisle, i, p. 200).

This Angevin initiative established a foothold in Normandy which was never lost, and from which over the next five years a series of expeditions set out to attempt the recovery of the duchy. For the moment further military progress could not be made. The invading troops, forced to live off the country, roused the hatred of the Normans; and a rebellion of Robert son of Lisiard of Sablé and other Angevin nobles forced Geoffrey to return and pacify his own county.[15]

Matilda remained in Argentan, where her third son, William, was born on 22 July 1136.[16] The scanty references to her movements that survive suggest that she remained in the Norman castles, probably spending most of the time at Argentan, until she set out for England in 1139. If she ever returned to Anjou it can only have been for short visits. She was needed in Normandy, to hold on to the one small fragment of her inheritance that she had been able to secure. Argentan was an important administrative centre for the collection of revenues; the castle became one of the repositories of treasure from the duchy.[17] Its proximity to the forest of Gouffern as well as its administrative importance had made it one of the favoured residences of Henry I, where he had been able to combine hunting with business. It was also an important military centre, where the king's hauberk-makers were privileged inhabitants. Henry had granted a plot of land there to Robert and Hamelin, his hauberk-makers (*loricarii*), towards the end of his reign;[18] and one of Matilda's few charters surviving from the period of her occupation was a writ addressed to Richard the vicomte and her officers and lieges of Argentan, granting a plot of land 'in the Caen road' to Robert *loricarius* and his heirs.[19]

Matilda is heard of in Normandy at the beginning of October 1136, when she brought a troop of men to give support to her husband at the unsuccessful siege of Le Sap. In Lent 1138 her retainers captured Ralph of Esson, one of the local lords fighting against her, and handed him over to her to be kept in fetters until he surrendered his castles.[20] One charter for the citizens of Saumur allows her family's movements to be traced with unusual precision. It was granted by Count Geoffrey in June

15 John of Marmoutier, *Historia Gaufredi*, pp. 206–7; Chartrou, *L'Anjou*, pp. 30–5.
16 *Chronicae S. Albini Andegavensis*, p. 34: '1136. Guillelmus natus est xi⁰ kal'Augusti'.
17 Haskins, *Norman Institutions*, pp. 105–7, 119, 124.
18 *Regesta*, ii, no. 1946 (1130–5).
19 *Regesta*, iii, no. 567. The editors dated this act 1126–35, but it must belong to the period 1136–9 when Matilda was based in Argentan. Two of the witnesses were certainly with her at Carrouges in June 1138 (Delisle/Berger, I*), and it probably belongs to the same period. The *mansura* granted *in vico Cadumensis* was not in Caen, where Matilda had no authority, but 'on the Caen road'; the identification in *Regesta*, ii, no. 1946 and *CDF*, no. 591 is to be preferred to that in *Regesta*, iii, no. 567.
20 Orderic, vi, pp. 512–15.

1138 before the doors of St Pierre-de-la-Couture in Le Mans; three days later he took it to his wife at Carrouges, a castle near to Argentan which had been captured and lost in 1137, and evidently recaptured by 1138.[21] She and her sons Henry and William added their crosses before witnesses; it was then carried back to Saumur, where her middle son Geoffrey was being brought up in the house of Goscelin *Rotonardi*, and he added his cross. Each of the three boys received a silver cup from the citizens of Saumur.[22] Her two-year-old son, William, had probably remained with her since his birth; Henry may have been brought to Normandy by his father with a view to claiming his Norman inheritance, but it is equally likely that he too had been with his mother for some time. Everything points to her residence in the one corner of Normandy she was able to hold rather than in Anjou during the years before she made the bid for the English throne.

Did she also attempt to win papal support for her claims after the death of her father?[23] Ulger, bishop of Angers, who defended Matilda's rights at a later date, is known to have been with Innocent II at Pisa between 12 and 25 January or longer, dealing with the business of his see. Since he had to travel in midwinter, when the days were short and the Alpine crossings slow, he must have left Anjou at latest very early in December, when the news of King Henry's death had only just been received, and nothing was known about Stephen's actions. Matilda could have briefed him to speak on her behalf before she left for Argentan in the first week of December. But would she have wished to seek papal support at this stage? She had an apparently straightforward claim to be her father's legitimate heir. Of the three Norman kings only her grandfather, William the Conqueror, had attempted to secure papal approval of a right to the throne before coronation; and William's claim was weak enough to need strong spiritual backing. The English monarch was not in the position of the German king, who needed papal coronation to ratify his imperial claims. Perhaps her German upbringing turned her thoughts to the pope at that moment; perhaps as a woman she already felt the need for the strongest possible approval from the church. Whatever the truth may be, there is no known evidence of any letters sent by her or received from Innocent in the months that followed Henry's death.

21 Orderic, vi, pp. 466–7.
22 Delisle/Berger, no. I*. The charter is dated 1138 without further detail, but Count Geoffrey is known to have invaded Normandy in June.
23 The evidence of the dates of appeals to the papal court is very well summarized by Giles Constable, *The Letters of Peter the Venerable* (2 vols, Cambridge, Mass., 1967), Appendix C, ii, pp. 252–6. For the time required to travel to Rome see R. L. Poole, *Studies in Chronology and History* (Oxford, 1934), p. 263; and for Ulger's presence in Pisa in January 1136, Migne, *PL*, 179, cols 261–5; JL, nos 7753, 7755.

On the other hand Stephen is known to have applied immediately to the pope, and while Ulger was in Pisa he could have met envoys arriving hotfoot from the English court. Papal support was necessary for Stephen because of the oaths that he and the other magnates had sworn to Matilda; however plausibly they may have argued that these were extorted and invalid or had contained reservations, it was more satisfactory to have papal approval for their violation. Indeed both the archbishop of Canterbury and the bishop of Winchester may have insisted on it. Couriers could have left London immediately after the coronation and travelled by way of Paris to arrive at Pisa before the end of January. They carried letters from the archbishop and bishops of the realm, and also obtained letters from the king of France and Count Theobald of Blois supporting Stephen.[24] Innocent may have decided hastily, impressed by the letters handed to him, without attempting to probe the question deeply. He had always dealt diplomatically with Henry I, sometimes giving way reluctantly to his demands in order to avoid conflict; he may have hoped that Stephen, supported by a powerful Cluniac bishop who was known to stand up for the rights of the church, would prove more amenable. In any case, Stephen had been crowned and anointed by the archbishop of Canterbury. Innocent accepted the strength of his position; at this stage anything Ulger might have said could not hope to carry much weight with him. Nothing as formal as a 'case' was heard at this early date. Ulger returned to Angers with the privileges for his see he had gone to obtain, but with nothing for his countess.

By Easter 1136 Stephen was able to produce a letter from the pope approving his elevation to the throne, and almost all the Anglo-Norman magnates were ready to accept the fact of his usurpation. A few argued later that they had done homage only conditionally; but Baldwin de Redvers was the only magnate of the first rank who never accepted Stephen.[25] His revolt in the West Country was a forlorn struggle, doomed from the outset. Matilda and Geoffrey were faced with a formidable task in attempting to advance beyond their frontier foothold in Normandy. They had only the forces of Anjou to back them, unless they could win support from the border lords. Men like Rotrou of Mortagne, Theobald of Blois and Roger of Tosny naturally had their own interests at heart, and hard bargaining was necessary to secure even a temporary truce from potential enemies. The loyalty of the Angevin lords too was questionable; Geoffrey had always to guard his rear

24 Richard of Hexham, *Chronicles of the Reigns of Stephen, Henry II and Richard I*, (RS) iii, pp. 147–8.

25 Davis, *King Stephen*, pp. 18–23; Round, *Geoffrey de Mandeville. A Study of the Anarchy*, (London, 1892), p. 19.

when he led his forces into Normandy. Stephen had his own troubles; apart from the rebellion of Baldwin de Redvers and minor outbreaks of disorder, he had to contend with a rising of the Welsh and an invasion of the Scots. He had, however, the accumulated wealth of Henry I and the resources of England at his back; and for two years his rivals were unable to do more than hold their first gains and make unsuccessful forays deeper into Normandy. They were immersed in the local politics of the Norman frontier.

The small handful of Matilda's charters that survive from this period show only a tentative assertion of her claims. After leaving Germany, where her title had always been 'queen of the Romans', she adopted the style 'empress' and kept it to the end of her life.[26] She preferred not to call herself 'countess of Anjou', and her husband showed some respect for her chosen magnificence in a few of his early charters. He once styled himself 'the husband of Matilda, daughter of the king of the English and former wife of Henry, Roman emperor',[27] and on another occasion called her 'Matilda, my wife, daughter of Henry king of the English, lawfully married to me after the death of Henry emperor of the Romans.'[28] In two charters that certainly belong to the years before 1139 she contented herself with 'Matilda, empress, daughter of the king of the English'.[29] One charter confirmed the grants of English churches by earlier Norman kings to St Nicholas, Angers, and therefore assumed that she had rights in England. She had, however, no English title until she was received as 'Lady of the English' in 1141; and though some right of inheritance was no doubt implied in 'daughter of the king of the English' she did not spell it out as 'rightful heir', as her young son sometimes did later. The charters are very few; even granting that some must have been lost, Matilda had very little patronage to bestow during

26 In a writ issued in London between 1126 and 1128 (*Regesta*, iii, no. 898), she uses this style. The editors give the wider dating limits of 1126–35; but Matilda was never in London after she left England to marry Geoffrey of Anjou in 1128, unless she passed through briefly on her way to Northampton in 1131, when she would scarcely have had time or authority to issue writs.

27 P. Marchegay and A. Salmon, *Chronique des Comtes d'Anjou* (Paris, 1856–71), i, p. xv n. 1. This charter was dated 29 June 1130, during the period of Geoffrey's estrangement from Matilda, and the language seems to indicate a wish for reconciliation.

28 Delisle/Berger, i, no. I* (June 1138); in this charter, however, Matilda's cross is identified as *Signum Matildis comitisse*. In July 1133 she confirmed another charter as *Mathildis uxor Comitis* (Chartrou, *L'Anjou*, p. 379).

29 *Regesta*, iii, no. 567, granting a plot of land in Argentan, was given at Argentan probably in 1138–9; *Regesta*, iii, no. 20 confirmed the gift of churches in England to St Nicholas, Angers. *Regesta*, iii, no. 805, given at Falaise, is dated by the editors as 1136–9; but Falaise did not fall to the Angevins until 1141, and unless Matilda granted the charter during the siege of Falaise in 1138 it must belong to the year 1148, when she is known to have been there (*Regesta*, iii, no. 794).

these years. Firm title to a plot of land in her own base at Argentan, or the confirmation of rights in English churches which an Angevin abbey had enjoyed for fifty years and which were hardly likely to be questioned, were realistic favours to bestow. She may have settled some of the knights who formed her household troops on land near Argentan by verbal grant. Her later practice in England showed that she provided for her knights on small estates round any castle where she established a base. Even if Orderic exaggerated when he described her arrival to help her husband at Le Sap as accompanied by many thousand knights, she had a considerable body of armed men at her command, capable of making forays and capturing enemy lords like Ralph of Esson, possibly even of storming small castles, since her knights had apparently captured Carrouges when Geoffrey joined her there in June 1138. Their captain, Alexander de Bohun, was somewhat grandiloquently described in one charter as *cohortis comitisse primipilus*.[30] He and his brother, Engelger de Bohun, were active in the service of the Angevins throughout the period of the struggle with Stephen.

Engelger, who lived until 1180, was one of the men who provided information about the events of these years to John of Marmoutier for his *History of Geoffrey, Count of Anjou*. In attempting to reconstruct the events of these years and understand the motives and methods of Matilda's husband, some cautious use may be made of this late source, though Orderic Vitalis, who wrote before 1141, is more accurate in detail and less tendentious. John of Marmoutier knew the outcome, and wrote to show how Geoffrey, combining boldness with prudence, worked for the succession of his son Henry as duke of Normandy. Stephen of Blois, the usurping king, was, wrote John of Marmoutier, Geoffrey's greatest enemy; but though Geoffrey and Matilda had a just claim to the kingdom that had been promised them, Geoffrey knew that he could not overpower Stephen because of the immense treasure he had seized from the late king's store and the number of supporters he had bought with it. He therefore negotiated for a two-year truce.[31] There is some truth in this, though John's chronology, here as elsewhere, is out of joint: the truce was not negotiated until 1137.[32] From the beginning Geoffrey was anxious to arrange a truce wherever possible with his potential rivals on the turbulent frontiers of Normandy.

30 Delisle/Berger, i, no. I*. He occurs elsewhere as one of the officers placed in charge of a district. According to the editors of *Regesta*, iii (pp. xxxv–xxxviii) he was 'put in charge of Argentan and Domfront by Count Geoffrey', and he certainly seems at times to have acted as one of Geoffrey's regional officers, but in 1138 his duty was clearly to command Matilda's knights.

31 John of Marmoutier, *Historia Gaufredi*, pp. 214–15 and note.

32 Orderic, vi, pp. 486–7.

There the traditional rival of the house of Anjou was the house of Blois.[33] The counts of Anjou had built up their power by their steady advance into Touraine, an acquisition even more important than Maine, where Geoffrey's father, Fulk, had finally established his authority against Normandy by marriage with the heiress Erembourg. Count Theobald of Blois had been one of the staunchest allies of King Henry; he was thought by some to harbour resentment because Stephen had seized authority in England and Normandy, to which, as his elder brother, he had in theory a better right.[34] As a result Geoffrey was constantly on the alert to make a truce with Theobald.

Initially his chief indirect help on the frontier came from Roger of Tosny, who was engaged in private war with Stephen's supporters, the Beaumont twins, holders of the honours of Breteuil and Beaumont. [35] Since William Talvas of Bellême was Geoffrey's friend, the hostility of his rival, Count Rotrou of Mortagne, was to be expected. With private warfare breaking out all along the Norman frontier, Geoffrey had to move cautiously whenever he made a military incursion into Normandy. He needed diplomatic no less than military skill to preserve what he had and hold off the threat of attack in the rear. Matilda gave him a base in Normandy and a right to claim the duchy on behalf of his son. There can be little doubt that the planning of the Norman campaigns even before she left for England was his rather than hers, even though Orderic Vitalis described him when he invaded for the third time in June 1137 as acting as his wife's stipendiary.[36]

In September 1136 Count Geoffrey invaded Normandy for the second time.[37] He had secured support from William, duke of Aquitaine, William, son of the count of Nevers, and Count Geoffrey of Vendôme, as well as from William Talvas of Bellême. He captured Carrouges, at least temporarily, persuaded Robert of Neubourg, a son of Henry earl of Warwick, who was in charge of the castle at Asnebec, to make a truce for a year, and advanced as far as Lisieux. Then Waleran of Meulan, who had been sent to organize the defence of Normandy, succeeded in consolidating Stephen's hold on eastern Normandy and leading a substantial army towards Lisieux. Geoffrey chose to withdraw; the arrival of his wife with fresh troops at Le Sap was not enough to change his fortunes. He himself was wounded in the foot,

---

33 John Gillingham, *The Angevin Empire*, pp. 6–7; O. Guillou, *Le comte d'Anjou et son entourage au xie siècle* (Paris, 1972), *passim*.

34 Orderic, vi, pp. 454–5.

35 Crouch, *Beaumont Twins*, pp. 31–5.

36 Orderic, vi, pp. 482–3.

37 See Orderic, vi, pp. 466–7; Torigny, *Chronicle* (ed. Howlett, p. 131; ed. Delisle, i, p. 205); Crouch, *Beaumont Twins*, pp. 33–5, for details of this campaign.

and an outbreak of dysentery in his army turned the retreat into a rout. This campaign, waged with the utmost savagery, left a legacy of lasting hatred. Orderic wrote: 'The Angevins remained in Normandy for thirteen days and made themselves hated for ever by their brutality.'[38]

In March 1137 Stephen was able to come to Normandy for the first and only time in his reign.[39] In the long run the visit probably did his cause more harm than good. He succeeded in meeting King Louis VI and reaching an agreement with him; Eustace, his son, did homage to Louis for Normandy. Count Geoffrey had lost one of his allies: William, duke of Aquitaine, who had gone on a pilgrimage to Compostela, died there on 9 April, after arranging to betroth his daughter and heir, Eleanor, to the future Louis VII.[40] Nevertheless Geoffrey raised a larger army than in the year before and invaded Normandy early in May. It was more than ever necessary to assert Matilda's rights, and he may have hoped to profit from the rifts which began to appear in the royal army. Stephen had brought with him his able mercenary commander, William of Ypres, with a large force of Flemings; and, by granting away castles, pensions and privileges lavishly, he attracted an impressive number of Norman magnates into his camp. This proved to be a dubious advantage, for rivalries of all kinds appeared in the motley army. Orderic, Robert of Torigny and John of Marmoutier stress the quarrels between Normans and Flemings and between their leaders.[41] William of Malmesbury thought that the major cause of dissension was William of Ypres's suspicion of the loyalty of Robert of Gloucester. Stephen was forced to give up hope of laying siege to Argentan or any other castle held by the Angevins; he decided to make a two-year truce and withdraw to deal with new disturbances in England. He took with him both the Beaumont twins and most of the Norman magnates with extensive honours in England. Robert of Gloucester, though outwardly reconciled to Stephen, remained in Normandy. He and the king each suspected the other, and with good reason. William of Roumare and Roger, vicomte of the Cotentin, were left behind to attempt the task in which Stephen had failed, of restoring order and justice to the Normans.[42] Stephen's failure in Normandy was the first real turning point in his reign.

38 Orderic, vi, pp. 470–1.

39 Orderic, vi, pp. 482–3; Torigny, *Chronicle* (ed. Howlett, p. 132; ed. Delisle, i, pp. 206–7); Henry of Huntingdon, p. 210.

40 *Chron. Morigny, RHF*, xii, p. 83.

41 Orderic, vi, pp. 484–5; Torigny, *Chronicle* (ed. Howlett, p. 132; ed. Delisle, i, p. 207); John of Marmoutier, *Historia Gaufredi*, p. 225.

42 Orderic, vi, pp. 494–5; Haskins, *Norman Institutions*, p. 127; L. Delisle, *Histoire du Château de Saint-Sauveur le Vicomte* (Valognes, 1867), pp. 27–31, 59–65.

Some months were to pass before Robert of Gloucester openly renounced his homage to Stephen and declared for his sister. He remained
in Normandy, firmly based in Caen and Bayeux, near to another region
of doubtful loyalty. Henry I's success in winning and holding England
against his elder brother had owed much to the support he had built
up among the Bretons and men of the Cotentin and Avranchin. The
region now provided a refuge for the few men who had defied Stephen
in 1136 and had been forced into exile. Baldwin of Redvers and his
friend Stephen of Mandeville rallied there under the leadership of
Reginald of Dunstanville, one of King Henry's many bastard sons.[43] The
Cotentin became a centre of disorder, with family feuds cutting across
dynastic rivalries; in one skirmish some knights in Baldwin's forces
turned against other knights fighting on their own side. The uneasy
truce broke down in less than a year, and in May Count Waleran and
William of Ypres were sent back to restore order in Normandy.[44]
Robert of Gloucester chose this moment to renounce his homage to
Stephen, claiming that Stephen had plotted against his life.[45] This
assured Count Geoffrey of the castles of Caen and Bayeux, and in June
he brought a strong army into Normandy. He entered by way of Carrouges and there joined his wife Matilda. On 1 October he laid siege
to Falaise and struck deep into Normandy as far as Bonneville-sur-
Touques, but he failed to capture Falaise and finally withdrew to Anjou
in November.[46] Though the Angevins failed to make headway in eastern Normandy, and the first rising of their supporters in England was
temporarily held in check by Stephen, they had merely withdrawn to
strike more forcibly. The charter of Matilda in favour of her armourer,
Robert *loricarius*, in Argentan was witnessed by her brother Reginald
of Dunstanville as well as by Alexander of Bohun, commander of her
knights, and Guy of Sablé, who was shortly to accompany her to
England. With its hint of military preparations under way, it must
surely belong to the year 1138–9.[47] Backed by Robert of Gloucester
and Reginald of Dunstanville, with her husband securely based in
Normandy, she was ready to mount a serious challenge for the English
throne.

43 Orderic, vi, pp. 510–13; for Stephen de Mandeville see L. C. Loyd, *The Origins of
Some Anglo-Norman Families*, ed. C. T. Clay and D. C. Douglas (Publications of the
Harleian Society 103, 1951), pp. 57–8.
44 Orderic, vi, pp. 514–15.
45 Malmesbury, *HN*, p. 23, 'after Whitsuntide'; Torigny, *Chronicle* (ed. Howlett,
p. 136; ed. Delisle, i, p. 205), 'about Easter'.
46 Orderic, vi, pp. 526–9.
47 *Regesta*, iii, no. 567; see above, n. 19.

A New Initiative

Matilda's appeal to the papal court early in 1139 should be seen as the first step in her challenge. She began at a disadvantage because, even if Bishop Ulger had attempted to put in an informal plea on her behalf in 1136, Stephen had already secured a letter of support from Pope Innocent II. There are two accounts of the proceedings. The first is by Gilbert Foliot, abbot of Gloucester and later bishop of Hereford, who as a young Cluniac monk attended the Lateran Council with his abbot, Peter the Venerable, and was present at the proceedings; he described them in a letter to Brian fitz Count, written to support the cause of the empress in 1143–4.[48] The other, by John of Salisbury, was written about 1167 to explain to his friend Peter of Celle why Stephen had never been able to persuade any pope to crown his son Eustace; it embodied the information he had gleaned in Rome between 1148 and 1154. While John's details are less reliable than Gilbert's his perspective of the case in the context of the whole struggle for the kingdom deserves serious attention.[49]

The second Lateran Council was opened on 4 April 1139. Both sources agree that Matilda challenged Stephen's usurpation of the throne and laid claim to succeed as her father's heir, on the grounds of hereditary right and the oaths sworn to her by the leading prelates and magnates of the kingdom, and that her case was presented by Ulger, bishop of Angers. Arnulf, archdeacon of Sées and later bishop of Lisieux, led Stephen's delegation and replied on the king's behalf. Arnulf was a nephew of John, bishop of Lisieux, one of Henry I's most loyal servants; but even Bishop John, along with the other Norman bishops had accepted Stephen after his coronation, and Arnulf, educated at Chartres as well as Sées, was on friendly terms with the family of the counts of Blois and Champagne.[50] He devoted himself to Stephen's service with the same thoroughness he was later to show in the service of Geoffrey of Anjou and his son. A skilled lawyer and advocate, he had no difficulty in countering Ulger's arguments with technicalities. If the principal point (*ius principale*) of law were invalid, he argued, the subsidiary *ius* would fail. He then attacked Matilda's hereditary claim, avoiding the awkward question of the oaths. His argument was the ingenious one that she was illegitimate because her

48 *Letters of Gilbert Foliot*, pp. 60–6.
49 *Historia Pontificalis*, Foreword and pp. 83–6
50 For his career see *Letters of Arnulf of Lisieux*, ed. F. Barlow (Camden Society, 61, 1939), pp. 83–6.

mother had been a nun. To this, according to Gilbert Foliot, no reply
was made. Ulger was probably unprepared for such a specious argument, and did not make the obvious reply, which Gilbert himself later
provided in his letter to Brian fitz Count: namely that the marriage had
been openly celebrated by archbishop Anselm, who was satisfied of its
legitimacy, and who was already being spoken of as a saint. By the time
John of Salisbury wrote, this had passed into accepted tradition as a
reply actually given at the time. John added for good measure a defence
of the validity of the oaths taken; whether or not Arnulf had thought
it necessary to defend Stephen and his supporters against charges of
perjury, the arguments on both sides were common knowledge in John
of Salisbury's circle. William of Corbeil had refused to consecrate
Stephen as king until he was persuaded by the oaths of Hugh Bigod and
others that their oaths to Matilda had been extorted by force and that
Henry had changed his mind and designated Stephen on his deathbed.
John, who hated Arnulf vehemently, imagined a scathing reply by
Ulger:

> As for your statement that the king changed his mind, it is proved false by
> those who were present at the king's death. Neither you nor Hugh could
> possibly know his last requests, since neither was there. The proof that
> you claim was accepted cannot injure the empress; for since she was
> neither present nor duly cited she could not be lawfully condemned, least
> of all by men who were not her judges, but her subjects, bound to her by
> oaths of fealty and involved in a common offence.

All this is a dramatic reconstruction, based on arguments built up on
both sides over the years. But John's further comment is important, and
is consistent with the evidence of Gilbert Foliot: 'Pope Innocent would not
hear their arguments further, nor would he pronounce sentence or
adjourn the case to a later date; but acting against the advice of certain
cardinals, especially Guy, cardinal priest of St Mark, he accepted
Stephen's gifts and in letters to the king confirmed his occupation of the
kingdom of England and the duchy of Normandy.'[51]
The hearing, in John's interpretation, had been suspended, and
although Innocent refused to go back on his acceptance of Stephen,
later popes insisted that no further action should be taken by the
English church because the question of the crown was still under dispute. In 1139, however, Matilda had to be content with a cynical
comment from Ulger about the venality of the papal Curia. She
prudently kept open the channels of communication with the cardinals
who opposed Innocent, and hoped for a more favourable outcome in
the future. Meanwhile she and her brothers Robert and Reginald laid

51 *Historia Pontificalis*, p. 84.

plans and prepared to raise arms against Stephen and carry their claim into England.

In the first two years of Stephen's reign the main threats to his authority came from the Welsh princes and the king of Scotland. Although the Norman advance into Wales had been largely the work of the great Norman families, the whole enterprise had been backed by royal power.[52] Henry I's two expeditions into Wales and his close watch on the internal rivalries of the princes had provided temporary stability. The news of his death was the signal for risings all over Wales. Richard fitz Gilbert of Clare, lord of Ceredigion, was killed in 1136; and a year later Payn fitz John, lord of Caus, also fell while repelling a border raid. Stephen was powerless to resist the dramatic recovery of Welsh control; it was Miles of Gloucester who led a raid to rescue Richard fitz Gilbert's widow from Cardigan. It was left to the marcher lords themselves to defend their Welsh conquests as best they might. One argument that may have induced Robert of Gloucester not to defy Stephen in 1136 and risk an attack on his honour was the threat to his recent conquests in Glamorgan and his need to keep in touch with the Welsh princes to avoid an attack in his rear. By the end of 1136 he had come to an agreement with Morgan, son of Owain Wan, and was more secure.[53] Similar considerations may have weighed also with Brian fitz Count, lord of Abergavenny, and William fitz Alan of Oswestry, who were both inclined to favour the empress had conditions been more propitious. Ranulf, earl of Chester, though threatened in Tegeingl and married to a daughter of Robert of Gloucester, was less ready to declare for the Angevins because he needed Stephen's support to uphold his claims in Lincoln and in his Cumbrian lands, threatened by the King of Scots.[54]

King David had lost no time in striking a blow for the rights of his niece, whilst at the same time furthering his own cause in the north.[55] On receiving the news of Stephen's coronation, he led an army into Northumbria and received the fealty of the lords holding the castles of Wark, Norham, Newcastle and Carlisle. Richard of Hexham said that he acted on behalf of his niece,[56] and his action so exactly parallels

---

52 For Wales see R. R. Davies, *Conquest, Coexistence and Change in Wales 1063–1415*, (Oxford 1987), ch. 2.

53 David Crouch, 'The slow death of kingship in Glamorgan, 1067–1158', *Morgannwg*, 29 (1985), pp. 32–3.

54 R. H. C. Davis, 'King Stephen and the Earl of Chester revised', *EHR* 75 (1960), pp. 654–60; Chibnall, *Anglo-Norman England*, pp. 95–6.

55 Barrow, *Kingdom of the Scots*, pp. 144–8.

56 Richard of Hexham, p. 72; see also Matthew Strickland, 'Securing the North ...', *Anglo-Norman Studies*, 12 (1990), p. 186 n. 62.

Matilda's instant occupation of her dowry castles in Normandy that this may be true. Stephen, however, acted swiftly; he led an army north and bought peace by ceding Cumbria, while David returned all the castles except Carlisle. He had now succeeded in restoring the northern border to its old place at the Rere Cross, but he did not abandon his niece's cause in principle. He allowed his son Henry to do homage for Cumbria, while refusing to compromise his oath to Matilda by himself doing homage to her rival. Stephen showed in these years that he could on occasion move quickly to deal with insurrection or invasion; but he relied greatly on winning support by grants of lands, money and privileges. By 1139 most of Henry I's wealth had melted away, the frontiers had been eroded, and his favours to men dispossessed by the old king's judgements had raised a new body of disinherited. Robert of Gloucester had every reason to hope that his renunciation of homage in 1138 would be the signal for a revolt by those who had lost lands; and, if this were not enough to spark off a general rising, Matilda's arrival to make her claims in person should suffice to tip the scales. We have, unfortunately, no means of knowing how far Matilda herself had any influence in deciding that the moment to strike had come.

Stephen succeeded in holding his own against the first wave of rebellion in 1138. His attempt to confiscate Robert of Gloucester's English lands and to take over his castles involved him in heavy fighting. With the aid of ships from Boulogne he was able to capture Dover castle from Robert's castellan, Walchelin Maminot. His army in the West Country took Castle Cary from Ralph Lovel and Harptree from William fitz John; but he failed to capture Bristol, and his forces were needed elsewhere to counter the outburst of fighting in the Severn valley, and regain the towns of Hereford, held by Geoffrey Talbot, and Shrewsbury, where William fitz Alan had come out openly for the empress.[57] Stephen won support by a lavish grant of earldoms: Derby to Robert of Ferrers, Pembroke to Gilbert of Clare, and Worcester to Waleran of Meulan.[58] He himself undertook the siege of Shrewsbury, and when it fell after refusing to surrender he ordered the execution without mercy of almost a hundred of the rebels. King David once again invaded the north, this time openly in support of Matilda; but here local loyalties and terror at the ravages of the Galweigians in his

---

57 Orderic, vi, pp. 520–3.

58 Davis, *King Stephen*, pp. 132–3, 154–6. Some of Stephen's grants (e.g. his grant of Hereford to Robert earl of Leicester in 1140) were exceptionally sweeping, as they included all the king's rights in the county as well as the earldom. For the difference implied in *comitatus* and earldom, see Paul Latimer, 'Grants of 'totus comitatus' in twelfth-century England: their origins and meaning', *Bulletin of the Institute of Historical Research*, 59 (1986), pp. 137–45.

army served to unite resistance without the presence of the king. The barons of Yorkshire, encouraged by Archbishop Thurstan of York, defeated and routed his army at the battle of the Standard near Northallerton.[59] Momentarily Stephen was in control of the situation, but he was justifiably apprehensive, with revolt smouldering in England, and Normandy almost out of control. Fear of treachery and invasion made him suspicious and over-anxious to have as many as possible of the great castles of the kingdom in his own hand.

Bishops no less than barons held great castles. In Henry I's reign they had held them in principle on the king's behalf; in any emergency the old king would certainly have insisted on having them manned by garrisons answerable to him. Stephen's actions suggested that he wished to emulate the uncle in whose court he had grown up by resisting the spread of private great castles. This must have been one reason for his sudden and ill-advised attack on Roger, bishop of Salisbury, and his nephews Alexander, bishop of Lincoln, and Nigel, bishop of Ely.[60] The *Gesta Stephani* asserted that they were plotting to hand over their castles to the empress,[61] and Stephen may have believed this. William of Malmesbury thought he acted on a mere suspicion of their siding against him;[62] and in view of the veiled hostility between Matilda and Roger of Salisbury in the last years of King Henry's life, and the bishop's insistence that his oath had been conditional, this is a little more likely to be true.[63] Court rivalries may also have played a part, for a rift was appearing between the powerful Bishop Henry of Winchester and the adherents of Waleran of Meulan, who were anxious to bring new men into the administration. Whatever the reasons, in June 1139 Stephen either provoked or took advantage of a brawl in his court at Oxford involving some of Bishop Roger's men in order to summon the three bishops to answer for the disturbance of the peace and to surrender their castles. When they refused, he seized and imprisoned Roger and Alexander, and laid siege to Devizes, where Nigel of Ely had taken refuge. The bishops were forced by threats and rough treatment to surrender their castles. Roger gave up Salisbury, Sherborne, Malmesbury and Devizes; and Nigel relinquished Newark and Sleaford.

---

59 Orderic, vi, pp. 520–3; John of Worcester, pp. 50–1; Ailred of Rievaulx, *Relatio de Standardo*, in *Chronicles of the Reigns of Stephen, Henry II and Richard I*, ed. R. Howlett (RS 1884–9), iii, pp. 181–99; John of Hexham in SD, ii, p. 293; Henry of Huntingdon, pp. 261–5.

60 Malmesbury, *HN*, pp. 26–8; Henry of Huntingdon, p. 266; Orderic, vi, pp. 530–5; *Gesta Stephani*, pp. 76–81.

61 *Gesta Stephani*, pp. 72–3.

62 Malmesbury, *HN*, p. 25.

63 See above, pp. 52–3.

Stephen had bought a measure of security at a heavy cost; he had finally
alienated his brother, the powerful Bishop Henry of Winchester, who
(probably unknown to Stephen) had just been appointed papal legate by
Innocent II. Though Henry, a prince of the church, had his share of
family pride, he was a convinced believer in church reform. He summoned a legatine council and demanded penance and reparation from
his brother. Although it is doubtful that he thought seriously of trans-
ferring his allegiance to the empress at this stage, some men thought
that he wrote to invite her to come to England.[64] Certainly he was
beginning to see that Stephen's promises to respect the freedom of the
church were empty words and that coercion might be necessary to
ensure that they were kept. So although Matilda failed at this time to
persuade Innocent II to depose Stephen, Innocent's legate in England
was beginning to waver. It was widely believed that prominent men in
England invited the empress to come; she later claimed that the legate
himself had sent letters to her.[65] The Gloucester chronicler asserted that
she had been invited by some magnates with an assurance that she
could gain possession of the country within five months.[66] In spite of
setbacks, her cause was far from hopeless when she and Earl Robert set
out for England in September 1139.

Baldwin de Redvers first landed at Wareham and entered Corfe castle
either in the hope of securing a port of entry in the West Country or
to distract Stephen's armies when Matilda landed in Sussex.[67] Most of
the Channel ports were in the hands of Stephen's adherents. Arundel
castle, however, was part of the dower of Matilda's stepmother, Queen
Adeliza, and she was there with her second husband, William of Albini
pincerna. Envoys had passed between the queen and the empress; amid
conflicting rumours it is certain that Matilda knew she could rely on a
friendly reception in an almost impregnable castle, even though William
of Albini was and continued to be a steady supporter of Stephen. She
and her brother landed on 30 September with a force made up partly at

64 Malmesbury, *HN*, pp. 63–4; *Gesta Stephani*, pp. 88–9.
65 Malmesbury, *HN*, pp. 63–4.
66 For the different recensions of the Worcester Chronicle see Antonia Gransden,
Historical Writing in England, i, p. 148. The Gloucester continuator of John of Worcester's chronicle claimed to have his information from Miles of Gloucester; but his chronology is confused. The statement that Miles renounced his fealty to Stephen and conspired
with Robert of Gloucester to invite the empress to England, inserted into the Worcester
chronicle just before the account of the battle of the Standard in 1138, cannot be correct;
Miles defected a year later, and Robert had already renounced his homage. Miles may
have misled the chronicler in an attempt to assert his loyalty to King Henry's children in
spite of his earlier support of Stephen. For the Gloucester interpolations, see John of
Worcester, pp. 51 n. 1, 54 n. 1; Florence of Worcester (ed. Thorpe), ii, pp. 110–11.
67 *Gesta Stephani*, pp. 84–5.

least of Angevin knights.[68] Almost immediately Earl Robert slipped away at night with a small bodyguard and made his way by devious byroads, evading Stephen's armies, to Bristol. Stephen found himself faced with a dilemma, which has not always been appreciated by those who have either condemned his action as weak and ill-advised or praised it as chivalrous. There were norms governing accepted conduct which could not lightly be disregarded. Matilda was a woman, an ex-empress and his cousin; she had been promised a safe refuge in the castle by a queen dowager, widow of Stephen's benefactor. He could not have captured her without undertaking a lengthy siege which would have tied down a considerable part of his army, while her brother Robert raised rebellion in the West Country. The harsher his conduct towards Matilda, the more likely he would be to alienate his vassals and drive them into Robert's camp. If he had captured the castle he might perhaps have attempted to send Matilda back to Normandy; but he could no more have imprisoned her at this stage without undermining his prestige and authority than Henry I could have imprisoned Robert Curthose's young son William Clito along with his father in 1106. Adeliza, the daughter of Duke Godfrey of Lotharingia, for whom Matilda had interceded as a child bride in 1110, would not willingly have surrendered her without some guarantee of her freedom, however alarming Stephen's warlike preparations. Chroniclers could only guess motives. William of Malmesbury complained that Adeliza had shown a woman's fickleness and had broken faith in not providing a more permanent refuge for Matilda. The author of the *Gesta Stephani* more plausibly claimed that Bishop Henry of Winchester persuaded the king that it would be wiser to let Matilda join her brother, so that they might more easily be attacked and overcome in one place. Whatever the arguments put forward, the outcome was that she was given a safe-conduct to travel to Bristol under the escort of Bishop Henry and Waleran of Meulan. Such escort, as William of Malmesbury wrote, 'it is not the custom of honourable knights to refuse to anyone, even their bitterest enemy.'[69]

In this phase of the conflict the motives of the men who joined Matilda's cause were either hope of material advantage, very strong moral principles, or a combination of the two.[70] Men like Baldwin de Redvers, disinherited by Stephen, had nothing to lose by supporting his

68 *Gesta Stephani*, pp. 86–9; Malmesbury, *HN*, pp. 34–5; Henry of Huntingdon, p. 266; John of Worcester, p. 55; Orderic, vi, p. 535. According to Malmesbury's *Historia Novella* Robert brought only 140 knights with him, and left with an escort of about 12.

69 Malmesbury, *HN*, p. 35.

70 Cf. Davis, *King Stephen*, pp. 38–40.

rival. Loyalty was probably a very strong motive determining the conduct of King Henry's two bastard sons, Robert of Gloucester and Reginald of Dunstanville. They owed their upbringing to their father, and Robert had already been enriched and ennobled by him and trusted with his confidence in the financial reorganization of the kingdom and the negotiations for Matilda's marriage. His initial acceptance of Stephen was the act of a practical man, who chose rather to wait for an opportunity to act effectively than to throw away his inheritance by a hopeless act of defiance. An experienced and pragmatic judge of men, he may have been one of the first to recognize in his nephew Henry a boy capable of rule, and to pin his hopes on the next generation. Reginald was much less prominent and had less to lose; he appeared only briefly at Stephen's court in 1136 and moved definitely into Matilda's camp with his brother in 1138.[71]

Miles of Gloucester, who held Gloucester castle under Earl Robert, took slightly longer to change his allegiance. He had done well during the four years that he supported Stephen; he was confirmed in his honours of Brecknock and Gloucester, and granted Gloucester castle to hold directly from the king.[72] When Earl Robert renounced his homage Miles remained outwardly loyal to Stephen. In the summer of 1138 he received Stephen with royal honours in Gloucester.[73] His motives are not clear; he may have been prepared to improve his position at the expense of Earl Robert, or he may have taken the practical line that it was useless to defy Stephen while Earl Robert, far away in Normandy, could offer him no support. William fitz Alan in Shrewsbury might have fared better if he had held his hand a little longer. Nevertheless, by strengthening his own hold on Gloucester, Miles was taking advantage of his lord, and some evidence suggests the possibility of tensions between them. In a later treaty, drawn up probably in June 1142, Earl Robert promised to help Miles to retain his territorial honour and castles, and Miles surrendered his son Mahel as a hostage; a necessity that hardly implies complete trust.[74] Outwardly, however, they acted together from the time that the empress landed in England. Miles declared for her as soon as she arrived. Perhaps he realized that Earl Robert in Bristol would be a threat to his Welsh no less than his Gloucester lands, perhaps tensions have been exaggerated, and he was only waiting for Robert to return from Normandy to follow him in renouncing his homage to Stephen.

71 See *Regesta*, iii, no. 944, where he witnesses as R. *filius regis Henrici*.

72 R. H. C. Davis, 'The treaty between William earl of Gloucester and Roger earl of Hereford' in *Medieval Miscellany*, pp. 143–4; David Walker, in *Trans. Bristol and Glouc. Arch. Soc.*, 77 (1959), pp. 64–84; 79 (1960), pp. 174–211.

73 Florence of Worcester (ed. Thorpe), ii, p. 105.

74 Davis, *Medieval Miscellany*, pp. 142–6.

As soon as Matilda reached Bristol, Miles went to declare his support. For what followed we have some evidence from the chronicles, notably one continuator of John of Worcester (probably a monk of Gloucester), and from short passages of narrative incorporated in a few of her charters. The Gloucester chronicler wrote that she 'spent more than two months at Bristol, receiving homage from all men and disposing freely of the royal rights; on 15 October she moved to Gloucester and there received the homage of the citizens and neighbouring lords.'[75] The date cannot be right, as it allows her only a day or two at Bristol, not two months, but the substance is true enough. One of Matilda's earliest charters described how, as soon as she came to England, Miles hurried to Bristol and received her as his lady, recognizing that she was the just heir to the kingdom of England; he then accompanied her to Gloucester and did liege homage to her against all men.[76] William of Malmesbury confirms that she went from Bristol to Gloucester, and the *Gesta Stephani* emphasizes the service that Miles gave her:

> He was so unquestioning in his loyalty to King Henry's children as not only to have helped them, but likewise to have received the Countess of Anjou herself with her men and always behaved to her like a father in deed and counsel, until at length the king was taken and imprisoned ... and he made her queen of England.[77]

This is an exaggeration; she never was queen of England, but it helps to confirm that from 1139 until after the victory of her supporters at Lincoln on 2 February 1141 her chief residence was in Gloucester, not Bristol.

Why was this? does it imply that she preferred the fatherly advice of Miles to the counsels of her brother Robert? The evidence could be read that way, but there were other reasons which may have been more compelling. The poet and historian, Samuel Daniel, writing in the early seventeenth century, may have put his finger on the fundamental reason when he spoke of her keeping Easter in 1141 at Oxford because it was 'her own town'.[78] Gloucester was a royal castle and had been a favoured residence of the first Norman kings: William I and William II had between them spent Christmas there at least five times.[79] Henry I followed a different pattern in his travels; but though before the end of his reign Gloucester was placed in the charge of Miles as castellan, to hold under Earl Robert, it had never been granted in fee. Bristol, on the

75 Florence of Worcester (ed. Thorpe), ii, pp. 117–18.

76 *Regesta*, iii, no. 391.

77 *Gesta Stephani*, pp. 96–7.

78 Samuel Daniel, *The Collection of the History of England*, revised edn (London, 1634), p. 74.

79 Martin Biddle, 'Seasonal festivals and residence', p. 53.

other hand, the chief seat of Earl Robert, did not come directly into the king's hand until the reign of Henry II; in 1139 it was very much the earl's castle. Gloucester may well have seemed to Matilda to be more 'her own'; of the greatest royal residences of the Norman kings it was the only one, at that date, firmly held by her supporters. It may have been a safer refuge than Bristol, though no place was entirely safe. At all events, in Bristol, where her brother already enjoyed all that royal favour could give him, she would have been a poor relation; in Gloucester she was a king's daughter, impoverished, but still able to dispose of a little patronage. She quickly enfeoffed Miles with the castle of St Briavel and the whole Forest of Dean;[80] later, when her power was greater, she made him earl of Hereford. Miles was to boast to the Gloucester chronicler that he alone had supplied her with provisions, and that she 'had received nothing for a single day except by his own munificence and forethought',[81] but whatever the extent of his provision, he was certainly well rewarded. The benefits were mutual; she for her part had good cause to be grateful. His service was invaluable; he was one of the ablest of her commanders until he met his death in a hunting accident at Christmas 1143.

Among her other first supporters, Brian fitz Count stands out as a man of strong moral principles. As lord of Abergavenny he may have seemed to have a material advantage in siding with Robert of Gloucester, the most powerful of the marcher lords in south Wales. His disinterestedness, however, was shown when he granted Abergavenny to Miles of Gloucester, to be held in return for the service of three knights, whom he used to defend his castle of Wallingford in the Thames valley.[82] By holding out there for the empress he risked all his lands, which were periodically ravaged by Stephen's men. He is unique among Matilda's lay supporters in having left a written justification for his actions in a letter to Henry of Blois, and having also sent a manifesto (now lost) to Gilbert Foliot, abbot of Gloucester. The learned Gilbert responded with a long and detailed summing-up of the arguments that might be used in her favour. The letters exchanged between Brian and Bishop Henry, probably in 1142–3, survive in the fourteenth-century letter book of Richard of Bury, a compilation containing many model as well as real letters.[83] Their authenticity has sometimes been questioned but, as Giles Constable has argued in the most recent summing-up of the evidence, if they were to some extent exercises in Latin

---

80 *Regesta*, iii, no. 391.

81 Florence of Worcester (ed. Thorpe), ii. 132–3; this part of the continuation was probably written at Gloucester.

82 *Regesta*, iii, no. 394.

83 Printed by H. W. C. Davis, 'Henry of Blois and Brian fitz Count', *EHR*, 25 (1910), pp. 297–303.

composition they 'show a remarkable sense of history' and must have been based on genuine letters.[84]

The details of the exchange between Brian and Henry of Blois relate to the circumstances of 1142–3, which will be considered later. Brian's letter shows his high regard for oaths, his wish to justify the oaths he had taken, and his motives for changing from his initial support of Stephen. It makes clear that, even if the losses he sustained on Matilda's behalf did not prove his disinterestedness, acting justly was of paramount importance to him. Gilbert Foliot's reasoned reassurance tells the same story; it is a careful statement of the justice of Matilda's cause, drawn up in response to a request from Brian for comment on his manifesto.[85] He begins by congratulating Brian on the manifesto he had composed out of devotion and loyalty to King Henry, his benefactor, and Henry's daughter and heir, and expresses wonder that a man who had never studied letters should have been able to compose it, and make a not unworthy showing in the field of letters. Then he proceeds to develop the more detailed and learned defence for which Brian had asked. Brian had proposed that everything that had belonged to King Henry was by right (*iure*) owed to his daughter begotten in lawful matrimony. Gilbert was prepared to show that this was so by divine, natural and human law. The evidence from divine law was to be found in the last chapter of the book of Numbers, where it was shown that daughters had a right to succeed if there were no sons: 'It seemed to some that because of the weakness of their sex they should not be allowed to enter into the inheritance of their father. But the Lord, when asked, promulgated a law, that everything their father possessed should pass to the daughters of Zelophehad. They might go where they wished.' This passage, he added, was one that Robert earl of Gloucester was fond of citing. He did not mention the somewhat less appropriate continuation of the citation; the injunction that the daughters were not to marry outside their tribe. We cannot know whether Robert of Gloucester had ever read the whole passage and knew this limitation, nor how it might have been twisted for or against Matilda's claims.[86] She had married into the house of Anjou, but she had also married a

---

84 Giles Constable, 'Forged letters in the Middle Ages', *Fälschungen im Mittelalter*, *MGH Schriften*, 1988, v, pp. 31–2. To my mind the style of Brian's letter is somewhat too rough to be a model of composition, and the copy is unlikely to be far removed from the original either in language or in substance. What writer of a literary exercise would have thought of replying to the bishop's injunction to remember Lot's wife and not look back, 'As for Lot and his wife, I never saw them nor knew them or their city, nor were we alive at the same time'?

85 *Letters of Gilbert Foliot*, pp. 60–6.

86 On this point my interpretation is different from that of David Crouch, 'Robert of Gloucester and the daughters of Zelophehad', *Journal of Medieval History*, 11 (1985), pp. 227–43.

kinsman so close that papal dispensation had been necessary for the marriage to be valid. The essential point was that justification for female inheritance could be found in a carefully selected passage from Scripture; that was enough for Gilbert, and probably for Robert also.

As for natural law, in man no less than in animals there is a closer love for a daughter than for a nephew. Human law consists of civil law and the law of nations, the one peculiar to a single city, the other to all peoples.[87] In neither may a father disinherit his child except for special reasons, such as striking him, plotting his death, or showing gross ingratitude for benefits. Matilda had been guilty of none of these. 'We have learned', he continues, in a graceful tribute to the empress,

> that in accordance with her father's wishes she crossed the sea, passed over mountains, penetrated into unknown regions, married there at her father's command, and remained there carrying out the duties of imperial rule virtuously and piously until, after her husband's death, not through any desperate need or feminine levity but in response to a summons from her father, she returned to him. And though she had attained such high rank that, it is reported, she had the title and status of queen of the Romans, she was in no way puffed up with pride, but meekly submitted in all things to her father's will and on his advice took a second husband, a man described to us as brave and resolute, lord of the Angevins, Manceaux and men of Tours, and now also conqueror of the Normans. In all this you will not find any cause why she should have been disinherited.

He then added the further argument that she had been assured of her inheritance in both England and Normandy by the oaths of all the bishops and leading men of the realm. Gilbert ended by describing the plea he had heard in the Lateran Council at Rome, and told how Arnulf of Lisieux had attacked the legitimacy of the empress on the grounds that her mother had been a nun. To this his own reply was that the marriage of her parents had been conducted openly by Archbishop Anselm himself – a man of such sanctity that miracles were being reported after his death.

Seen retrospectively, Arnulf had scored a quick point by an ingenious piece of legal casuistry. Murmurs against the marriage had not been heard before this time; shortly afterwards Hermann of Tournai suggested that the misfortunes of Henry's offspring were divine punishment for a marriage that, though lawful, lacked divine sanction.[88] Yet the

87 Gilbert had some knowledge of Roman law, and the division he made between natural law, civil law and the law of nations was derived from the *Institutes* and the *Digest*. See Morey and Brooke, *Gilbert Foliot and his Letters*, pp. 63–4; *Letters of Gilbert Foliot*, p. 61 n. 2, p. 62 n. 5.
88 See above, p. 40.

argument was never more than special pleading; it is quite wrong to describe the case as an example of bastardy proceedings,[89] and the later actions and pronouncements of Arnulf of Lisieux showed quite clearly that he did not even convince himself. Gilbert's letter is important for the information it gives of how Matilda's case appeared to her various supporters, amongst whom were both semi-literate laymen and sophisticated ecclesiastics. It rested on inheritance rights; rights which were central in the thinking of men concerned with their own property and its division in their own families. In particular the inheritance rights of women mattered to them in deciding where their allegiance ought to lie. Questions such as designation or 'election' were not at this time so important; they were, indeed, comprehended in Henry's insistence on the oaths to his daughter and the complaisance of the bishops and earls who accepted her and swore allegiance. Gilbert thought it necessary only to demonstrate that she had never given him grounds for changing his mind, or disinheriting her. Laymen at least were less concerned with the rights to which most importance was attached in the highest ecclesiastical courts – the rights conferred by coronation and unction. In the long run it was the fact of Stephen's coronation that saved his throne up to the end of his life in spite of all the mistakes he made. But in the years following 1139 the problems that perplexed men of conscience, uncertain where their duties lay, were those that Gilbert discussed at length. It must be remembered that the norms of conduct that held society together were of some importance alongside short-term material interests in influencing those who changed sides once or more in the following years. Few were as high-minded as Brian fitz Count, who was particularly indebted to King Henry and had no heirs to whom he might have wished to bequeath an inheritance; but few were utterly indifferent to social pressures.

89 This suggestion was made by Frank Barlow, *The English Church 1066–1154* (London and New York, 1979), pp. 169–71.

5
Lady of the English

Almost a Queen

If Matilda had indeed been led to believe that when she arrived in England the country would rise in support of her claims, she was soon disappointed. Stephen too was deceived in his hope that by allowing her to join her brother at Bristol he would be able to concentrate his attack on one district and win an easy victory. For more than fifteen months the opposing forces fought a war of sieges and attrition, with no more than local gains for either side. Stephen had the advantage of greater resources in men and money. The wealth amassed by King Henry was depleted but not exhausted; he could afford to hire troops and had a strong army of Flemish mercenaries. His wife enjoyed control of the Boulogne inheritance and, thanks to her ships, could maintain contact with Flanders. He still controlled most of England apart from the Welsh marches and some of the West Country. So he was able to mount major attacks on rebel strongholds and, even when these could not be captured, his quick movements of troops across the country could contain local rebellions and prevent any general uprising, as the empress was to learn to her cost.

Nevertheless her supporters were too numerous and belligerent to be crushed. Robert of Gloucester, Miles of Gloucester and Brian fitz Count were a sufficiently powerful coalition to keep Stephen at bay. The king was never able to gain a foothold in Earl Robert's marcher principality. The earl's vassals remained loyal to their lord and helped him to make some advances. He had too a contingent of Flemish mercenaries and a small group of Angevins who had landed with the empress; but he knew he could never risk his slender resources in a major battle and had to confine himself to attacks on individual castles. William of Malmesbury observed that in the closing months of 1139, 'the whole district around Gloucester as far as the depth of Wales, partly under compulsion and partly from goodwill, gradually went over to the lady empress.'[1] Miles of Gloucester's early capture of Hereford further strengthened Matilda's grip on the Welsh marches; his son-in-law, Humphrey de Bohun, successfully held Trowbridge. Both Miles and Robert knew how to find allies among the warring princes in Wales.

An initial success was won in Cornwall, where Matilda's brother, Reginald of Dunstanville, succeeded in gaining a foothold he never completely lost. With the support of William, the son of Richard fitz Turold, a powerful subtenant whose daughter he married, he gained entry to several of the royal castles, and was rewarded with a grant of the earldom of Cornwall. Chroniclers disagree on events, particularly on the granting of the earldom.[2] The author of the Gesta Stephani alleged that William fitz Ralph 'committed the whole earldom of Cornwall to him', but this cannot possibly mean more than that he provided the territorial base that enabled Reginald to establish himself, albeit precariously, in the earldom. William of Malmesbury, only a little more plausibly, claimed that Robert earl of Gloucester 'made his brother Reginald earl of Cornwall.'[3] This has led some historians to speculate on why Robert 'usurped his sister Matilda's rights',[4] but the alleged usurpation rests only on the word of Malmesbury, whose wish to exalt his hero led him to attribute to him a controlling voice in grants which, though he may have contributed the means to make them possible, must have been authorized by the empress. Stephen fought back vigorously, recovered some lost ground and left his own nominee, Alan, count of Brittany and earl of Richmond, as earl of Cornwall. Reginald held on tenaciously against all odds. He was excommunicated by the bishop of Exeter for destroying the tower of St Stephen's church in Launceston during the fighting, and his wife (according to the Gesta Stephani) went mad; but he succeeded at least in retaining one castle and continued to keep the Angevin cause alive in a small corner of the county.[5]

Some other dissidents came to Matilda's court. William fitz Alan, who had escaped from the siege of Shrewsbury, joined her forces. The bishop of Ely took refuge with her, until King Stephen found an

1 Malmesbury, HN, p. 36.
2 Gesta Stephani, pp. 100-3.
3 Malmesbury, HN, p. 42.
4 K. Schnith, Journal of Medieval History, 2 (1976), p. 144; Davis, King Stephen, p. 136.
5 Gesta Stephani, p. 103; The Cartulary of Launceston Priory, ed. P. L. Hull, Devon and Cornwall Record Society, new ser. 30 (1987), p. xi. Either in 1140 or 1146 he made reparation to Launceston Priory with a grant out of the farm of 'Dunheved' castle (ibid., pp. 10-11, no. 12).

ingenious way of involving him in litigation which compelled him to go to Rome in person.[6]

She had one bastion in the Thames valley, where Brian fitz Count held the impregnable castle of Wallingford, supported by vassals who were throughout the years of war as unshakably loyal to him as he himself was to his lady. Besieged on several occasions, the castle never fell to Stephen's forces. Such conduct was exceptional; as the rivals manoeuvred for position there were many who hesitated between them. William of Malmesbury aptly summed up the situation in 1140:

> The whole year was troubled by the brutalities of war. There were many castles all over England, each defending its own district, or, to be more truthful, plundering it. The war, indeed, was one of sieges. Some of the castellans wavered in their allegiance, hesitating which side to support, and sometimes working entirely for their own profit.[7]

Some of them kept the balance so delicately that even their contemporaries were uncertain which side, if any, they supported at a particular time. Henry I's able marshal, John fitz Gilbert, who held Marlborough castle, at first followed Stephen; but John of Worcester thought he still backed the king at a time when the *Gesta Stephani* wrote of him as a supporter of the empress.[8] Once he had changed sides he remained as loyal to Matilda as he had been to her father. Others waited longer before committing themselves. In East Anglia Hugh Bigod revolted and held his castles of Bungay, Framlingham, Thetford and Walton against the king, though without as yet openly declaring for the empress.[9] The mercenary captains were the least reliable. Robert fitz Hubert, a Fleming who 'feared neither God nor man', double-crossed his master, Robert of Gloucester, after capturing the castle of Devizes, and tried to hold it for himself. He was outwitted by John fitz Gilbert and met an ignominious end, but the castle itself was for a time recovered by Stephen's men.[10]

We have very little information about Matilda's activities during this year of stalemate and growing anarchy.[11] No charters issued by her

6 Davis, *King Stephen*, pp. 77–8.

7 Malmesbury, *HN*, p. 40.

8 John of Worcester, p. 62; *Gesta Stephani*, p. 105.

9 *Waverley Annals*, in *Annales Monastici* (RS), ii, p. 228; R. A. Brown, *Castles from the Air* (Cambridge, 1989), p. 43.

10 John of Worcester, pp. 61–2; Malmesbury, *HN*, pp. 43–4; *Gesta Stephani* pp. 104–7.

11 Cf. H. W. C. Davis, 'Some documents of the Anarchy', *Essays in History presented to Reginald Lane Poole* (Oxford, 1927), pp. 168–89, esp. p. 179; Kenji Yoshitake, 'The arrest of the bishops in 1139 and its consequences', *Journal of Medieval History*, 14 (1988), pp. 107, 111 n. 29.

survive from the period, although there is evidence that she made some grants, including that of the castle of St Briavel and the Forest of Dean to Miles of Gloucester. Her confirmation of a grant of Kingswood in Gloucestershire to Tintern Abbey, made by William de Berkeley, may belong to 1139.[12] She may have made some small grants of land in Cornwall in the following year; a lost charter to her chamberlain, Drogo 'of Polwheile', is said, on somewhat dubious evidence, to date from 1140.[13] The patronage she could control was limited to royal demesne in the territory held by her supporters. She was not yet strong enough to buy support with grants that would have amounted to no more than a licence to conquer, or to be approached by religious houses wishing for general charters of confirmation.[14] At best she might have made anticipatory promises, as she did later. Both she and Stephen were obliged by the uncertainties of the time to keep most of their garrisons on a permanent war footing, and if the laments of the chroniclers carry any weight they lived partly by plundering the country round about. It cannot be assumed that either her knights or her household officers were rewarded with small grants of land in the vicinity of a castle, as might have been expected later; and such rewards might in any case have been life grants made without charters.

As the months passed it began to seem increasingly unlikely that the succession question would ever be settled by force of arms. Matilda felt strong enough to be prepared to negotiate and see if a satisfactory solution could be found to put an end to the miseries of the protracted civil war. Proposals for negotiation were put forward twice by the papal legate, Henry, bishop of Winchester. He had played a major part in securing the throne for Stephen, but however strong his family and personal loyalties and however lofty his personal ambitions, he was a Cluniac monk with a genuine belief in the importance of church reform. His motives, like those of many others in this time of conflicting loyalties, are not easy to interpret. Undoubtedly he believed that his duty, as the pope's representative in England, with a higher status even than his own archbishop, was to work for peace; but though his

---

12 *Regesta*, iii, nos 391, 419; but Yoshitake, 'The arrest of the bishops', n. 10 suggests February–March 1141 as a possible alternative date for both charters.

13 The charter was still extant in the early nineteenth century, when R. Polwhele, *The History of Cornwall* (Falmouth, 1803, 2 vols and supplement), ii, pp. 22–3, stated that it began, 'Drogoni de Polwheile camerario meo ... '. He added, 'this family document bears date 1140'; but since he described it as given after the battle of Lincoln, which he dated in 1140, no reliance can be placed on this date. Unfortunately the charter was shortly afterwards 'sent to a gentleman to peruse' and never returned (Tonkin's note in J. Polsue, *Lake's Parochial History of the County of Cornwall* (Truro, 1867–73, reprinted 1974), i, p. 209). See also *The Gentleman's Magazine*, 93 (Jan–June 1823), pp. 24–6, 98.

14 See below, pp. 127–34.

intentions were honourable and Christian, his political judgement was not of the highest order. He had become disenchanted with Stephen's treatment of the church, particularly after his attack on the bishops of Salisbury, Lincoln and Ely. He had been disappointed in Stephen's interference in church elections, partly no doubt on principle, partly because his own influence – which he believed to be exercised in the best interests of the church – was diminished. In addition he had been personally disappointed in his hopes of election to the archbishopric of Canterbury.[15] He was believed by some to have encouraged the empress to come to England, and he acted as one of her escorts when she was given a safe-conduct from Arundel to Bristol. All the same there is no reason to suppose that his efforts to find a settlement that would put an end to war and incipient anarchy were motivated by personal resentment.

At Whitsuntide, 1140, Henry succeeded in arranging a meeting between representatives of both parties. Earl Robert of Gloucester and 'the rest of her advisers' acted for the empress, and the legate himself, the archbishop of Canterbury and Queen Matilda for the king. The empress, according to William of Malmesbury, 'sent a message that she did not fear an ecclesiastical judgement', but the king's envoys 'were entirely opposed to this as long as they could hold the upper hand to their own advantage.' In September the legate tried again; he went to France to confer with the king of France, Count Theobald and many churchmen, and returned with proposals at the end of November. What these proposals were we do not know: 'the Empress and the earl agreed at once; the king put off a decision from day to day and finally made the whole plan of no avail.' The legate then abandoned the attempt, 'watching, like others, to see the outcome of events.'[16] Within a few weeks events unexpectedly turned in favour of the empress, because of the rebellion of Ranulf, earl of Chester, and his uterine brother, William of Roumare.

They were the sons of the great Lincolnshire heiress, Lucy, daughter or niece of Thorold of Lincoln, by her second and third husbands.[17] She was married first of all to Ivo of Taillebois, then to Roger fitz Gerold of Roumare, and finally, after Roger's death in about 1097, to Ranulf le Meschin, vicomte of Bayeux and lord of Carlisle, who became earl of Chester when his cousin, Richard of Avranches, went down with the

---

15 For a discussion of the 1138 Canterbury election see M. Chibnall, 'Innocent II and the Canterbury election of 1138', *Medievalia Christiana xie-xiiie siècles*, ed. C. E. Viola (Paris, 1989), pp. 237–46.

16 Malmesbury, *HN*, pp. 44–5.

17 For her career see *Complete Peerage*, vii, App. J, pp. 743–6.

White Ship. After Ranulf died in 1129, Lucy paid the king for the right not to marry again, and survived until at least 1138. Her sons considered that they had claims to extensive lands and offices in both England and Normandy. Ranulf le Meschin apparently surrendered some of his wife's lands and possibly his own lordship of Carlisle when he was given the county of Chester.[18] Rights of inheritance by either of the half-brothers in the face of more distant kinsmen or royal favourites were sufficiently complicated for both to feel at times cheated and to cherish a wish to recover everything that their mother Lucy could at any time have claimed.[19] William of Roumare had served Henry I as castellan of Neufmarché until he was disappointed by Henry's disposal of his mother's lands after his stepfather became earl of Chester. He had rebelled in support of William Clito in 1124, but had later made his peace with the king, recovered the greater part of his possessions, and served him faithfully for the remainder of his reign. His principal interests were initially in Normandy, in the Roumois and on the eastern frontier at Neufmarché; and it is not surprising that he accepted Stephen in 1135. He was one of the men whom Stephen left to act as justiciar and try to keep the peace at the end of his only visit to Normandy in 1137. The death or entry into religion of Countess Lucy in 1138 or 1139 probably brought him to England, where he and his half-brother actively pressed their claims on the king.

Ranulf of Chester, though married to Robert of Gloucester's daughter, still remained outwardly loyal to Stephen; his interests were so widespread that it was almost impossible for him to decide which of the contestants could best satisfy his claims, and perhaps he did not entirely trust either of them. He bitterly resented the grant of Carlisle to Henry, son of King David, and even tried to kidnap Henry on his way north from London to Carlisle. He still hoped that Stephen might be induced to restore the lordship to him, yet his Norman lands were threatened by the Angevins. Moreover he believed that he had a valid claim of some kind through his mother to the castle of Lincoln. William of Roumare also felt aggrieved by Stephen's grant of the earldom of Lincoln to William of Aubigny in 1139. This was an improvident move by the king, since he was indebted to Roumare for service in Normandy; and though he tried to compensate him with a grant of the earldom of

18 Orderic, vi, p. 332; H. A. Cronne, 'Ranulf de Gernons, earl of Chester, 1129–1153', *TRHS* 4th ser., 20 (1937), 105. Sally Thomson, *Women Religious* (Oxford, 1991), p. 160, suggests that Lucy may have become a nun at Stixwould.

19 For their interests see Cronne, 'Ranulf de Gernons', pp. 103–34; *Complete Peerage*, vii, pp. 667–70, 743–6; I. J. Sanders, *English Baronies* (Oxford, 1960), pp. 17–18; F. A. Cazel Jnr, 'Norman and Wessex charters of the Roumare family', *Medieval Miscellany*, pp. 77–88; Davis, *King Stephen*, pp. 129, 134–5, 161–5.

Cambridge the concession was unrealistic. Roumare had very extensive inherited lands in Lincolnshire, and nothing at all in Cambridgeshire. Perhaps if Stephen had been wise enough at the start to make d'Aubigny earl of Arundel and Roumare earl of Lincoln, as he did later, he might have avoided the rising that nearly cost him his throne.[20]

At the beginning of December 1140 Stephen made some concessions to the brothers. Either then or a year later he granted William of Roumare the title of earl of Lincoln, but, whatever the terms of the grants he made, they did not include the castle of Lincoln, which remained a bone of contention. Evidently he believed that the brothers were satisfied, and he went off to keep Christmas at Windsor, leaving the castle only lightly garrisoned. The disgruntled brothers were able to seize possession of it by a trick. No English chronicler explains how the castellan was caught off his guard; Orderic Vitalis, in distant Normandy, heard the story from followers of William of Roumare, a patron of Orderic's abbey of Saint-Evroult, whose household knights would have been on friendly terms with the monks. Orderic could never resist a good story, even if it had been embellished by jongleurs before it reached him, as this one probably had, and he told it in good faith.[21] According to him the two earls chose a time when the troops of the garrison were widely dispersed, and sent their wives to the castle under the pretext of a friendly visit to the wife of the castellan. When the earl of Chester arrived, unarmed and accompanied by only three men, ostensibly to escort them home, he aroused no suspicion; but as soon as his little party was inside the castle they seized all the weapons they could lay their hands on and drove out the guards. Meanwhile William of Roumare burst in with a force of armed knights, and took control of the castle and the whole city. There are elements of literary commonplace in this; but it is clear that Stephen's garrison was caught unawares. Perhaps too the earls did not expect Stephen to react as quickly as he did. The citizens of Lincoln, who favoured the king, at once sent news to Stephen, who hurried north with an army and laid siege to the castle.

The earls were not prepared to submit. Ranulf, who was 'both the younger and the more resourceful and daring', managed to escape with

20 The exact date of Stephen's grant of the earldom of Lincoln is uncertain; it must have been made either in an attempt at appeasement in December 1140, in which case William may have resented not receiving the castle of Lincoln, or to attempt to persuade him to return to allegiance after Stephen was released from captivity, and there is no clear evidence that he did return. As Davis, *King Stephen*, pp. 134–5, has argued, December 1140 is the most plausible date.

21 Orderic, vi, pp. 538–41, discussed by M. Chibnall, 'Orderic Vitalis on castles', *Studies in Medieval History presented to R. Allen Brown*, ed. Christopher Harper-Bill et al. (Woodbridge and Wolfeboro, 1989), pp. 54–6.

a few men and make for Chester, where he mustered his vassals and Welsh allies and sent to his father-in-law, Robert of Gloucester, promising fealty to the empress.[22] Robert joined him with his own troops and together they advanced to Lincoln. Stephen did not fear a pitched battle and, believing his own forces to be stronger, accepted the challenge. The result was his defeat and capture on 2 February 1141. The combined forces of the two earls, augmented by a considerable number of knights disinherited by Stephen, and supported by their formidable Welsh allies, proved too much for the army the king had considered adequate for the siege. He was taken as a prisoner to the empress at Gloucester and imprisoned in Bristol castle. At first he was allowed moderate freedom within his quarters; later, because he was suspected of trying to escape, he was fettered. Meanwhile his bewildered vassals and the churchmen of the realm debated what to do next.[23]

There were questions both of force and of right. Matilda needed to win the support of Stephen's vassals with their men if she was to control the kingdom and its resources. Her husband, Count Geoffrey, immediately struck a blow on her behalf by coming to Normandy and consulting the wavering magnates and the bishops on the best course to take. They first proposed offering the kingdom and the duchy to Stephen's older brother, Count Theobald, but Theobald renounced his claims in favour of Geoffrey, provided the king were set free and granted the possessions he had held in his uncle's lifetime.[24] These conditions were never met, but Geoffrey set about establishing his lordship. A number of castellans surrendered to him, and Robert earl of Leicester, though not renouncing his allegiance to Stephen, negotiated a truce with the Angevins for himself and his brother Waleran. So material interests gradually forced all those who valued their Norman patrimonies to think again about their allegiance. Geoffrey's slow conquest of Normandy was crucial in deciding the ultimate success of the Angevin party.

In England, meanwhile, resistance to the Angevins was kept alive by Stephen's wife, Queen Matilda, a woman as resolute and indomitable as the empress herself. The queen still had the resources of her honour of Boulogne; and the mercenary force of Flemings led by William of Ypres had withdrawn from the battle of Lincoln when it became clear that the

22 Orderic, vi, pp. 438–41.

23 For the battle of Lincoln see Orderic, vi, pp. 540–7; Henry of Huntingdon, pp. 268–74; Malmesbury, HN, p. 49; John of Hexham in SD, ii, pp. 307–8; John Beeler, Warfare in England 1066–1189 (Ithaca and New York, 1966), pp. 110–14. For Stephen's imprisonment, Florence of Worcester, ii, p. 129; Malmesbury HN, pp. 50, 66. Malmesbury says he was fettered by Earl Robert's orders, but the initiative may have come from Matilda.

24 Orderic, vi, pp. 546–51.

field was lost, and so lived to fight another day. Her cause was strong in Kent, Sussex and Essex, and the Londoners were traditionally on her side.[25] The king was held a close prisoner but that in itself did not justify the deposition of an anointed king, whatever the circumstances in which he had originally seized the crown. So the attitude of the church was important if the claim of the empress was to be justified.

The church at that time was under a dual leadership. Theobald, archbishop of Canterbury, a monk of Bec, was (like Anselm before him) a man of peace who appreciated the realities of political life, but was never prepared to compromise on principle. He must have known Matilda before his election, when he was prior of Bec and she had been a devoted patron of the abbey and a frequent visitor to its priory of Notre-Dame-du-Pré at Rouen.[26] But he would never allow any personal feelings to stand in the way of his duty as a churchman, and only when Stephen gave him permission to act as the times required did he give his voice cautiously in her support. In any case he was uncomfortably subordinate to his own suffragan, Henry of Winchester, the papal legate; and it was the legate who took the lead in what followed. He entered into negotiations with the empress, while also acknowledging that he owed allegiance to a higher authority; and at some date during the spring or summer he wrote to consult Pope Innocent II.[27] This reliance on papal sanction must be remembered if we are to understand Bishop Henry's double change of allegiance in the course of the year 1141.

With the capture of Stephen, Matilda moved into the most active years of her personal struggle for the succession. She was now called upon to take the lead in political and military decisions, to assess the character and reliability of the men who were sometimes urging her to different courses of action, and to act decisively without alienating those who supported her largely out of self-interest. As a woman she suffered from two disadvantages. One was the reluctance of many magnates, in spite of their oaths, to accept a woman ruler. It is noteworthy that during the negotiations in Normandy there had been no

25 Davis, *King Stephen*, pp. 54–5.

26 Chibnall, 'The Empress Matilda and Bec-Hellouin', pp. 41–3.

27 Malmesbury, *HN*, p. 62. The outlook and motivation of Henry of Blois in his capacity as papal legate may be compared and contrasted with those attributed to Pius XII in the Second World War by the British Minister to the Holy See, Sir d'Arcy Osborne: 'The Pope and his advisers do not consider and resolve a problem solely in the light of its temporary and obviously apparent elements. Their approach and survey are by habit and tradition unlimited in space and time ... They reckon in centuries and plan for eternity and this inevitably renders their policy inscrutable, confusing, and on occasion reprehensible to practical and time-conditioned minds.' Quoted by Owen Chadwick, *Britain and the Vatican during the Second World War* (Cambridge, 1986), pp. 315–16.

suggestion that she personally should hold the duchy; when Theobald of Blois declined to be considered it was taken for granted that Geoffrey should be the next choice. He at least could do homage in his wife's right. Homage was not the only stumbling block. The advice given by St Bernard to Queen Melisende of Jerusalem after the death of her husband Fulk at about this time was to 'show the man in the woman; order all things ... so that those who see you will judge your works to be those of a king rather than a queen.'[28] Matilda certainly tried to show the man in the woman; unfortunately the comments of hostile chroniclers make plain that what might in a man have passed for dignity, resolution and firm control were condemned in her as arrogance, obstinacy and anger. Her second difficulty was the virtual impossibility of leading knights in battle. We never hear of her donning a hauberk and riding as a knight among the knights, as Isabel of Conches is said to have done,[29] and even Isabel did not lead armies. During the Norman fighting Matilda once brought troops to help her husband at the siege of Le Sap, and she was in grave danger during the sieges of Winchester and Oxford; but she remained as far as possible in the background during battles, both from total inexperience in military leadership and because her capture would have meant the end of her cause. She could never hope to conduct the kind of dashing campaigns that her son Henry undertook with conspicuous success as soon as he was old enough to bear arms. These handicaps must be borne in mind in assessing her responsibility for failing to win the crown in 1141.

The first essential was to legitimize her position by securing the support of the legate. Bishop Henry was in a quandary; he was in no position to resist the triumphant forces of the Angevins, but in spite of his anger at his brother Stephen's treatment of the church he was reluctant to renounce him altogether. The author of the *Gesta Stephani*, writing later with knowledge of his double change of allegiance, suggested that he made a pact of peace and friendship with the Angevins only to win time in which to assess the strength of his opponents. This is probably no more than special pleading; Henry may have believed that the empress would prove more pliable to the wishes of reformers in the church, and he certainly wanted time to consult the pope on what he ought to do. He therefore agreed to meet the empress and her principal supporters.[30] The meeting took place at Wherwell, near Winchester, on 2 March, just a month after Stephen's defeat at Lincoln.

28 Bernard, *S. Bernardi Opera*, ed. J. Leclercq, C. H. Talbot, H. M. Rochais (8 vols in 9, Rome, 1957–77), viii, pp. 297–8 (ep. 354).

29 Orderic, vi, pp. 212–25.

30 *Gesta Stephani*, pp. 118–19; Malmesbury, *HN*, p. 51.

William of Malmesbury noted that it was a rainy and cloudy day, which he took to be an ominous sign. There the empress swore and gave security that she would consult him on all major business in England, particularly on the gift of bishoprics and abbeys, if he would receive her in holy church as his lady and always preserve his fealty to her.[31] Robert earl of Gloucester, Brian fitz Count, Miles of Gloucester and some others were with her. The legate then received her as 'Lady of England' and gave pledges that he would keep faith with her as long as she was true to her undertaking. Next day he received her ceremonially in his cathedral at Winchester. She walked in procession, supported by the legate on her right and her mother's former chancellor, Bernard, bishop of St Davids, on her left, and accompanied by the bishops of Lincoln, Hereford, Ely, Bath and Chichester, and a number of abbots, including Ingulf of Abingdon, Edward of Reading, Peter of Malmesbury, Gilbert of Gloucester and Roger of Tewkesbury.[32] Archbishop Theobald was not there; he came to her a few days later at Wilton, but put off swearing fealty until he had been to visit Stephen in his prison and obtained his consent to act as the difficulties of the time required. Easter was spent with her circle of loyal supporters at Oxford.

The legate's next step was to summon a church council to Winchester. William of Malmesbury, who was present, has left an eye-witness account of proceedings. The legate rested his case on the need for peace and for the freedom of the church, so justifying his initial support for Stephen and his present proposal to transfer allegiance to Matilda because of the king's failure to save the realm from civil war and disorder, and his oppression of the church. The ecclesiastics were persuaded, but the citizens of London, invited to attend because of the importance of the city, showed more reluctance and asked for time to consider their reply. A further obstacle was provided by the queen, who sent a letter denouncing the imprisonment of her husband and demanding his release. Although the council agreed to accept the empress as 'Lady of England and Normandy' and the treasure and royal crown were handed over to her, it must have been clear to the waverers that her cause hung in the balance. Two more months were needed to persuade the Londoners to receive her and allow her to be crowned at Westminster.[33]

How solid was the support given her in the hour of her triumph? The chroniclers spoke in sweeping terms of 'almost all England', but hard

31 Malmesbury, HN, pp. 50–1.
32 Davis, King Stephen, pp. 52–3 adds the name of Seffrid of Chichester to those given by William of Malmesbury.
33 Davis, King Stephen, pp. 53–5; Malmesbury HN, pp. 52–6.

evidence is scanty. The longest list of names was given a year or two later by Brian fitz Count, in a letter to Henry of Blois justifying his continued support of the empress.[34] 'You yourself,' he wrote, 'who are a bishop of holy church, ordered me to support the daughter of your uncle King Henry and assist her to recover her right, which had been taken from her by force', and he explained why he felt justified in seizing goods from men travelling to the fair at Winchester in order to feed his garrison:

> Be assured that neither I nor my men have done this for money or fee or land, either promised or given, but only because of your command and for my honour and that of my men. And I call the following to witness that what I say you commanded is true: Theobald, called archbishop of Canterbury, Bernard, bishop of St Davids, Robert, bishop of Hereford, Simon, bishop of Worcester, the bishop of Bath (whose name escapes me), Robert, bishop of Exeter, Seffrid, bishop of Chichester, Roger, bishop of Chester, Adelolf, bishop of Carlisle, Everard, bishop of Norwich, Robert, bishop of London, Hilary, dean of Christchurch, David, king of Scotland, Robert, earl of Gloucester, Miles of Gloucester, Ralph Paynel, Earl Ranulf of Chester, William Peverel of Nottingham, William de Roumare, Earl Hugh of Norfolk, Aubrey de Vere, Henry of Essex, Roger of Valognes, Gilbert fitz Gilbert, Geoffrey de Mandeville, Osbert Eightpence and all the Londoners, William of Pont de l'Arche and all the men of Winchester, Robert of Lincoln, Robert Arundel, Baldwin de Redvers, Roger de Nonant, Reginald the son of your uncle,[35] William de Mohun, William de Curcy, Walter de Chandos, Walter de Pinkeney, Elias Giffard, Baderon, Gilbert de Lacy, Robert de Euias, William de Beauchamp, Miles de Beauchamp, John de Bidun, Robert de Aubigny, William Peverel of Dover, William de Sai, William fitz Richard, Roger of Warwick, Geoffrey de Clinton, William fitz Alan. These are the men who heard.

Some concrete evidence of support is provided by the witness lists to her surviving charters, but even the longest include only a handful of bishops and earls.[36] Archbishop Theobald was with her for a few weeks in the summer, but he reserved his position and carried most of the church with him. Robert of Hereford's see was in the heart of the territory she controlled; Bernard of St Davids was an old friend, who, moreover, was cherishing an ambition to secure a pallium for his see and was willing to act independently of Canterbury. Alexander of Lincoln and Nigel of Ely were still smarting from the treatment they had received at Stephen's hands; Seffrid of Chichester made only a brief

34 H. W. C. Davis, *EHR*, 25 (1910), pp. 298–303.
35 Reginald of Dunstanville, earl of Cornwall.
36 *Regesta*, iii, *passim*.

appearance. She was able to secure one election, that of Robert de Sigillo to London, and she abetted her uncle King David in his unsuccessful attempt to intrude William Cumin into the see of Durham.[37] Lay witnesses to her charters include some of her household officers and the commanders of her forces. Robert de Courcy and Humphrey de Bohun, her stewards, had joined her in 1138 or 1139, and John fitz Gilbert, her marshal, followed a little later. William Pont de l'Arche, formerly Stephen's chamberlain, deserted to her early in 1141.[38] Mercenary leaders who sometimes witnessed included the Angevin, Robert fitz Hildebrand, who was playing for his own advantage; and others who appeared were household knights like William Defuble, and vassals disinherited by Stephen, including Ernulf de Hesdin and William fitz Alan.

The secular magnates most constantly with her were those who had been faithful from the time of her arrival: her brothers, the earls of Gloucester and Cornwall, Baldwin de Redvers, Miles of Gloucester, and Brian fitz Count. King David joined her for a few weeks in the summer; possibly his presence kept Ranulf of Chester (his rival in Cumbria) and William of Roumare away from court. They were still only lukewarm supporters; the military assistance they gave at Winchester was minimal. Their rebellion and seizure of Lincoln castle had led directly to her triumph and the capture of the king, yet for a time they hesitated; they may already have committed themselves against the king far more than they had originally intended when they asserted their rights in Lincoln.

David, king of Scots, was a man of honour, conscious of his duties both to his niece and to his country, and it was not always easy to reconcile the two. He was punctilious in never violating the oath he had taken to Matilda at her father's behest, and was careful never to swear fealty to Stephen, though he allowed his son Henry to do so. As king of Scots he had a keen eye to Scottish interests in the north of England. He came south probably in the hope of seeing his niece crowned, and was with her for a short time at Oxford, where he appears as a witness to a handful of her charters. Apart from a charter granted on 25 July creating Miles of Gloucester earl of Hereford, all were concerned with small grants to churches in which he may have had an interest, as he undoubtedly did in Tiron.[39] He once acted with Earl Robert of Gloucester as guarantor (*obses*) of a grant made by the empress.[40] Known only from a brief cartulary notice, it recognizes the right of

37 See below, pp. 137–9.
38 See *Regesta*, iii, pp. xxix–xxxii for her officers and household.
39 *Regesta*, iii, no. 393 for Miles of Gloucester; nos 328, 377, 629, 899 for Fontevraud, Haughmond, Osney and Tiron.
40 *Regesta*, iii, no. 429.

Gilbert de Lacy to disputed lands, some of which were in Yorkshire. David had an interest in securing these for a supporter of his cause, and was in a position to give an effective guarantee. To some extent his power in northern England, where he continued to hold Cumbria in spite of his defeat at the battle of the Standard, helped to provide at least a modicum of order in a troubled region: William of Newburgh later contrasted conditions in the lands under his control favourably with those prevailing further south.[41] But his influence was not always in Matilda's best interests; William Cumin was his candidate for the see of Durham, and he must be held more than a little responsible for the troubles that followed the disputed election there. He was never effective as a leader in battle, and outside his own sphere of interest he was not able to give her very much help at this time, though his presence provided moral support and added to the dignity of her court.

The charters of the empress that contain the longest witness lists are those granting earldoms and shrievalties: to Miles of Gloucester, Aubrey de Vere, Geoffrey de Mandeville, and William de Beauchamp.[42] Matilda never issued any general charter of liberties, such as Stephen's Oxford charter of March 1136, which shows the strength of support he had been able to muster in the first weeks of the reign. Her court, in the brief period as she moved from Winchester towards London and back to Oxford and Winchester, was at best a small affair. The charters issued at the time of her most desperate bid for support in July 1141, which show the longest lists of witnesses, are evidence less of a court than of an army on the march. Earldoms were granted either to reward loyal service or to win over waverers. The grant of the earldom of Devon to Baldwin de Redvers, like that of Hereford to Miles of Gloucester and Cornwall to Reginald of Dunstanville, was no more than a recognition of deserts; and all these were counties where the empress had some control and hoped to extend it. At first sight it seems surprising that Brian fitz Count never received such an honour. Possibly he did not want it. He had no heirs to inherit and seems to have been without personal ambition. Several of Matilda's charters record her consent to gifts which he had made. King Henry had given him the lordship of Abergavenny, but at the request of Brian himself and of his wife she granted the castle and honour of Abergavenny to Miles of Gloucester in 1141 or 1142, to be held of them by the service of three knights.[43] Lands were given to Reading Abbey at Brian's request.[44] He was

41 William of Newburgh, i, 69–70.
42 *Regesta*, iii, nos 274, 275, 634, 68.
43 *Regesta*, iii, no. 394.
44 *Regesta*, iii, no. 703.

apparently satisfied with his office as constable of Wallingford; and recognizing the strategic importance of his castle he concentrated his resources on holding it.

Matilda had not been proclaimed queen; her title of 'Lady of the English' or 'Lady of England' was an ambiguous one, accepted in unprecedented circumstances. It may have been intended as a recognition of her right to the throne: an intermediate stage before Stephen could be persuaded to renounce his title and she could be crowned queen.[45] Leopold Delisle thought that she favoured the title because she regarded herself as regent for her son;[46] and it is true that she ceased to use it after 1148, when she left England and handed over the initiative in the struggle to young Henry Plantagenêt. But that does not prove her to have been ready for this renunciation in April 1141, when she began to make preparations for a crown-wearing in London and possibly (though the evidence for this is slight and very dubious) had a seal prepared with a new legend describing her as queen.[47] Until circumstances forced her to think again, she probably considered that the title marked a preliminary step to the throne.

In spite of her acceptance by the legate and a small group of magnates and bishops as Lady of the English, her progress towards London was slow. Some castles still held out (she had to avoid Windsor and go round by St Albans), and the Londoners, threatened by the forces of the queen under William of Ypres, who were devastating the lands on the south bank of the Thames, hesitated to offer her a welcome.[48] It was essential for her to secure the support of Geoffrey de Mandeville, castellan of the Tower. Geoffrey's career had been a long hard struggle to recover the lands and offices forfeited by his father, who in 1101 had failed in his duties as castellan when he allowed Ranulf Flambard to escape from the Tower of London. The way of the young man's advancement lay, as with many other aspirants to wealth and favour during Henry I's reign, through service in the royal household troops.

---

45 Round, *Geoffrey de Mandeville*, pp. 70–5; A. L. Poole, *From Domesday Book to Magna Carta 1087–1216* (Oxford, 1951), p. 3 and n. 1. Round points out that Queen Adeliza was called by the same title before she was crowned queen as the wife of Henry I.

46 Delisle, *Introduction, Recueil des Actes d'Henri II*, p. 171.

47 The evidence for a second seal is critically examined by J. C. Holt, review of *Regesta*, iii and iv, in *Economic History Review*, 2nd ser., 24 (1971), pp. 481–3. He concludes that there was no clear evidence that the seal which the two antiquaries claimed to have seen was genuine or had not been tampered with, and commented, 'If Matilda anticipated her coronation and changed her seal, as Round suggests, it was apparently unknown or unimportant to her Chancellor or to her greatest secular supporter, Earl Robert of Gloucester.'

48 Christopher Brooke et al., *London 800–1216: The Shaping of a City* (London, 1975), pp. 36–8.

He served well, received some of the forfeited estates and became close enough to the king's counsels to begin to witness charters before Henry died.[49] It had been a hard struggle; the chronicle of Walden Abbey, which he founded, speaks of his gratitude to William, the first prior of Walden, who had previously been prior of Bradwell, for the hospitality shown him when he had been a poor knight following the king's court.[50] Ambition to recover all and more than all his father had lost drove him on, combined with a determination not to go on his travels again. Up to 1141 he served Stephen well, and he was rewarded with the earldom of Essex and a restoration of the custody of the Tower. He wished at all costs to come out on the winning side. This has been somewhat dubiously described as service to the Crown;[51] though a concept of the Crown can certainly be found in the more sophisticated assumptions of clerical theorists at this date, the baronage still thought rather in terms of personal loyalty and personal advantage. The empress seemed, in the summer of 1141, to be gaining ground, and she needed Geoffrey's support. Because of his strength in London and Essex, where the lands of the honour of Boulogne were extensive, he alone could provide a counterpoise to the influence of the queen; without him she could not hope to be crowned at Westminster or to hold London.

By midsummer Matilda had reached Westminster and was negotiating with the Londoners for entry into the city. Plans were being made there, possibly for coronation and unction, or at least for a ceremonial crown-wearing followed by a triumphal procession into London. It was here that Geoffrey swore fealty to her and she issued a charter for him. In it she granted the earldom of Essex to him and his heirs, together with the custody of the Tower and another castle in London, the sheriffdom and justiciarship of Essex, and other lands and rights.[52] The grants were made without reference to Stephen's previous grants, which she did not recognize, but they equalled and surpassed those made by Stephen. The charter itself was hastily drawn; written by a former royal scribe, it departs in many ways from the phraseology one would expect from an experienced chancery scribe and the seal, lost and known only from a very rough sketch, is puzzling. The legend was said by two antiquaries to be MATILDIS IMPERATRIX ROM. ET REGINA ANGLIAE, but the seated, crowned figure is the same as that on her usual seal as queen of the Romans, and in the charter itself Matilda

49 C. Warren Hollister, 'The misfortunes of the Mandevilles', *Monarchy, Magnates and Institutions*, pp. 117–28.

50 British Library, MS Arundel 29, p. 79.

51 J. O. Prestwich, 'The treason of Geoffrey de Mandeville', *EHR*, 103 (1988), p. 300.

52 *Regesta*, iii, no. 274; Stephen's charter is ibid. no. 273.

calls herself simply 'daughter of King Henry and Lady of the English', not queen. It is just conceivable that a new seal had been hastily cast in anticipation of coronation, and that it was affixed to this one charter, issued at Westminster on what should have been the eve of the coronation. But it may be a forgery, or a battered seal with the legend imaginatively reconstructed.[53] We cannot be sure that Matilda ever called herself queen of England, though some chroniclers gave her the title.

During the few weeks when the crown was almost within her grasp she still faced formidable obstacles, and she made mistakes which helped to lose the support of waverers. In making church appointments she began prudently; her candidate for the see of London was Robert de Sigillo, a man of good character, acceptable to the archbishop, and a former household officer. But her actions in the Durham election were ultimately disastrous; she supported William Cumin, whom her uncle David was attempting to intrude into the see of Durham against the wishes of the Durham monks and the legate himself, who refused to accept such an obviously uncanonical election.[54] This may have been the moment when he appealed to Pope Innocent II for guidance; certainly the intrusion helped him to justify himself later when he returned to Stephen. It was one of the errors of judgement that tipped the scales against her; the other was her alienation of the Londoners by demanding money from them when they asked for their financial burdens to be reduced. The *Gesta Stephani* may have exaggerated the haughtiness and anger with which she was said to have received their request; but her own experience should have taught her to go softly.[55] She had travelled with her first husband through northern Italy, and had seen the good effects of the concessions that he was making to the wealthy and powerful Italian cities to win their support. She would have been wise to follow his example, especially if the news of the concessions she had already made to Geoffrey de Mandeville had reached them, for they deeply resented the domination of their city by the castles of feudal magnates.[56] The result of her mismanagement of the situation was that the citizens, threatened as they were by the armies loyal to Stephen and with nothing to hope for from the empress, decided to throw in their lot with the queen. As preparations for a ceremonial entry into the city were being made at Westminster on 24 June, they rang their bells as a

53 J. H. Round, *Geoffrey de Mandeville*, p. 300, argued that it was impossible to misread the legend, but see above, n. 47.
54 M. Chibnall, 'The Empress Matilda and church reform', *TRHS* 5th ser., 38 (1988), pp. 114–17; and see below, pp. 137–9.
55 *Gesta Stephani*, pp. 120–3.
56 Chibnall, *Anglo-Norman England*, pp. 153–7.

call to arms and swarmed out of the gates.[57] The empress and her supporters, forewarned just in time, retreated hastily to Oxford, leaving the Londoners to plunder their lodgings and eat the remains of the banquet. William of Malmesbury loyally insisted that they withdrew in good order; the *Gesta Stephani* described the retreat in colourful language as a rout.[58]

Declining Fortunes

In Oxford Matilda mustered her principal adherents and their household troops and vassals. A month of preparation and bidding for support followed a setback that had been severe, but was not yet necessarily fatal. In Normandy the Angevins were strongly established. Though Geoffrey had not yet conquered across the Seine and neither the archbishop of Rouen nor the king of France recognized him, he was so deeply entrenched that the magnates whose greatest estates lay in Normandy were being pulled by self-interest away from Stephen.[59] The attitude of William of Roumare during these months is enigmatic; after the battle of Lincoln he never appeared with the empress, and there is no record of him doing homage to her. He may have gone to Normandy for a time; he apparently succeeded in not embroiling himself any further with Stephen without endangering his Roumare inheritance, while he weighed up the prospects of ultimate Angevin victory. By 1144 he had no doubts, and after a pilgrimage to Compostela he openly appeared in the Angevin camp in England.[60] His half-brother, Ranulf earl of Chester, was more in the public eye, and his hesitation is more clearly documented. By September 1141 his support for the empress was wavering, and apparently nothing prevented him from veering to the queen's side except the refusal of her army to trust him.[61] His interests pulled both ways: no concessions the empress had the power to give could have held him more firmly, yet he knew that he had much to lose by returning to Stephen. The magnates who most clearly saw the

57 There is confirmation for the date 24 June, tentatively accepted by Round, *Geoffrey de Mandeville*, pp. 117–18, in an unpublished version of the Merton Annals, Corpus Christi College, Cambridge, MS 59, f. 163v; 'a London' expulsa est in die Sancti Johannis Baptiste.' I owe this reference to Dr Martin Brett.

58 Malmesbury, *HN*, pp. 56–7; *Gesta Stephani*, pp. 122–7; see also Florence of Worcester, ii, p. 132 (the Gloucester continuation).

59 Haskins, *Norman Institutions*, pp. 128–30.

60 *The Charters of the Anglo-Norman Earls of Chester c. 1071–1233*, ed. Geoffrey Barraclough (Record Soc. of Lancs. and Cheshire 126, 1988), no. 70, note.

61 Davis, *King Stephen*, p. 59 n. 25 and App. VII.

writing on the wall in Normandy were Waleran of Meulan and his brother Robert, the powerful and canny earl of Leicester. Robert was the first to visit Normandy, and by May he had made his peace with Count Geoffrey, but, having less to lose on that side of the Channel, he was content to leave Waleran to look after his interests in Normandy while he himself supported Stephen in England. He made a truce with Geoffrey which included Waleran.[62] Waleran held out for a few months longer; he was not with the empress in July, but by September at the latest he had recognized that he had no choice but to submit to her.

During the month of July Matilda was busy rallying her forces. King David remained with her, and she was in close communication with her husband in Normandy. The names of a few Angevin and Manceaux lords appear in her charters at this time (and at no other) during the war in England. Juhel de Mayenne, who had first promised support in 1135 when she entrusted the castles of Ambrières, Gorron and Châtillon-sur-Colmont to him, Alexander de Bohun, Guy of Sablé and Pagan of Clairvaux appear as witnesses and *obsides* at Oxford in July. Their presence is an indication of the discussions that must have been taking place on the future role of Count Geoffrey. Given his triumphs in Normandy, his assent to any grant involving lands on both sides of the Channel was clearly necessary; and it is hard to believe that there was no discussion about whether he should be associated with his wife in grants in England. When Pagan and Guy witnessed Matilda's charters confirming grants to Fontevraud and Tiron, and her charter creating Miles of Gloucester earl of Hereford they may have acted as Geoffrey's representatives. Also in the treaties with Geoffrey de Mandeville and Aubrey de Vere they acted as *obsides*, and Count Geoffrey's assent is regularly invoked in these documents.[63]

The exact sequence of events in July 1141 is uncertain, but one Oxford charter dated 25 July, creating Miles of Gloucester earl of Hereford, provides a focal point which makes it possible to establish a rough chronology.[64] During the early part of the month both the queen and the empress appealed for support, with some success on both sides. The legate, Henry of Winchester, was already wavering, and now a further cause for disagreement arose; he pressed the empress to give the counties of Boulogne and Mortain to Stephen's son Eustace while his father was held a prisoner and she resolutely refused his request. She

62 Crouch, *Beaumont Twins*, p. 50.

63 Pagan of Clairvaux and Guy de Sablé witnessed *Regesta*, iii, nos 328 and 899 in July 1141, and were also *obsides* with Juhel de Mayenne in the *conventiones* with de Mandeville and de Vere, nos 275 and 634; Pagan of Clairvaux also witnessed no. 393 on 25 July 1141, with Alexander de Bohun.

64 *Regesta*, iii, no. 393.

had, indeed, already promised them to others. The result was that he kept away from her court and had a meeting with the queen. From this time he was seriously contemplating a return to Stephen's party, but at first merely withdrew to Winchester without openly breaking with the empress. Robert of Gloucester's suspicions were aroused, and after visiting Winchester without achieving anything he returned to his sister at Oxford. They resolved to advance to Winchester with as large a force as could be mustered.[65] It was at Oxford, with much of her army encamped around her, that the empress granted a number of important privileges.

One new recruit to her cause was William de Beauchamp. His family had held the sheriffdom and castle of Worcester long enough to regard their position as hereditary, and he bitterly resented Stephen's grant of the earldom of Worcester to Waleran of Meulan, and his insistence that William become Waleran's vassal.[66] Matilda refused to concede that the grant of the earldom had ever been valid; when William came to her at Oxford she received him as her liege man and restored him to the position he considered his by right. The strength of his feelings and his bitterness towards Waleran break through the formal language of the charter. She had 'given and restored' to him and his heirs, to hold by hereditary right of her and her heirs, Worcester with its castle and the sheriffdom and forest rights, to hold at the same farm as his father had paid. In return he had become her liege man against all men and specifically against Waleran, count of Meulan, who was never to be suffered to make fine with her or to oust William without his permission.[67] Waleran still held off, but his capitulation followed within a few weeks. She never recognized that he had any right to the earldom of Worcester, and his position was too weak for him to attempt to bargain with her.

Other earldoms were conferred at this time. Miles of Gloucester was rewarded for his service with the earldom of Hereford. Baldwin de Redvers had already been made earl of Devon. According to the *Gesta Stephani* Matilda now made William de Mohun earl of Dorset.[68] Geoffrey de Mandeville was already earl of Essex, but he successfully urged the claims of his brother-in-law, Aubrey de Vere, to an earldom, and obtained at the same time a document from his patroness setting out in much greater detail than in her former hastily drafted charter exactly what he himself and some of his vassals were to receive.

---

65 Malmesbury, *HN*, pp. 57–8; *Gesta Stephani*, pp. 126–7.
66 Davis, *King Stephen*, pp. 155–6; Crouch, *Beaumont Twins*, pp. 39, 52.
67 *Regesta*, iii, no. 68.
68 *Gesta Stephani*, pp. 128–9 and n. 3; he was usually called earl of Somerset and probably held both counties.

The 'charters' granted at this time to Geoffrey de Mandeville and
Aubrey de Vere have provoked long discussion, and they are indeed of
exceptional interest.[69] While cast in the form of charters they record
undertakings that were in effect sworn treaties. Documents of this kind
belong to a passing phase of feudal society; the need for them, apparent
in many different regions at different dates, lasted for too short a time
for any recognized common form to appear in the documents, but the
ceremonies behind them represented an attempt to deal with very real
problems. How were obligations to be enforced when no authority
existed with the power to coerce both the parties? A compromise or
conventio reached in the court of a lord caused no difficulty, but
agreements were frequently made between independent princes or between vassals of different lords, and these involved pacts of friendship.
The language of chroniclers shows that these were well known in
England, France and Normandy in the early twelfth century. Orderic
Vitalis speaks of such pacts between the kings of England and France,
between the duke of Normandy and the counts of Maine and Anjou,
and between the dukes of Normandy and Brittany.[70] The terms of these
concords do not survive; but we have the texts of the 1101 and 1110
treaties between Henry I and the count of Flanders, detailing the military service the count would undertake and the payment to be made for
it.[71] They contain the names of guarantors or hostages as well as witnesses. Whereas the witnesses merely testified to the facts, the guarantors (*obsides*) undertook to do their best to compel the parties to carry
out their obligations. If they were vassals, they might coerce a recalcit-
rant lord by withholding the service they owed him; whether vassals or
not they might offer an indemnity in cash if he reneged, or as a last
resort they might surrender their own bodies to imprisonment, as did
hostages in times of armed conflict. A churchman might appear in the
list as a vassal; but the practice of seeking to put concords under the

69 The dates have been a matter of controversy for many years. J. H. Round (*Geoffrey
de Mandeville*, ch. 8) dated the charters between Christmas 1141 and June 1142. R. H. C.
Davis, EHR, 79 (1964), pp. 302–7, argued that the date must be between 25 July and 1
August 1141, and this date is given in *Regesta*, iii, nos 275, 634. J. O. Prestwich in two
articles (EHR, 103 (1988), 283–312 and 960–7) argued for a return to Round's dating.
The main case he made was convincingly refuted by R. H. C. Davis (EHR, 103 (1988),
313–17 and 967–8). The discussion is summarized by Davis, *King Stephen*, App. VI. I
have adopted Davis's date as the one most acceptable historically.
70 Orderic, vi, pp. 14, 56, 60, 80, 180, 196; see also M. Chibnall, 'Anglo-French
relations in the work of Orderic Vitalis', *Documenting the Past: Essays in Medieval
History presented to George Peddy Cuttino*, ed. J. S. Hamilton and Patricia J. Bradley
(Woodbridge and Wolfeboro, 1989), pp. 13–19.
71 *Diplomatic Documents preserved in the Public Record Office*, 1 (1107–1272), ed.
Pierre Chaplais (London, 1964), no. 1.

protection of ecclesiastical jurisdiction seems to have been adopted only gradually, in England at least, during the early twelfth century. For that reason it is not to be expected that Matilda would necessarily have involved any of the bishops in her court at the time that she made an agreement that was essentially feudal, and was witnessed in the midst of an army mustering for an offensive. Her position was unprecedented, and legal forms were fluid.

Matilda's two charters to Geoffrey de Mandeville are best understood if they are considered not so much as a chronological sequence, after the fashion of J. H. Round, but as two parts of a single very important transaction.[72] The second document, drawn up at Oxford, complements the first issued at Westminster; the concessions are enlarged and made very much more explicit, and his vassals are included. In the Oxford treaty more was said about grants in Normandy; inevitably, Geoffrey of Anjou, fresh from his triumphs over Stephen's supporters, was brought into the picture, and for the first time he appears behind Matilda in England too. His agreement to the treaty was necessary, and the men acting as pledges undertook to seek it. Young Henry, the 'just heir' was also to be asked to pledge his support. Though the count of Anjou was not yet recognized as duke of Normandy he was carefully avoiding open defiance of King Louis VII, since his position could be legitimized only by the king. Louis had gone off to lay siege to Toulouse[73] and could not be consulted during the negotiations; Matilda could not be sure that he would be persuaded to confirm the Angevin claims in Normandy, but it was expedient for her to recognize his rights. Her own promises to de Mandeville were explicit: in addition to the powers she had already granted him in Essex by her first charter she expressly granted him the sheriffdom and justiciarship of London, Middlesex and Hertfordshire, promised him the bishop of London's castle at Bishop's Stortford, and allowed him to keep one new castle already built and build another. Whereas her first charter had stated only in general terms that she gave him all the land which his grandfather Geoffrey de Mandeville had held in England and Normandy, she now expressly mentioned all the land formerly held by Eudo the Steward, who was his maternal grandfather, in Normandy, and confirmed his stewardship as well as other fiefs, some of which were of more recent gift. The holdings of some of his vassals were specified, among them

72 Cf. the comments of Frederic L. Cheyette on the so-called 'sale' of Carcassonne ('The 'sale' of Carcassonne to the counts of Barcelona (1067 – 1070) and the rise of the Trencavels', Speculum, 63 (1988), p. 838): 'Many of the problems disappear if we take [the documents] as one complex transaction laid out in five documents rather than an explicit sequence of conveyances in which rights are moved back and forth.'

73 Orderic, vi, pp. 550–1 and n. 3.

those of his eldest, probably illegitimate, son Ernulf de Mandeville, who was serving in his household troops.[74] She agreed to make no peace with the burgesses of London without his consent, 'because they are his mortal enemies.' Probably she regarded them, after their recent rejection of her, as her own mortal enemies; but the importance of this concession was that it strengthened his grip on the constableship of the Tower, which his father had forfeited. It marked the complete recovery by Geoffrey of all that his family had lost.

The recovery was still partly theoretical; like some of the grants of the first Norman kings to their predatory vassals, it was no more than a licence to conquer. Matilda was in no position to put Geoffrey in possession of the Tower or many of the estates in Essex, and it was still uncertain whether she would ever be able to do so. Here the *obsides* became important. The absence of King David's name from the list is not surprising; he was no better placed than Matilda to secure the grants to de Mandeville. Whereas the witnesses simply swore to something they had seen and heard, the function of the *obsides* was to attempt to secure the fulfilment of promises, in the parts of England still held by Stephen's supporters no less than in Normandy. Whether or not they were all actually present at the time, and some of them certainly were, there was bound to be an element of uncertainty in their undertaking.[75] Hence the language of the document: they 'ought to be pledges by their faith.' The position of the church is imprecise for much the same reason; the deed ends with the unusually vague clause that 'the church (*christianitas*) of England which is in my power shall hold this convention to be observed for Earl Geoffrey and his heirs by me and my

74 Round, *Geoffrey de Mandeville*, p. 227, called Ernulf Geoffrey's 'son and heir', but gave no authority for the title; he believed that Ernulf was 'disinherited' because of his rebellion and excommunication with his father. *Complete Peerage*, v, pp. 116–17, while following Round in many details, suggests that Ernulf and the second Geoffrey de Mandeville may have had different mothers. Ernulf's position in his father's household troops, serving to earn lands and wealth as Henry I's bastard sons, Robert and Richard, had once served, suggests that he was probably illegitimate. He could well have been born in the years when Geoffrey, himself serving as a poor knight in the king's household troops, was in no position to marry.

75 The argument of Prestwich (*EHR*, 103 (1988), p. 287 n. 2) that Geoffrey de Mandeville was not present as one of the *obsides* for the charter granted to Aubrey de Vere is flawed. He suggests by comparing it with the charter for Geoffrey (M 2), that 'in the otherwise identical list in the Vere charter 'Geoffrey Earl of Essex' is a scribe's error for 'Henry of Essex', who appears in this position in the M 2 list.' But in fact the list is not otherwise identical; it is one name shorter. 'Comes Gaufridus de Essex' replaces 'Comes Albericus et Henricus de Essex'. It is far more likely that the eye of a scribe copying a list containing the names 'Comes Gaufridus de Essex et Henricus de Essex' should have missed the words 'et Henricus de' and omitted one entry altogether than that he should have misread 'Henricus' as 'Gaufridus' and also omitted one name.

heirs.' Later, named bishops were sometimes asked to enforce treaties,[76] and the implication was that breaches of them would bring the matter into the ecclesiastical courts. Matilda was making concessions in regions she did not control, and was in no position to demand a guarantee from all the bishops. The final clause, acknowledging the jurisdiction of the church courts as a last resort if other guarantees broke down, was little more than a formal gesture. Her ability to make her concessions effective depended on feudal loyalty and secular power. Geoffrey may have believed that she could win the day as her forces assembled round her at Oxford. It was not long before he had cause to doubt her ability.

On the same occasion, in a similar document, Matilda bestowed favours on Geoffrey's brother-in-law, Aubrey de Vere, who had not yet arrived with his men.[77] He had already been granted his father's chamberlainship in a lost charter; she now granted him the earldom of Cambridge if the king of Scots did not hold it. This clause suggests that King David was probably not present when the grant was made, but that does not mean that the charter cannot be dated in late July 1141. Aubrey de Vere himself was not there, and de Mandeville apparently did not arrive until after 25 July when Miles was granted the earldom of Hereford. The last week of July was a time of hectic preparations for a march on Winchester; King David may have moved south with his men while Matilda awaited the arrival a day or two later of other contingents summoned to her aid. The practical difficulty of organizing supplies for a sizeable army discouraged large bodies of troops from remaining encamped in one place and living off the country for a day longer than was necessary.[78] In any case the position of Cambridge was complicated. King David's son Henry had received the earldom of Huntingdon (which possibly included Cambridge) from King Henry, but had forfeited it when the Scots invaded England in 1138, and it was then given to William of Roumare. Because of William's interest, it may not have been restored to Earl Henry with his forfeited lands and the earldom of Huntingdon by the treaty of Durham (9 April 1139).[79] The

76 See for example the *conventio* between the earls of Chester and Leicester (1148–53) in F. M. Stenton, *The First Century of English Feudalism 1066–1166* (2nd edn, Oxford, 1961), pp. 249–53, 285–8, where the earls pledged their faith in the hand of Robert bishop of Lincoln. No clergy were involved in the earlier *conventiones* between the earls of Gloucester and Hereford, printed by R. H. C. Davis, *A Medieval Miscellany*, pp. 144–6.

77 *Regesta*, iii, no. 634.

78 The practical problems involved in provisioning an army are discussed by Bernard S. Bachrach, 'Some observations on the military administration of the Norman conquest', *Anglo-Norman Studies*, VIII (1986), pp. 1–21.

79 Davis, *King Stephen*, pp. 129–30, 135.

position would be clearer if we knew exactly when Roumare exchanged Cambridge for Lincoln. Understandably in such circumstances Matilda did not know whether it was vacant or not, and she offered Aubrey as an alternative a choice of the counties of Oxfordshire, Berkshire and Dorset. Presumably she did not consider that her grant of Somerset to William de Mohun included Dorset.[80] Aubrey subsequently chose Oxfordshire. Geoffrey de Mandeville immediately sent one of his vassals, Hugh of Ing, to Normandy to obtain from young Henry and probably also from Geoffrey of Anjou a sworn undertaking to observe the treaty. A transcript of Henry's charter survives. He granted all his mother's concessions, in the same words, as 'rightful heir of England and Normandy' (rectus heres Anglie et Normannie), and pledged his faith, putting his hand in that of Hugh of Ing, as his mother had pledged hers in Geoffrey de Mandeville's hand.[81] He was now in his ninth year, and for the first time he became actively associated in the struggle for his inheritance.

Strengthened by promises of allegiance, Matilda advanced to Winchester at the beginning of August. She was received by the citizens and took up residence in the royal castle. From there she sent a message to Bishop Henry in his palace at Wolvesey, summoning him to her presence. Henry prevaricated; he was already planning desertion, and he claimed later to have been afraid of her because she had marched against him with an army. He was either negotiating with the queen or waiting for letters from Innocent II which, when they came, authorized him to use all means of coercion, ecclesiastical and secular, to restore his brother to the throne. According to William of Malmesbury he told the empress that he would get ready to come, and meanwhile sent out messages to all those believed to favour Stephen.[82]

One new recruit to the Angevin cause probably joined Matilda at that time. Waleran of Meulan recognized that his few English possessions were threatened, and that unless he came to terms with the empress the truce arranged by his brother would expire in Normandy, and he would lose his principal inheritance there. He humbled himself and became her vassal; he also patched up his quarrel with William de Beauchamp.[83] Most probably he left almost immediately for Normandy; there is no mention of him in the fighting around Winchester in the following month. The author of the Gesta Stephani claimed that Matilda had a very strong force with her; he named King David and the earls of

---

80 He was, however, called 'earl of Dorset' in the Gesta Stephani, pp. 128–9.

81 Regesta, iii, no. 635. See Round, Geoffrey de Mandeville, App. T.

82 Malmesbury, HN, p. 58; Gesta Stephani, pp. 128–9. Henry of Huntingdon, p. 275, also says that Henry of Blois sent for the queen and William of Ypres and almost all the magnates of England.

83 See above, pp. 106–7.

Gloucester, Chester, Exeter, Cornwall, Hereford, Warwick and Dorset, and other 'men of valour and distinction', including Brian fitz Count, John the Marshal, Roger d'Oilli, Roger de Nonant, William fitz Alan, and many others 'whom it would be tedious to name.'[84] Perhaps there were not so many others; William of Malmesbury, anxious to explain away the defeat, mentioned only King David, the earls of Gloucester and Hereford and 'a few barons', adding that Ranulf earl of Chester's arrival was late and ineffective, and that Geoffrey de Mandeville again went over to the king's party.[85] Waleran does not appear to have taken any part in the fighting, and there is no mention of William of Roumare. Both may have been in Normandy.[86] As the *Gesta Stephani* referred to the forces that arrived, and Malmesbury to those that finally retreated, the discrepancy may be partly due to defections. Certainly William of Mohun soon returned to Stephen, and Roger de Beaumont, earl of Warwick, kept a cautiously low profile until his defection at a date not yet ascertained.

Matilda replied to the legate's prevarication by besieging his castle to compel his attendance. It was strongly held, and the forces loyal to Stephen, advancing from London, in turn laid siege to her castle, while the legate's supporters, throwing firebrands, burnt much of the town of Winchester and two of its abbeys. It was probably the action of Henry of Blois in this conflict that led Henry of Huntingdon to brand him indelibly as 'a new kind of monster, compounded of purity and corruption, a monk and a knight.'[87] The Londoners sent out their militia to join in the siege, and so found themselves fighting on the same side as their bitter enemy, Geoffrey de Mandeville. Both hoped to further their own interests by being on the winning side, and the balance was already tipping visibly towards Stephen. The besieging armies were able to bar the roads leading to Winchester and cut off food supplies. William of Ypres captured and burnt the borough of Andover and prevented the empress establishing a 'castle' at Wherwell, where the nunnery was burnt in the fighting.[88] By that time it had become apparent that the empress must at all costs be got away from Winchester. While her supporters fought a delaying action, she slipped out of the city under the escort of Reginald of Cornwall and Brian fitz Count, with the aim

84 *Gesta Stephani*, pp. 128–9.
85 Malmesbury, *HN*, p. 59.
86 Barraclough, *Chester Charters*, no. 70 note. William of Roumare was a friend of Waleran's and appears to have gone on a pilgrimage to Compostela with him in 1144.
87 Henry of Huntingdon, p. 315 (*Epistola de Contemptu Mundi*).
88 The clearest and most balanced reconstruction of the fighting that led up to the rout of Winchester and the capture of Robert of Gloucester is by Rosalind Hill, 'The battle of Stockbridge 1141', *Studies in Medieval History presented to R. Allen Brown*, pp. 173–7. See also Davis, *King Stephen* pp. 59–60.

of escaping to Ludgershall and from there to Devizes. They travelled along the Stockbridge road, riding at full speed. This was the occasion when the empress was forced by the urgency of the pursuit to ride astride, like a man.[89] The highly dramatized account later given in the poetic life of John's son, William the Marshal, cannot be taken at its face value; she could not have gone with John the Marshal by way of Wherwell, occupied by the Flemish mercenaries of William of Ypres, and though John the Marshal fought indomitably and lost an eye in the battle, he was not with the party that accompanied her along the Stockbridge road. Robert of Gloucester fought the rearguard action at the ford of Stockbridge and delayed pursuit long enough for her to 'disappear into the folds of Danebury Down and put the waterlogged marshes of the Test between her and her pursuers'[90] before he was captured along with a number of knights, including William of Salisbury and Humphrey de Bohun.[91] The retreat turned into a rout, with knights throwing away their armour and accoutrements and escaping alone. Miles of Gloucester got back home safely in sorry plight, and King David was said to have been captured three times but each time to have purchased his release.

Meanwhile the empress reached Ludgershall for the first night, and then hurried on to Devizes. By this time she was so exhausted that she was carried in a litter between two horses, and arrived 'more dead than alive'.[92] These no doubt were the circumstances which led to a later story that she had been smuggled out of Winchester in a coffin. Much, but not all, that had been won at Lincoln was lost at Winchester. Yet one of Matilda's severest critics, writing the *Gesta Stephani*, had only praise for her and her faithful vassal Brian in the crisis:

> The countess of Anjou, who was always above feminine softness and had a mind steeled and unbroken in adversity, fled ahead of the others to Devizes, accompanied only by Brian and a small escort; thereby she and Brian gained a title to boundless fame, since, as their devotion to each other had before been unbroken, so even in adversity, beset by the greatest dangers, they were in no wise divided.[93]

Matilda's ambiguous title, 'Lady of the English', may have been intended as the appropriate title for an acknowledged heir to the throne before coronation.[94] Whatever the truth of this, by the early autumn of

89 Florence of Worcester, ii, pp. 134–5; *L'histoire de Guillaume le Maréchal*, ed. Paul Meyer, i, pp. 7–11, esp. vv. 208–24.
90 R. Hill, op. cit. supra n. 88, p. 177.
91 Malmesbury, *HN*, p. 67.
92 Florence of Worcester, ii, p. 135.
93 *Gesta Stephani*, p. 134.
94 See above, p. 102.

1141 it was becoming clear to the more far-sighted among her supporters that she would never be crowned queen of England. It may have
taken her a few more months to realize this; but it seems to have been
clear to Robert of Gloucester, whose influence on the long-term strategy
of the Angevin party was steadily increasing. Matilda had shown at the
height of her power that she had neither the political judgement nor the
understanding of men to enable her to act wisely in a crisis. She was a
focus for genuine loyalty and a woman of courage and determination,
but Earl Robert had the strength and skill to exercise the rule from
which his illegitimate birth debarred him. He was probably the first to
see clearly that all efforts must now be directed to preparing young
Henry to take up the challenge, and the sooner his claims were associated with those of his mother the better. Matilda may already have
accepted this view; she certainly did so within a year or two.

For the moment, however, Earl Robert had to negotiate his release on
the best possible terms. He was kept in honourable captivity at Rochester, resisting all attempts to persuade him to abandon his sister's cause,
and even taking advantage of the place to receive money from his men
in Kent and purchase horses there. Threats to send him overseas to
perpetual imprisonment in Boulogne were ineffective; he knew (according to William of Malmesbury) that his wife and her men would
immediately send the king to Ireland if any wrong were done to him.[95]
The obvious solution was an exchange of prisoners. Robert argued in
vain that an earl was of less importance than a king, and that the
magnates who had been captured at Winchester should be released with
him. This was unacceptable to the queen's supporters, who demanded
their ransoms; Gilbert of Clare had taken William of Salisbury, and
William of Ypres, Humphrey de Bohun. Robert did win the important
concession that no castles or lands that had come into the hands of the
empress and her adherents after the king's capture should be restored. A
complicated exchange of hostages was agreed. When the king was freed
at Bristol on 1 November, the queen and two magnates remained as
hostages until, on 3 November, the earl too was released, leaving his
son as surety for the queen. He too was set free once the queen was
back at Winchester, and Earl Robert joined his sister, who had set up
her headquarters at Oxford and was holding her court there.[96] The
other captives duly paid their ransoms and returned home.

On 7 December the legate held a council at Westminster to justify his
double change of allegiance, and to assure waverers that they were not
bound by any oaths they had taken to Matilda.[97] There the letters he

95 Malmesbury, HN, pp. 66–70.
96 Davis, King Stephen, p. 60.
97 Malmesbury, HN, p. 62.

had earlier received from the pope were read out, mildly rebuking him for abandoning the king's cause, and urging him to procure his release by any means in his power. The legate charged the empress with breaking her pledges to respect the freedom of the church and with using armed force and threats against him. Countercharges were made by an envoy of the empress, who alleged that the legate himself had urged her to come to England and had connived at the king's capture. It was a battle of propaganda and angry words. The legate had the advantage of being able to threaten with excommunication all, except the empress herself, who continued to defy the king and to offer a kind of justification to the waverers whose material interests were pulling them back to the king's side. He failed to convince a few; Brian fitz Count, when later charged with plundering merchants on their way to the fair at Winchester, was to point out that in supporting the empress he was only obeying orders issued by the legate at Easter to help her to recover what was rightly hers.[98]

On balance, since the new recruits to her cause were chiefly those with Norman interests who, like Waleran, had taken themselves off to their lands in Normandy, she probably lost some of her vassals in England. It was becoming clear that her resources were equal only to holding on to the castles already controlled by her supporters, and that the only hope of achieving another major victory was to secure reinforcements. Early in Lent, 1142, she held a council of her followers at Devizes, more convenient than Oxford as a general meeting place, and a resolution was taken to send to the count of Anjou to ask for military aid. The envoys returned to Devizes at Whitsuntide and reported to another council: the count of Anjou was cautiously favourable, but did not know them and would negotiate only with the earl of Gloucester, whom he knew personally.[99] Earl Robert hesitated to leave his sister in Oxford with only a small following but, as Stephen had been seriously ill since Easter and may have seemed unlikely to attack, he decided to go. At the end of June he sailed from Wareham with a small force of knights. He found that the lords of some Norman castles were holding out against Count Geoffrey, and agreed to stay and help him in a mopping up operation within the region between Falaise, Caen and Avranches. Between them they captured ten castles: Tinchebrai, St Hilaire d'Harcourt, Briquesard, Aunay-sur-Odon, Bastonbourg, Trévières, Castel-de-Vire, Plessis Grimoult, Villers-Bocage and Mortain. William of Malmesbury, our only detailed source for these events, complained bitterly of Geoffrey's conduct, though if his figures are

98 H. W. C. Davis, *EHR*, 25 (1910), pp. 297–303.
99 Malmesbury, *HN*, pp. 71–2.

1   The coronation of the Emperor Henry V. The emperor, holding a sceptre and wearing a diadem, receives an orb from Pope Paschal II (Corpus Christi College Cambridge, MS 373, fo. 83: by courtesy of the Master and Fellows of Corpus Christi College Cambridge)

ꝯꞩꞩ dm ꝏ· ē ·xııı· Impꝛ· henrı̄c̄· natalē
dm̄· babenꞩ· celebꝛauıꞇꝟ·dıꞩpoꞩıꞇıꞩ nupꞇıꞩ ꞩuıꞇꝫ

2   The wedding feast of Henry V and Matilda (Corpus Christi College Cambridge, MS 373, fo. 95b: by courtesy of the Master and Fellows of Corpus Christi College Cambridge)

3   Arundel castle (Courtauld Institute, B74/2553: by courtesy of the Conway Library, Courtauld Institute of Art)

4 Charter of the empress for St Martin des Champs, Paris, with seal (King's College Cambridge, Muniments, SJP/19: by courtesy of the Provost and Fellows of King's College Cambridge)

5 Seal of the empress, from a charter for Bordesley Abbey. The empress is seated, crowned and holding a sceptre in her right hand. Legend: S + MATHILDIS DEI GRATIA ROMANORUM REGINE (BL Add. Ch. 75724: by permission of the British Library)

6a Coin of the empress, struck at the Cardiff mint. Obverse, [M]ATILLIS : IM[PER], crowned bust holding sceptre, right (National Museum of Wales, Cardiff: by permission of the National Museum of Wales)

6b Coin of the empress. Reverse, [+BRIC]MER : CAERDI: cross moline and lilies (National Museum of Wales, Cardiff: by permission of the National Museum of Wales)

7a   Oxford castle: the twelfth-century crypt. Engraving by Joseph Skelton, 1843

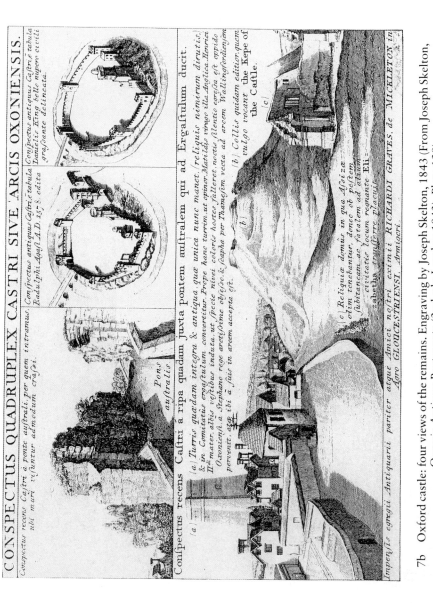

7b Oxford castle: four views of the remains. Engraving by Joseph Skelton, 1843 (From Joseph Skelton, *Oxonia Antiqua Restaurata* (2nd edn London 1843), Plate 129)

8 Coronation of the Virgin, Reading Abbey capital (Courtauld Institute 42/
   50(33): by courtesy of the Conway Library, Courtauld Institute of Art)

9 St Julian's chapel. Petit Quevilly (Courtauld Institute L45/33/17: by courtesy of
   the Conway Library, Courtauld Institute of Art)

10 St Julian's chapel, Petit Quevilly. Painting of the flight into Egypt. The Virgin rides side-saddle, as the empress rode when not escaping from Winchester (Courtauld Institute L45/33/16; by courtesy of the Conway Library, Courtauld Institute of Art)

11 St Julian's chapel, Petit Quevilly. Painting of the Nativity (Courtauld Institute, L45/33/15: by courtesy of the Conway Library, Courtauld Institute of Art)

correct Geoffrey must have provided some knights for Matilda's needs. Malmesbury states that, owing to a storm, only two of Earl Robert's ships reached Normandy on the outward journey, carrying 'knights ready for action' and presumably their horses too. He returned with between three and four hundred men, in fifty-two ships.[100] Some of the knights who accompanied his return may have been men from his own Norman lands; but if any credence can be given to these figures the small force he took with him from England must have been augmented in Normandy. Significantly he also brought back his nephew Henry, a boy of nine.

Malmesbury's bitterness is partly explained because, during Earl Robert's absence, the empress had fared badly. Stephen had captured Wareham castle, so threatening communications with Normandy, and was also laying siege to Matilda in Oxford. Robert attacked Wareham, hoping to draw Stephen away from Oxford; as a diversion the manoeuvre failed, but when no relief arrived the garrison in Wareham was forced to surrender, and possession of the castle was recovered. The Angevin party was thus assured of a Channel port. Meanwhile Stephen continued to press Matilda; he burnt much of the town of Oxford and invested her closely in the castle, where supplies were running out. While Robert was mustering his men in Cirencester in order to ride to her relief, she made one of the most dramatic and daring escapes of her perilous career. The winter was hard, and the Thames was frozen. At night, accompanied by only three or four knights, she slipped out of the castle, probably by a postern gate. Wearing white cloaks as camouflage, the little party crossed the frozen Thames and walked some seven or eight miles through the snow to Abingdon. Thence, having passed through the enemy's lines, she and her escort proceeded on horseback to Wallingford, where she was under Brian's protection until it was safe for her to move to Devizes.[101] Here, in Bishop Roger of Salisbury's mighty castle, she was to make her headquarters until she left England in 1148. Her son Henry, as was normal for any young prince or aspirant to knighthood, remained with his uncle in Bristol, occasionally visiting Devizes, until 1144. Before he returned to his father in Normandy, to prepare himself for taking over the duchy when he was of age to do so, he had begun to receive homage with his mother from his English vassals. Increasingly, Matilda's task was to prepare the way for his entry into his inheritance.

100 Malmesbury, *HN*, pp. 72–4.
101 *Gesta Stephani*, p. 142; Malmesbury, *HN*, p. 77. The *A-SC* s.a. 1141 states that she was let down from the tower by ropes. The statement on a seventeenth-century engraving of Oxford (see Plate 7b) that she travelled by boat is pure fiction (the river was frozen).

6

Lordship and Governance in a Divided Realm

Secular Governance

The rout of Winchester was a fatal blow to Matilda's hopes of ever wearing the English crown. She was nevertheless in a better position than before being recognized as Lady of the English. Until then she had been forced to live under the protection of the greatest of her vassals, Earl Robert and Miles of Gloucester, and had little but prospective conquests to offer her adherents. At Oxford, until she was driven out in December 1142, and at Devizes, which she then made her base until she retired to Normandy in 1148, she was in her own castle. Oxford was a royal castle; Devizes, built by Bishop Roger of Salisbury and confiscated by Stephen, was captured from him by Matilda's forces and kept for the time being in her own hands. In both places she was able to keep a small court and begin to settle her own supporters on royal demesne and confiscated estates within easy reach. She had to provide for her household officers and household troops and compensate the dis-inherited who had joined her cause as far as her limited resources allowed. Wherever she was able effectively to appoint sheriffs she could hope to receive some of the revenues of the county. They were never enough to enable her to launch a major offensive against Stephen, but they reduced his resources, already depleted by his dissipation of all the treasure of Henry I in years of war. The rivals were more evenly matched. From time to time isolated castles were stormed by both sides, and changes in the allegiance of one of the greater vassals might at any moment tip the balance indecisively one way or the other; but Matilda was never driven out of her heartland. For the most part the distribu-tion of property made by her and later by her son was to prove lasting. As J. C. Holt pointed out, the 'great belt of demesne lands, forests and royal castles which stretched from Corfe northwards to Marlborough and Ludgershall, and then east to the Thames at Wallingford . . .

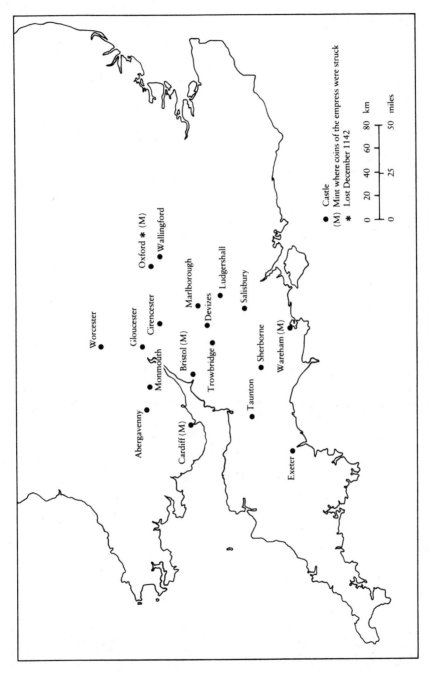

MAP 2 Principal castles held for the empress, 1142–8

Castle

(M) Mint where coins of the empress were struck

* Lost December 1142

0   20   40   60   80   km

0   25   50   miles

Worcester

Gloucester

Cirencester

Oxford * (M)

Wallingford

Marlborough

Devizes

Ludgershall

Salisbury

Monmouth

Bristol (M)

Trowbridge

Abergavenny

Sherborne

Wareham (M)

Taunton

Cardiff (M)

Exeter

was the territorial foundation of the Angevin power from the days of Matilda and the young Henry of Anjou.'[1]

Matilda's role during the next six years was very much what it had been in Normandy from 1136 to 1139, on a larger scale. With a firm base in a strong castle she provided a focal point of resistance that could be held for her party. She received vassals, granted charters, and occasionally took charge of captives; one of these was Walter de Pinkeney.[2] Sometimes her personal troops took part in local fighting. Unfortunately for her, the Flemish mercenaries were expensive to maintain and of doubtful loyalty. Robert fitz Hildebrand, sent to relieve William Pont de l'Arche in the castle of Porchester, betrayed his trust, imprisoned William, took the castle for himself and made peace with the bishop of Winchester.[3] Her own household knights, particularly the Bretons, were more reliable though never very numerous. Her vassals behaved unpredictably; Earl Robert's younger son, Philip, when put in charge of the castle of Cricklade, defected for a time to Stephen;[4] the greater magnates on both sides carried on with the war of sieges, partly in their own interests, partly in those of their lords. Matilda played a waiting game; her husband continued his successful offensive in Normandy; and it was Stephen himself, in his effort to drive home his advantage in England, who made all the mistakes.[5]

The first phase of the struggle was dominated by Geoffrey de Mandeville who, after his return to Stephen, was apparently favoured and trusted. Probably the chroniclers who called him 'second only to the king' should not be taken too literally; the phrase was a literary topos apt to be used of a man like Ranulf Flambard or Roger of Salisbury, who rose high only to fall low. Stephen may never have fully trusted him: as R. H. C. Davis has shown, he made use of Geoffrey while he was attacking the bishop of Ely, but in 1143 felt strong enough to turn on him, throw him into prison and demand the surrender of his castles. Geoffrey was forced to comply, but on being released he immediately rebelled, occupied and fortified the abbey of Ramsey, and held out against Stephen until he was killed in the fighting in September 1144. Thereafter much of the keenest fighting moved to the north Midlands, where Ranulf, earl of Chester, found himself in much the same position

1 J. C. Holt, *The Northerners* (Oxford, 1961), p. 212.
2 *Gesta Stephani*, pp. 178–81.
3 *Gesta Stephani*, pp. 150–2.
4 *Gesta Stephani*, pp. 178–80, 186–7.
5 For a good account of this period see Davis, *King Stephen*, ch. 7. There is much useful information in Round, *Geoffrey de Mandeville*, but a number of his statements have been corrected and he distorts the history of the reign by overemphasizing the role of de Mandeville.

as de Mandeville. In 1146, after long hesitation, he defected to Stephen, and the same scenario was re-enacted. Both men suspected the other of treachery. Stephen took Ranulf prisoner after provoking a quarrel in his court; Ranulf surrendered some castles, including Lincoln, to recover his freedom and, on being released, immediately returned to the empress. He did not desert again; this time he remained one of the most powerful magnates in her party until his death in 1153.

Matilda herself made one attempt at negotiation with Stephen, in 1146, acting through Reginald, earl of Cornwall. Her representatives insisted on her hereditary right to the kingdom, while Stephen maintained that his possession was lawful but, as neither side would yield an inch, the negotiations came to nothing.[6] For the most part she kept a low profile and husbanded her resources, welcoming as her vassals all who felt themselves unjustly treated by Stephen. After the attack made on her by Bishop Henry of Winchester in 1141 no one accused her of failing to keep her word, let alone proved that she had done so. Stephen was frequently accused, especially for his treatment of the earls of Essex and Chester. His occasional acts of chivalrous generosity were offset by others of deceit and perfidy, and this made him suspect. On the whole Matilda kept to the accepted rules of conduct and combat in a harsh society. She could be hard when necessary; she was prepared to imprison Walter de Pinkeney in close fetters, but not to order his execution (or even go through the grim mockery of ordering an execution, countermanded at the last minute) and she respected sworn oaths. Active and effective in a limited sphere, she continued to attract much lasting loyalty.

For the whole of Matilda's eight and a half years in England the solid core of her authority was in the great marcher lordship of Robert of Gloucester. There, even before the battle of Lincoln, coins were struck in her name at Bristol, where Stephen's moneyer, Thorketill, continued in her service, and at Cardiff, where a new mint was set up. She also had mints at some date at Wareham and briefly at Oxford. The new dies carry on the obverse an image of the empress, in profile, possibly taken from the life.[7] It is clear and individual, though rough, for the die cutters were inexperienced and the silver, though of good quality, varied in thickness and was not always properly annealed. Such coins

6 *Gesta Stephani*, pp. 186–7.

7 George C. Boon, *Coins of the Anarchy 1135–54* (National Museum of Wales, Cardiff, 1988), pp, 10–12, 21 no. 9, 24–5. See Plate 6a. On the coinage of this period see also R. P. Mack, 'Stephen and the Anarchy 1135–1154', *British Numismatic Journal*, 35 (1960), pp. 38–112; Edmund King, 'Anarchy of Stephen's reign', *THRS*, 5th ser., 34 (1984), pp. 147–52; George C. Boon, *Welsh Hoards 1979–81* (Cardiff, 1986), pp. 43–60.

were able to circulate within the region securely controlled by the earl of Gloucester. They were acceptable in her main port of entry into the kingdom, Wareham, and in the territories of the Welsh allies of the earl. A hoard discovered in 1980 at Coed-y-Wenallt, just over the border from Norman Cardiff, contained a large number of coins from the mints of the empress. Some of these coins circulated far more widely throughout the kingdom; others, particularly those of the Class B type issued in the name of some baron (never of the highest rank), but still bearing her image, apparently had a more local circulation. The royal prerogative was respected, either in her person or in that of one of her Norman ancestors, for some have images of a crowned King William or King Henry, while at the same time being authenticated by a military leader known to the mercenaries or others who were paid in coin.[8] After the battle of Lincoln Stephen's coinage partially collapsed; the London dies were replaced in the mints of Lincoln, Nottingham, Leicester and Northampton by locally cut dies. The coins are some of the most graphic and convincing illustrations of what kind of authority prevailed in different regions during the Anarchy. They exemplify even more clearly than the charters, far more clearly than the chronicles, the intermeshing of Matilda's authority with that of the men who were fighting on her behalf. They are a warning not to believe too hastily that her prerogative was disregarded, even when her practical influence was weak, and an indication of the great difficulty in determining just how much was due to her personal influence.

In the Gloucester heartland the party of the empress controlled, besides the mints, the sheriffs. Some of the local officials had been trained under earlier kings, and her principal supporters included Earl Robert and Brian fitz Count, the two men who had presided over King Henry's reform of the exchequer. Nigel, bishop of Ely, was for a time at her court and brought with him his unrivalled experience of the practical workings of the exchequer. Retrospective evidence from the Pipe Roll of 1155–6 shows that, although the practice of assessing the sheriff's farm by counting the coins ('tale') had been largely superseded by a more refined process to determine their actual silver content ('blanc'), some counties had reverted to the cruder method during the Anarchy.[9] These were the counties of Norfolk, Suffolk, Essex, Sussex, Shropshire, Somerset and Devon – all of which were either disputed

---

8 Boon, *Coins*, pp. 29, 44. No. 24 is a coin almost certainly issued by Brian fitz Count at Wallingford. In the north coins were minted for King David and his supporters at Bamborough, Carlisle, Corbridge and Newcastle. At Carlisle he took over Stephen's moneyer, William son of Herebald (Boon, *Coins*, p. 8 (map) and no. 40).

9 Kenji Yoshitake, 'The exchequer in the reign of Stephen', *EHR* 103 (1988), pp. 950–9; King, 'Anarchy of Stephen's reign', pp. 143–7; Davis, *King Stephen*, pp. 83–6.

territories or at least removed from the heartlands of both protagonists. Gloucestershire, Herefordshire and later Wiltshire were all closely controlled, and must have provided the most stable elements in the resources of the empress and the vassals who were closest to her. In more distant parts of the realm, like the earldoms of Chester, where Earl Ranulf was (apart from 1146) nominally an Angevin vassal, or even Norfolk and Suffolk, where Hugh Bigod was consistently opposed to Stephen, she had no control of either administration or coinage, or effective patronage. The most that could be said was that Stephen's assets in these regions were never more than limited and uncertain.

The most solid gain from the few months of her triumph was the extension of her sphere of influence from Gloucester and Hereford more firmly towards the south Midlands. Oxford was lost in 1142, but she held Devizes, dominated much of Wiltshire, and maintained fairly firm contact through Berkshire with Wallingford. This greatly enriched her store of patronage. At the height of her power she had distributed notional earldoms with a generous hand, but the gifts did not always carry effective control of the county administration or resources. After Earl Robert successfully negotiated that the conquests of 1141 should be retained, she had the firmer disposal of extensive royal demesnes in Oxfordshire for a time and later in Wiltshire. She was able to provide for her household and to do something for the disinherited. When Ralph son of Pichard lost everything in the rout of Winchester she could give him only some small rents and a house in Gloucestershire, and had to rely on Miles of Gloucester for more substantial endowments.[10] Now she could establish her household knights and officers in small estates of their own. J. H. Round noted the extent of Wiltshire *terrae datae* in the first Pipe Rolls of Henry II's reign; [11] and the gifts in several counties recorded in these rolls link up with the patchy evidence of charters to show that a number of the gifts date from the time that the empress was active in England, before she withdrew and left the struggle to her son.

There were a number of disinherited, or at least dispossessed, lords to be provided for. After the fall of Shrewsbury, Stephen held on resolutely to Shropshire, in spite of attempted encroachments by the supporters of the empress. William fitz Alan, who had succeeded to the estates of Henry I's Breton follower, Alan fitz Flaald, and had married into the family of Ernulf de Hesding, had to seek refuge at her court. Joce de Dinan, the 'obscure Breton adventurer' made castellan of Ludlow by

10 David Walker, 'Ralph son of Pichard', *BIHR*, 33 (1960), pp. 195–8; *Regesta*, iii, no. 316a.

11 Round, *Geoffrey de Mandeville*, p. 230.

Stephen, turned against the king and held Ludlow castle against him.[12] So independent was he that Stephen at one time exempted his fee from a comprehensive grant to Robert earl of Leicester, with the proviso that Robert might have it if he could persuade Joce to hold it as his vassal.[13] In the end the castle fell, and Joce retreated to Lambourn with his Breton knights. Two of them married his daughters: Fulk fitz Warin married Hawise and went into the service of Robert of Gloucester, so needing relatively little from the empress;[14] Hugh de Plugenai or Plucknet, who married Sibyl, came directly into her service. She first granted him the manor and hundred of Headington to hold for life.[15] The grant, known from his charter making a gift out of the land to St Frideswide's Priory, must have been made during the time she held Oxford, and may have been held precariously for some years afterwards. Whatever the fate of Headington in the years after 1142, Hugh was in possession of *terrae datae* worth £42 there from the beginning of Henry II's reign until his death in 1200.[16] The hereditary lands of his family were in Berkshire and Wiltshire, at Lambourn and Chippenham, and were comprised partly of royal demesne, given most probably after the fall of Oxford, and partly of his wife's dowry lands.[17] Several other beneficiaries of Matilda's Oxford period are known from lands later held in the neighbourhood. Henry of Oxford had *terrae datae* in Headington and Bensington.[18] Roger of Sandford acknowledged that land in Brill, on the borders of Buckinghamshire and Oxfordshire, had been granted him by the empress and her son for his service.[19] One of her clerks,

12 *Fouke le Fitz Warin*, ed. E. J. Hathaway, P. T. Ricketts et al. (Anglo-Norman Texts, 1975), pp. x-xiii; Eyton, *The Antiquities of Shropshire* (12 vols, London, 1856–60), v, pp. 244–8.

13 *Regesta*, iii, no. 437.

14 Eyton, *Shropshire*, vii, pp. 68–70; *VCH Berks.*, iv, p. 254; *Gloucester Charters*, nos 118, 119; in the returns of 1166 he held 1 fee of the new enfeoffment out of the demesne of the earl of Gloucester (*Red Book of the Exchequer*, p. 292).

15 *The Cartulary of the Monastery of St Frideswide at Oxford*, ed. S. R. Wigram (2 vols, Oxford Hist. Soc., 1896), ii, 20, no. 705.

16 *PR 2 H II*, p. 36; the entry continues regularly up to *PR 2 John*. In *PR2 John*, p. 206 there is a reference to the land in Headington formerly belonging to Hugh de Plugenai; and p. 195 his widow, Sibyl, is holding the Lambourn lands.

17 *Pipe Rolls, passim; VCH Berks.*, iv, p. 253; W. de G. Birch, 'Collections of the Cistercian abbey of Stanley', *Wilts. Arch. and Nat. Hist. Magazine*, 15 (1875), pp. 258–60, 263.

18 *PR 2 H II*, p. 36; *3 H II*, p. 82; *4 H II*, p. 149. It was in Bensington too that in 1212 Reginald the Angevin held 10 pounds worth of land which the empress had given to his ancestors for the service of half a knight at the castle of Wallingford (*Book of Fees*, i, p. 104).

19 W. H. Turner and H. O. Coxe, *Calendar of Charters and Rolls preserved in the Bodleian Library* (Oxford, 1878), p. 293 (Charter 8).

Adam of Ely, was given land in Boarstall by her; he also served at different times in the households of Earl Robert of Gloucester and his son Earl William, and received, possibly from young Henry, lands in Somerset, Cambridgeshire and Surrey.[20]

At Devizes she had over five years to establish her servants and vassals around her. She gave twenty-eight pounds worth of land in Westbury, a royal manor, to Humphrey fitz Odo, the constable. This was evidently a hereditary grant, as a hundred years later one of his descendants produced a charter in which she had granted the land to him and his heirs.[21] Westbury also provided for one of her leading knights, William Defuble, who witnessed several of her charters.[22] He received thirty pounds worth of land from her; and before his death granted a third part of this to her favoured priory of Notre-Dame du Pré.[23] Among her household officers Drogo 'of Polwheile', her chamberlain, who had earlier received estates in Cornwall, was given land at Loxwell (*Fons Drogonis*), which later provided the first endowment of a Cistercian abbey subject to Quarr.[24] The gift may have been to maintain this Cornish vassal near to Devizes; possibly his Cornish estates were temporarily out of his control owing to the civil war. Later generations of the family remained firmly rooted in Cornwall well into the nineteenth century.[25] Unless his gift to Quarr Abbey was a deathbed gift or he entered a monastery, Drogo may have surrendered the Wiltshire lands because his service to the empress had ended and he wished to return and settle in Cornwall after she left England.

The disinherited found pickings to support them in the former royal demesnes within reach of Devizes. Ernulf de Mandeville, Geoffrey de Mandeville's presumably bastard son, had demesne lands worth £11. 10s. in Wurth (Wiltshire) and at Bratton in Westbury.[26] William fitz Alan was able to find a foothold in land inherited from his kinsman Ernulf de Hesding at Keevil.[27] Joce de Dinan was established at Lambourn with Hugh de Plucknet. Jocelin de Balliol began his career in Matilda's service; he witnessed her charters from 1141, always at Devizes, and was rewarded with land worth £36 in the hundred of

20 *VCH Bucks.*, iv, p. 13; *Gloucester Charters*, p. 12.
21 *VCH Wilts.*, viii, p. 148; PRO J I 1/996 m. 11.
22 *Regesta*, iii, nos 115, 116, 372, 581, 702.
23 *VCH Wilts.*, viii, pp. 148, 154.
24 *Regesta*, iii, no. 666.
25 See above, ch. 5, n. 13. Since the lost charter cited by Polwhele referred to 'Drogoni de Polwheile camerario meo' he is clearly the same person as Drogo, chamberlain of the empress, mentioned in the charter for Quarr Abbey.
26 *VCH Wilts.*, viii, 160.
27 *VCH Wilts.*, viii, 252.

Mere in Wiltshire.[28] He also held some lands in Gloucestershire; in 1166 the feudal returns of Henry of Neufmarché noted that Jocelin de Balliol had half one knight's fee and 'four parts' of another by the king's command, and that Henry could get no service from them.[29] This seems an echo of grants made during the civil wars, possibly initially by the empress and later confirmed by Henry II. The 1166 returns of Humphrey de Bohun included one fee held by Manasser Bisset of the new enfeoffment,[30] but since Manasser was young Henry's steward this was probably a later grant. The same is probably true of Warin fitz Gerold, Henry's chamberlain, who held lands in Sparsholt and witnessed Henry's charters from about 1148.[31]

John fitz Gilbert, Matilda's marshal, proved to be a tower of strength in Wiltshire. He had been firmly established there in her father's time. Marlborough castle was his principal base; he also held Ludgershall and Newbury, and from all three he ravaged the lands of Stephen's supporters round about and threatened their lines of communication.[32] Initially he had clashed with Patrick, constable of Salisbury castle; but peace was made between the two when John, apparently repudiating his first wife Aline, daughter of Walter Pipard, married Patrick's sister Sibyl. He may have been responsible for bringing Patrick over to the empress, who in time rewarded her new supporter with the earldom of Salisbury. These two great barons gave her the solid backing in Wiltshire that she had previously had from Miles of Hereford and Robert of Gloucester in her earlier base. John's military prowess was all the more vital for her cause after Miles was killed in a hunting accident at Christmas, 1143. Both of them had a solid core of knights enfeoffed in the neighbourhood or maintained in their household.[33] John's praises were later to be sung in the poem celebrating the life of his more famous son, L'Histoire de Guillaume le Maréchal; but Sidney Painter probably did not exaggerate when he wrote that it was to him that the empress owed her control of northern Wiltshire and the adherence to her party of Patrick of Salisbury.[34]

Some at least of the grants made in these years were life grants. Many were made in the royal forests or out of the royal demesne, but some certainly came from the captured lands of Stephen's supporters. Some

28 *Regesta*, iii, nos 115, 116, 372, 632, 702; later he passed into Henry's service, ibid., nos 64, 65, 492, 495, 496, 837; Lees, *Templars*, p. 207 n. 6; *PR 2 H II*, p. 57.
29 *Red Book of the Exchequer*, p. 296.
30 *Red Book of the Exchequer*, p. 244.
31 *PR 2 H II*, p. 57; *Regesta*, iii, p. xxxv and *passim*.
32 For John the Marshal see *Complete Peerage*, x, App. G, pp. 93–5; *L'histoire de Guillaume le Maréchal* (3 vols, Société de l'histoire de France, Paris, 1981–4), ed. P. Meyer, vol. 1, vv. 168–269; S. Painter, *William Marshall* (Baltimore, 1933), pp. 8–12.
33 *Red Book of the Exchequer*, pp. 239–41, 300, 304, 307, 309.
34 Painter, op. cit. supra n. 32, p. 12.

even came from church lands; the heirs of William fitz Alan had one knight's fee in Wiltshire for which they did service to the bishop of Salisbury.[35] The church had reason to complain of all parties during the civil war; supporters of both Stephen and Matilda plundered church lands to requisition food for their garrisons, and repeatedly took advantage of stone-built churches to use as strongpoints during a siege or campaign, so turning them, as churchmen bitterly complained, into fortresses.[36] Scripture readily provided the language of denunciation: the house of God was turned into a den of robbers. There was nothing to choose between the sides; churches were left hoping for deathbed penitence and reparation, or for restitution whenever peace returned.

Matilda did, however, show herself more careful than Stephen not to antagonize the church. She had experienced the consequences of her first husband overstepping the bounds of prudence, and had watched the skill with which her father upheld his interests while making just enough concessions to the demands of reforming churchmen to avoid an open breach. She herself made one bad mistake, over the Durham election, but apart from that her relations with the church show that she had a better grip of the realities of papal politics than many of her contemporaries. She never deserved the reputation, foisted upon her by many historians, of an old-fashioned opponent of church reform.

Relations with the Church; Monastic Endowment

Before 1135 Matilda had little, if any, land of her own in England. The only small endowment offered to the church that may have come from her personal revenue was her gift of 9s. worth of land at Eastrop to the abbey of Tiron, probably made in her first widowhood between 1126 and 1128.[37] Her father associated her with his grants to Cluny and Fontevraud out of the farms of London, Lincoln and Winchester, and she made a point of insisting on the payment of the farm to Fontevraud after she became Lady of the English.[38] There is little record of her

35 Red Book of the Exchequer, p. 234.

36 Gesta Stephani, pp. 61–2, 91–2; Malmesbury, HN, pp. 42, 48; D. F. Renn, Norman Castles in Britain, 2nd edn (London, 1973), pp. 49–50.

37 Regesta, iii, 898. The editors give a wide date; but the charter was issued in London, and Matilda was only in England during the years between her return from Germany in 1126 and her marriage in 1128, and for a very few weeks or days in late August and early September 1131.

38 See above, pp. 58–9, Regesta, iii, no. 328, for Fontevraud. King Henry's grant of 100 marks annually out of the farms of London and Lincoln, with Matilda's signum is calendared in Regesta, ii, no. 1691. Stephen granted the royal demesne manor of Letcombe Regis to Cluny in place of the cash pension. Matilda apparently gave a charter (now lost) to supersede Stephen's: this was confirmed by her husband (Regesta, iii, no. 205) and later Stephen's was confirmed by her son Henry (Regesta, iii, no. 206).

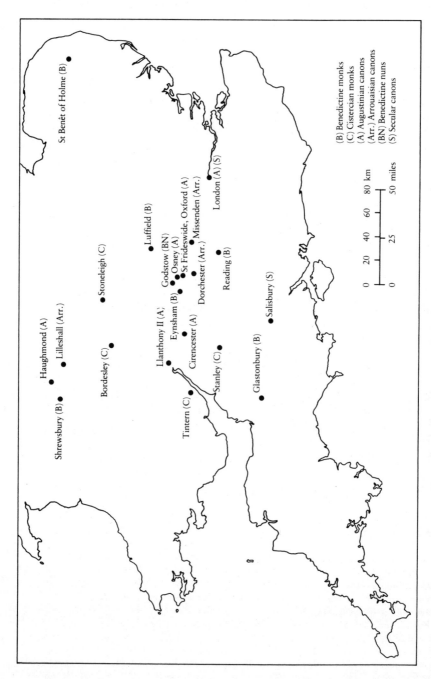

MAP 3 Religious houses in England which received charters from Matilda

St Benêt of Holme (B)

Luffield (B)

Stoneleigh (C)

Godstow (BN)
Osney (A)
St Frideswide, Oxford (A)
Missenden (Arr.)
Dorchester (Arr.)

Reading (B)

London (A) (S)

Haughmond (A)
Lilleshall (Arr.)

Llanthony II (A)
Eynsham (B)
Cirencester (A)

Bordesley (C)

Stanley (C)

Salisbury (S)

Glastonbury (B)

Shrewsbury (B)

Tintern (C)

(B) Benedictine monks
(C) Cistercian monks
(A) Augustinian canons
(Arr.) Arrouaisian canons
(BN) Benedictine nuns
(S) Secular canons

0   20   40   60   80 km

0   25   50 miles

almsgiving in the first eighteen months after she arrived in England, when her authority was restricted and her patronage not widely sought. Only one known charter for any church comes from this period; probably in 1139 she confirmed William de Berkeley's gift of Kingswood (Gloucestershire) to Tintern for the foundation of a Cistercian abbey. Her charter, modestly addressed to all the faithful subject to her, places her gift firmly in the context of an authority still limited in practice to her brother Robert's marcher lordship of Gloucester.[39]

After the battle of Lincoln and especially after her recognition as Lady of the English she assumed a right to make grants out of the royal demesne; and for a time at least, as her charters make plain, she treated all grants of demesne made by Stephen as invalid. Since she had no wish to deprive churches of any lands which they held, her normal method was to issue charters making the grants, or confirming those of her father, in her own name, without reference to Stephen. The geographical distribution of the religious houses which received charters from her suggests that much depended on where she set up her residence and which houses actually applied to her for a charter. The initiative in seeking a charter for any except family monasteries normally lay with the petitioner rather than the monarch; the appearance of a handful of charters in regions where she never established a firm foothold was probably due to the wish of particular individuals to be on the safe side, and not depend solely on grants received from Stephen. Henry of Winchester secured on behalf of his abbey of Glastonbury a general charter of confirmation which explicitly restored Uffculme, taken by William I.[40] Henry also held, among his various benefices, the office of dean of St Martin Le Grand in London, previously held by Bishop Roger of Salisbury; after Roger's disgrace some properties passed into other hands, and Matilda, in one of her rare interventions in London, ordered their restoration to Henry of Winchester.[41] This charter was issued during the first few weeks of the summer of 1141 when her writ ran in London. Another charter for a London religious house granted at the same time was one in favour of Holy Trinity Priory, which superseded an earlier grant by Stephen and added new pasture rights.[42] The

39 *Regesta*, iii, no. 419; the charter is said in the abbreviation to be addressed to 'omnibus sancte matris ecclesie filiis tam clericis quam laicis sue subjectionis.'

40 *Regesta*, iii, 343; the charter was granted *c*.3 March 1141, as soon as Bishop Henry made his peace with the empress. Stephen had previously granted a similar charter (ibid., no. 341).

41 *Regesta*, iii, no. 529.

42 *Regesta*, iii, no. 518; the charter in its present form is suspicious, but the substance is sufficiently characteristic to indicate that a genuine charter was granted. Stephen's charter is ibid., no. 517.

general confirmation for St Benêt of Hulme, which is her only known charter for Norfolk, belongs if genuine to March 1141, when her success at Lincoln made her a desirable benefactress.[43] The wording is almost identical with that of Stephen's 1140 confirmation, and the monks may have been taking out an insurance policy.[44]

One other charter granting a concession in a region where she never maintained a firm hold probably also belongs to the year 1141. Waltham, with the service of the canons there and all their property, had been granted by Henry I successively to both his wives, Matilda and Adeliza.[45] It was evidently intended to be in the queen's dower and Stephen granted it to his queen, presumably dispossessing Adeliza. The empress, who owed her first foothold in Arundel to her stepmother and was determined to respect her father's wishes, granted it to Queen Adeliza, with all the customs the canons had enjoyed in the time of Queen Matilda, as King Henry's charter had confirmed them. Her own hold on Essex was tenuous, but Adeliza's second husband, William of Aubigny, was a powerful landholder in the district and seems, from the account in the Waltham Chronicle, to have kept a firm grip on Waltham. It is possible that Stephen conceded Adeliza's right in order to retain William's support against Geoffrey de Mandeville.[46]

Most of Matilda's gifts and confirmations to churches were confined to houses in the neighbourhood of castles that she held. Many of them were founded either by her ancestors or by her vassals. Reading was one of the first to seek and obtain her favour. She visited the abbey, where her father was buried, in March 1141. The presence of the former master of her father's writing office, Robert de Sigillo, among the monks of Reading may have encouraged them to apply for favours. Five of her charters for Reading are extant for the period from March to July in that year. Three of these superseded, in part at least, grants made by Stephen.[47] The charter concerning Stanton Harcourt church was, however, a confirmation of a charter of Queen Adeliza, and may have replaced her earlier grant of 100s. in Stanton, which Stephen had

43 *Regesta*, iii, no. 400.

44 *Regesta*, iii, no. 399.

45 *The Early Charters of the Augustinian Canons of Waltham Abbey, Essex 1062–1230*, ed. Rosalind Ransford (Woodbridge and Wolfeboro, 1989), p. xxiv, and nos 3, 16; *Regesta*, ii, no. 525; iii, nos 916, 918.

46 W. Stubbs, *The Foundation of Waltham Abbey: the tract 'De invencione Sanctae Crucis nostrae in Monte Acuto'* (Oxford, 1861), ch. 29. A new edition is being prepared by L. Watkiss and M. Chibnall for OMT. The chronicler describes a local struggle between Geoffrey de Mandeville and William d'Aubigny, during which Waltham was burnt by Geoffrey, but he does not mention Stephen's queen and treats Waltham as Adeliza's dower.

47 *Regesta*, iii, nos 697–701; for Stephen's charters see ibid., nos 675, 679, 690.

confirmed. The empress was clearly anxious that Adeliza's gifts should be recognized; a few years later, between 1144 and 1147, she confirmed the gift of Berkeley church which apparently had originated with the dowager queen and her clerk, Serlo.[48]

The empress made one new grant to Reading for a special reason; most probably in 1144 she gave the monks the royal manor of Blewbury, for the souls of her ancestors and for the love and loyal service of Brian fitz Count.[49] The lands of Reading lay in the thick of the fighting, and the abbey suffered loss from the partisans of both sides. Brian fitz Count, holding out in Wallingford, was often desperate for the means to feed his garrison and was driven to plunder when his own lands had been ravaged.[50] Matilda seems in this gift to be making reparation for the wrong done to the church by her loyal vassal fighting in her cause; he had lost too much to be able to offer anything of his own. A year or two later Stephen, equally guilty of plundering the lands of Reading, ignored Matilda's gift and gave Blewbury to the monks for his soul and the souls of his wife and sons.[51] Not to be defeated, young Henry in the course of his English campaign in 1147 or 1149 confirmed his mother's charter and granted Blewbury in words almost identical with hers, so showing their determination that the faithful Brian was not to be deprived of the prayers of the monks.[52]

Matilda's period of residence at Oxford produced another crop of charters. Four for Osney Abbey and five for St Frideswide's Priory were dated at Oxford; these included some new grants out of the royal demesne.[53] One later charter, given at Devizes, confirmed the grant to Osney of the church of St George in the castle of Oxford, made in her presence by Henry d'Oilli and John of St John.[54] Stephen retaliated, it seems, by giving the lands of these men to two of his supporters,

48 Regesta, iii, no. 702; B. R. Kemp (ed.), Reading Abbey Cartularies (2 vols, Camden 4th ser., 31, 33, London, 1985–6), no. 267. This gift was a cause of confusion, as the same church was also given to St Augustine's Abbey, Bristol, by Robert fitz Harding, and Duke Henry had later to resolve the conflict with the help of Archbishop Theobald (Regesta iii, nos 706–9).

49 Regesta, iii, no. 703, 'et pro amore et legali servitio Brientii filii comitis quod mihi fecit.' Brian fitz Count acted as a protector of Reading Abbey as far as he was able; his relationship has been described as 'quasi-patronal' (Kemp, Reading Cartularies, ii, 345, no. 1276; Barrow, Kingdom of the Scots, pp. 185–6).

50 In his letter to Henry of Blois he stated that although King Henry had given him lands he could harvest nothing from his ravaged fields; see above, pp. 99, 116.

51 Regesta, iii, no. 694; cf. the charter of Stephen's son Eustace, ibid., no. 694a.

52 Regesta, iii, no. 704, 'et pro amore et legali servitio Briencii filii comitis quod domine Mathildi matri mee imperatrici et mihi fecit.'

53 Regesta, iii, nos 628–31, 644–8; three of the charters for St Frideswide's were witnessed by Archbishop Theobald.

54 Regesta, iii, no. 632, dated between 1142 and 1148.

William Chesney and Richard de Camville, and confirming their grant of the same church to Osney.[55] The Knights Templars at Cowley received one grant from Matilda of forest rights at Shotover; this was possibly intended to supersede and augment one of Stephen's grants.[56] Apparently she recognized the legitimacy of the grant of Temple Cowley made by Stephen's queen out of her own Boulogne lands, and she may not have been asked to take any action over Stephen's gifts and confirmations of lands in Essex and Hertfordshire, many of which came from his queen, and were in counties where the empress was powerless.[57] Most of her charters for the Oxfordshire nunnery at Godstow were granted at Devizes. She spoke of the house as being of her father's and her own foundation, but John of St John was regarded as its patron.

The Shropshire abbeys were favoured, although Matilda never won a firm foothold in the county. William fitz Alan, the leading landholder and former sheriff, belonged to a family of unshakable loyalty to King Henry and his lawful heirs. He was one of those who revolted prematurely in 1138, and was disinherited by Stephen after the siege and capture of Shrewsbury, when his father-in-law, Ernulf de Hesdin, was executed. William took refuge with the empress and was frequently with her at Devizes. Although she was unable at first to regain a strong foothold in Shropshire, she was prepared at least to enrich the abbeys of which he was a benefactor. Her gifts of three carucates of land and the mill of Walcot to Haughmond Abbey, founded by William fitz Alan, were witnessed by both William and his brother Walter, and possibly made at their request. Stephen, in a charter probably later than Matilda's, reasserted his rights by granting the same property. It was left to Duke Henry in 1153 to reclaim the gift by confirming his mother's charter.[58] Shrewsbury Abbey had been founded by Roger de Montgomery; after the fall of Robert of Bellême it came into the protection of the crown, and William fitz Alan was only a minor benefactor.[59] Matilda's grant of Acton, near Wellington, out of royal demesne may have been made to assert her rights in Shropshire and to indicate that

---

55 *Regesta*, iii, 633, dated between 1149 and 1152; see H. E. Salter (ed.), *Facsimiles of Early Oxford Charters in Oxford Muniment Rooms*, (Oxford, 1929) no. 61.

56 *Regesta*, iii, 854; Stephen's charters are ibid., nos 851, 853.

57 See Lees, *Templars*, p. 176; *Regesta*, iii, no. 850.

58 *Regesta*, iii, nos 377 (June–July 1141), 378 (1141–3); cf. *The Cartulary of Haughmond Abbey*, ed. U. Rees (Cardiff, 1985), nos 1250, 1251, 1252, where Stephen's charter (*Regesta* iii, no. 376) is dated after Matilda's.

59 *The Cartulary of Shrewsbury Abbey*, ed. Una Rees (2 vols, Aberystwyth, 1975), i, pp. x–xii.

the abbey was now regarded as being of the royal patronage.[60] By 1144, the most likely date of this gift, Shropshire may have seemed to be territory that could be recovered. Certainly both she and her son showed their determination to assert their demesne rights there in the late 1140s.

The new house for regular canons that Richard Belmeis established at Donnington, on the Shropshire border with Staffordshire, had been endowed with the prebends of the former royal chapel of St Alkmund's in Shrewsbury, of which Belmeis was dean. Stephen confirmed the gift in 1145.[61] In June 1148, just after leaving England, Matilda addressed a writ to William fitz Alan, Walter his brother, and all her faithful men of Shropshire, granting protection to Abbot William and the canons, now moved from Donnington and established at Lilleshall.[62] By that date, with Ranulf earl of Chester back in her camp after his brief flirtation with Stephen, and her son Henry beginning to plan an expedition to make a bid for his inheritance, it was worth her while to reassert her royal rights in Shropshire, and to prepare the way by establishing an ecclesiastical foothold. In the bitter local struggles being fought in these years of weak royal control, many lords used monastic foundations as a means of pushing their claims into disputed territory. The strategy was an old one, and it was used at all levels. Motives of genuine piety, a wish to make reparation for the occupation of church property and monastic buildings and to escape from excommunication after such violation, all contributed to the exceptionally large number of new houses founded in these years; strategic considerations often determined the sites chosen. Matilda was no stranger to such devices, and her son pursued the same policies even more purposefully.

King Stephen may have taken the first step in establishing a hermitage in Cannock forest in Staffordshire, as a charter of Roger, bishop of Chester, testifies.[63] Matilda characteristically granted the site of the hermitage to God and St Mary of Radmore and the monks there serving God, without reference to Stephen. It seems most convincing to date this grant about 1147, when Earl Ranulf was emerging from a period of vacillation to become the mainstay of the Angevin party in north-west England and parts of the Midlands, even if Ranulf himself made no

60 *Regesta*, iii, no. 820, dated *c*.1144 by U. Rees, *Shrewsbury Cartulary*, no. 50. Matilda also issued a general confirmation of her father's confirmation charter (*Regesta*, iii, no. 821), ignoring Stephen's (*Regesta*, iii, no. 819).

61 *Regesta*, iii, no. 469; *VCH Shropshire*, ii, 70–1.

62 *Regesta*, iii, no. 461.

63 For Bishop Roger's charter see *Regesta*, iii, no. 838; *Stoneleigh Leger Book*, ed. R. H. Hilton (Dugdale Society 24, 1960), p. 10.

grants until a few years later. In 1153 Duke Henry confirmed the foundation of a Cistercian abbey at Radmore to replace the hermitage, and gave his consent to a charter of Earl Ranulf granting Cannock.[64] This was the community which, shortly afterwards, moved to Stoneleigh in Warwickshire, with the approval of Henry as king.[65] Radmore and Lilleshall together indicate a movement of Angevin patronage into the west Midlands; the gifts of Matilda and her son suggest that they were preparing to strike out from their established base in Wiltshire and link up with the earldom of Cheshire.

Other new foundations were more closely connected with the struggle in Wiltshire. After briefly losing Malmesbury in 1140, Stephen successfully held on to the castle, which was a threat to the communications between Gloucester and Devizes. Matilda made the most of the forest of Chippenham to establish her knights and keep an effective presence almost at the gates of Malmesbury. One of her men, Drogo 'of Polwheile', her chamberlain, had received land at Loxwell or Drownfont from her and her son; after his death or by his consent they later used it for the foundation of a Cistercian abbey. In April 1149 Duke Henry gave the place to Quarr Abbey in the Isle of Wight, which sent a community of monks.[66] Later they moved five miles to a new site at Stanley and received further royal grants of pasture in the forest. Several of the vassals of the empress also contributed to its endowment. In particular Hugh of Plucknet gave a hide of land in Lambourn and also land at Godswell in the manor of Westbury; his kinsfolk continued to be generous benefactors throughout the twelfth and into the thirteenth century.[67] The mutual interests of lords and vassals extended beyond castle and court into the religious houses which they combined to endow, and where they were commemorated together by generations of monks. These foundations helped to strengthen their interests in a particular region, and to demonstrate their rights to the lands and customs given to the monks.

It was not to be expected that the empress would tolerate the foundation of a religious house on royal demesne given by Stephen when she could prevent it. Often she was obliged to acquiesce; but she could force a surrender from anyone hoping to be her vassal. This explains her treatment of the abbey of Bordesley, founded by Waleran of Meulan on royal demesne lands he had received from Stephen in the

---

64 *Regesta*, iii, nos 840, 841.

65 Knowles and Hadcock, pp. 125–6.

66 *Regesta*, iii, nos 666, 836; the place was first called *Fons Drogonis*.

67 *Regesta*, iii, no. 837; *VCH Wilts.*, viii, 161; W. L. Bowles, *Parochial History of Bremhill in the County of Wiltshire* (London, 1828), pp. 89–91; Birch, 'Cistercian abbey of Stanley', pp. 249–65, gives a calendar of records from the archives of Stanley Abbey.

county of Worcester. When Waleran recognized in the summer of 1141 that his predominantly Norman interests compelled him to make peace with the empress, she exacted a price before receiving his homage. Bordesley was to be given up, and the patronage taken over by her and her son. She did not attempt to remove the abbot he had approved; but her first charters to Bordesley, witnessed by Waleran, refer to it as her foundation, made for the souls of her parents and ancestors, and for the salvation of herself and her husband Geoffrey, Henry her heir, and her other sons.[68] Waleran may have kept some shadow of patronage through his friendship with the abbot, particularly after the grip of the empress on Worcestershire weakened; but by the time Henry II became king there was no doubt that Bordesley was an abbey of royal foundation.[69] The general charters of confirmation which, in 1156, both Matilda and Henry granted to Bordesley confirmed the gifts of several benefactors; although Waleran witnessed both charters at Rouen he was not mentioned among the donors.[70] Matilda never conceded that he had any valid right to the demesne lands which made up the abbey's first endowment.

Her conduct over Bordesley shows her reluctance to allow the secularization of royal demesne lands given by her enemies to religious houses; this is also shown in the wording of a charter granted by her son Henry to the abbey of Stanley after he became king. Worth, a member of his manor of Faringdon, had been given to the abbey of Thame by Stephen; Henry took it back on gaining the throne. But because it had once belonged to a religious house, at the request of his mother and the abbot of Citeaux, he gave it to the abbey of Stanley, which his mother and he had founded.[71]

Some of Matilda's gifts to religious houses, particularly grants of revenue, have left no charters; others clearly inspired by her were given by her supporters. Throughout the whole of her life after 1125,

68 *Regesta*, iii, nos 114, 115, 116; no. 116, dated by the editors between 25 July 1141 and June 1142, is unlikely to have been later than August 1141, when Waleran probably left England for good. For a discussion of the charters see Edmund J. King, 'Waleran, count of Meulan, earl of Worcester (1104–1166)', in *Tradition and Change,* ed. Diana Greenway et al. (Cambridge, 1985), pp. 170–2.

69 Crouch, *Beaumont Twins,* pp. 39–40 gives an account of the foundation of Bordesley which tends to be overcritical of the empress. Her actions were entirely consistent with her belief in her just rights; she would have weakened her claims by allowing that Stephen had the power to give away the royal demesne.

70 *Calendar of Charter Rolls,* ii, 63–4.

71 Delisle/Berger, i, no. 682; Dugdale, *Monasticon,* v, 564–5; facsimile in Charles Johnson and Hilary Jenkinson, *English Court Hand* (Oxford, 1915), pt. ii, Plate VIId. The charter was granted in 1186 or 1188, long after the concession had been made at Matilda's request.

whatever benefactions she made to other religious houses out of either piety or policy, the monks of Bec had a special place in her devotion. Even during her eight and a half years in England she was not cut off from them. The abbey was generously endowed in England, and had manors and churches scattered from Devonshire to Norfolk, from War-wickshire to Sussex. Several English conventual priories had been founded, and there were also one or two small priory cells that were centres of administration for the far-flung estates.[72] Bec's Norman priory of Notre-Dame-du Pré had a small cell at Steventon, given by Henry I; so monks Matilda may have known in Rouen were living just south of Oxford. Even though the disturbed state of the country made travel difficult and it was practically impossible to send produce back to Bec, monks were still able to come and go across the Channel. Changes in the administration of the estates made in the middle years of the twelfth century probably resulted from conditions prevailing during the Anarchy. The small cell of Ruislip in Middlesex was at first the adminis-trative centre for the English estates, but at about this time a second centre appears in Ogbourne, which looked after properties in the south-west of England. Ruislip and the eastern manors were in Stephen's sphere of influence. Ogbourne St Andrew had been given to Bec for the wardrobe of the monks by Matilda of Wallingford and her husband Brian before the death of Henry I; at some time in the 1140s they confirmed the grant of the manors and churches of both Ogbourne St George and Ogbourne St Andrew.[73] Monks from a cell established at Ogbourne could travel by easy stages through Chisenbury, Brixton Deverill, Milburne and Povington, which were all Bec manors, to the port at Wareham, where the abbey owned a mill. They, or their atten-dants, may have taken messages. Matilda of Wallingford granted a virgate of land in Ogbourne to one of her humbler kinsmen, Richard, in return for light services which included letter-carrying.[74] Although neither monks nor their companions always enjoyed immunity from attack, as the canons of church councils condemning their assailants prove, they were probably safer messengers than merchants or lay servants. Letters were certainly smuggled through hostile territory by friendly monks. William, prior of Ste-Barbe-sur-Auge, who died in 1153, used to send letters to the empress and her son to warn them of imminent danger by folding them tightly and hiding them in the long,

---

72 For the history of Bec's possessions in England see M. Morgan, *The English Lands of the Abbey of Bec* (Oxford, 1946).

73 *Select Documents of the English Lands of the Abbey of Bec,* ed. M. Chibnall (Camden 3rd ser., 73, 1951), pp. 10, 34–5.

74 *Ibid.*, p. 24.

flowing beard of one of the lay brothers.[75] While the reference in the *Chronicle* of Ste Barbe may be to letters sent after 1150 in Normandy, the priory had a dependent cell at Beckford in Gloucestershire, so communication with England was easy for the monks.[76] Matilda showed her gratitude to them by giving some revenues and promising to build either a cloister or a dormitory for them.[77] Her gift may be one of those made by her in England for which no charter is known.

Relations with the Church: Episcopal Elections

When Matilda made her peace with Henry of Winchester after the battle of Lincoln she promised to respect his wishes in the gift of bishoprics and abbacies; later, when he reverted to Stephen's side, he complained that she had persistently broken her pledges relating to church rights.[78] How far was this true? She was violently attacked by the Durham chronicler, whose word has been too readily accepted by many historians; but the facts do not bear out the charges of hostility to church reform made against her by her enemies in their propaganda.

The only two episcopal elections Matilda was able to influence directly were those to London and Durham. As soon as she was recognized as Lady of the English she took steps to provide a bishop for the see of London, vacant since the abortive election of Anselm of Bury St Edmunds had been quashed in 1138. Matilda's choice was Robert de Sigillo, the master of her father's writing office. He had retired and taken the monastic habit in the abbey of Reading, where he was respected as a man of good character; and his abbot consented to the election.[79] Clearly the choice was Matilda's, but the election was evidently canonical and acceptable to both Henry of Winchester and Theobald, archbishop of Canterbury. Theobald blessed him as bishop, probably in late June or early July 1141, and he made the customary profession of obedience to the church of Canterbury.[80] His only trouble came later, when Stephen was restored to power and resented finding a

75 R. N. Sauvage, 'La chronique de Sainte-Barbe-en-Auge', *Mémoires de l'Académie Nationale ... de Caen* (Caen, 1906), Documents, p. 51. The letters were sent 'per quemdam conversum, cui barba festivior erat.'

76 *VCH Gloucs.*, viii, pp. 253–4.

77 Sauvage, op. cit. supra note 75, p. 51.

78 Malmesbury, *HN*, pp. 50, 63.

79 Florence of Worcester, ii, p. 131. Henry of Huntingdon, p. 316, called him 'vir animo magnus'.

80 *Canterbury Professions*, ed. M. Richter (Canterbury and York Society, 67, 1973), p. 42, no. 84.

bishop from the inner circle of his rival established in his capital city. He demanded an oath of fealty which Robert, possibly because he had already sworn fealty to Matilda and had been consecrated and invested with his see, was unwilling to give. When Stephen angrily excluded him from his bishopric, help came from the most exalted men in the church. In 1142 St Bernard himself wrote to Pope Innocent II on behalf of Robert, whom he described as a friend of long standing, a faithful servant and a devoted son, lawfully occupying a see which had fallen to his lot by the will of God.[81] Later, when Robert was further persecuted by Stephen, Eugenius III wrote of him as 'a wise and upright man, a lover of true religion.'[82] There was nothing in his election to give offence to even the most ardent reformers in the church.

The Durham election, which has proved so fatal to Matilda's reputation, was a different matter. King David of Scotland had an interest in a see where the prince bishop's territory adjoined provinces he either held or claimed, and commanded his best route into England. When the see fell vacant through the death of Geoffrey Rufus on 6 May 1141 he had, it seemed, a suitable candidate. William Cumin, one of bishop Geoffrey's former clerks, had become King David's chancellor, and the king attempted to force his election on the cathedral chapter. The Durham monks thought otherwise and refused to accept the election unless the legate, Henry of Winchester, gave his assent. Both parties sent envoys to Westminster at breakneck speed. When they arrived the legate was not there. Matilda gave her consent, but when Bishop Henry arrived he declared the election irregular and refused to confirm it. Matilda, backed by her uncle, stood her ground. She may at some point have received William's fealty and restored the temporalities to him; but it is not credible, in view of her past experience and future conduct, that she would ever have invested him herself with ring and staff, as the Durham chronicler (writing at the other end of England) alleged she was preparing to do.[83] Her conduct may have helped to keep King David's friendship; unfortunately for her it also provided ammunition for Henry of Winchester when he began to regret his change of sides, and was fatal to her later reputation in many quarters. William Cumin

81 Bernard, *S. Bernardi Opera*, viii, p. 70 (ep. 211).

82 Migne, *PL*, 180, cols 1248–9 (ep. 199).

83 A detailed but biased account is given by the Durham chronicler, SD, i, pp. 143–8 (*continuatio prima*); there is a shorter account written about 30 or 40 years later, ibid., pp. 161–7. See also G. V. Scammell, *Hugh du Puiset, Bishop of Durham* (Cambridge, 1956), pp. 8, 129. The general statement of R. L. Benson, *The Bishop Elect*, p. 256, n. 20, that 'most of the evidence for investiture with ring and staff after 1133 is questionable' could be applied to Matilda's conduct in the Durham election, as well as to elections elsewhere.

behaved tyrannically in his attempts to gain possession of the temporalities, and he was permanently excluded from the see. It was an unhappy, but unique, chapter in the history of Matilda's relations with the church.

Thereafter she was never in a position to claim a direct voice in any episcopal election. Even before Henry of Winchester's legateship had lapsed with the death of Innocent II in 1143, Theobald began to emerge as the true leader of the English church. He was able to hold the bishops together in the divided realm, and to keep them loyal to the anointed king, Stephen, without forfeiting the respect of the empress and her son. The areas where there was most danger of friction were those controlled, or partly controlled, by Matilda's supporters. The bishopric of Salisbury was a particularly sensitive area, where the opposing factions divided the territory among themselves; and the empress, after her flight from Oxford, made her headquarters in the former episcopal castle of Devizes. The bishopric had already been the scene of a conflict of wills between Stephen and his brother Henry after the death of Roger of Salisbury in 1139. Stephen rejected Henry's candidate, his nephew Henry of Sully, and proposed instead his own new chancellor, Philip of Harcourt, whom Henry refused to consecrate.[84] Not until Philip was provided with the bishopric of Bayeux was the way clear for a new election. This time a convenient compromise candidate was found: Jocelin of Bohun, an archdeacon of Winchester and friend of Henry of Blois, who was also a kinsman of Robert earl of Gloucester. Jocelin was, in the words of David Knowles, 'a somewhat irresolute man', who held office from 1142 to 1184 and 'was destined to play an important, if not very glorious, part in the long series of disputes.'[85] A worldly churchman rather than a reformer, he was elected at a time when there was fighting near to Salisbury and some divisions in the cathedral chapter; but his election was never challenged as irregular and he was duly consecrated by the archbishop.[86]

Church elections in Normandy were outside Matilda's direct influence. There the support of the bishops for Stephen crumbled as Count Geoffrey's armies advanced. For a time in 1141 they hesitated, uncertain which way to turn. John, bishop of Lisieux, died on 21 May 1141, shortly after recognizing Geoffrey;[87] but Arnulf, archdeacon of

84 Orderic, vi, p. 536; S. E. Gleason, *An Ecclesiastical Barony of the Middle Ages* (Cambridge, Mass., 1936), pp. 27–31.

85 For his career and family see David Knowles, *The Episcopal Colleagues of Archbishop Thomas Becket* (Cambridge, 1951), pp. 17–22; King, 'The Anarchy of Stephen's reign', pp. 139–40.

86 *Letters of Gilbert Foliot*, no. 31; Richter, *Canterbury Professions*, p. 43, no. 85.

87 Orderic, v, pp. 550–3.

Sées, who was elected to succeed him before the end of the year, came from a family which supported Stephen strongly, and he refused to swear fealty to the count of Anjou. Since he had been consecrated without Geoffrey's consent, the latter retaliated by refusing to admit him to the temporalities and appealing to the pope. By 1143 Arnulf could hold out no longer; he paid a fine of nine hundred livres, was granted the temporalities, and began to date his charters from Geoffrey's, not Stephen's, reign.[88] Thereafter the two men worked harmoniously together, and Arnulf pressed Geoffrey's claims wherever possible. A second election to Sées in 1144 ran into difficulties for a different reason. There were some irregularities in the election which led to an appeal to Rome, and Geoffrey sent some of his officers to prevent the bishop elect, Gerard, being intruded until the appeal was settled. The officers behaved with such brutality that Geoffrey disowned them and agreed to allow the matter to be settled in an ecclesiastical court.[89] He was prepared not to challenge a properly conducted election and to allow ecclesiastical justice to take its course, provided that he could retain his right to give the licence to elect and invest the new bishop with the temporalities.[90] In this he was upholding in Normandy the rights claimed by Henry 1, just as Matilda tried to uphold them in England. The two may have acted in consultation, or they may have followed the course marked out by King Henry independently. Both succeeded in upholding the royal prerogative without seriously offending the pope.

When Geoffrey first asserted his rights he was roundly denounced by Bernard of Clairvaux as a hammer of good men and a destroyer of the peace and freedom of the church;[91] but he was soon able to appease Pope Eugenius, whom he met in Paris in 1147, by accepting the rights claimed for the church courts,[92] and he gave Bernard no further cause for complaint. Matilda was even more careful to act circumspectly in her relations with the pope, and the gifts that she and her brother Robert made to the Cistercians may have helped to sweeten their relations with the formidable abbot of Clairvaux. When Earl Robert founded a Cistercian abbey at Margam in 1147 Bernard's brother, Nivard, travelled to south Wales to be present at the inauguration ceremony.[93] He seems to have met Matilda on his journey and enlisted

88 Barlow, *Letters of Arnulf*, pp. xix–xx, 209; *RHF*, xv, pp. 582–5, 603–4.

89 Barlow, *Letters of Arnulf*, pp. 4–5, no. 3, 21–2, no. 16.

90 See H. Böhmer, *Kirche und Staat in England und in der Normandie im xi et xii Jahrhundert* (Leipzig, 1899), pp. 310–25.

91 Bernard, *S. Bernardi Opera*, viii, pp. 291–3 (ep. 348).

92 H. Gleber, *Papst Eugen III* (Jena, 1936), p. 71.

93 *Gloucester Charters*, no. 119.

her support for the monks of Cerne, who were involved in an appeal to Rome arising from a violent quarrel with their newly elected abbot. The elect had previously been a prior of Gloucester, and Matilda wrote to the abbot of Gloucester, Gilbert Foliot, in support of the monks. Gilbert replied respectfully but firmly, that the monks had misrepresented the facts to Nivard, for the pope himself had instructed him to have them removed to another monastic house, and although he would obey the empress in everything that was lawful, he could not defy the pope's authority.[94] Apparently she accepted his defence; she had at least acted diplomatically and tactfully, giving what help she could to the influential Cistercians, but acquiescing in the papal mandate. Both Stephen and his brother Henry, on the other hand, by their actions lost favour with both Pope Eugenius and St Bernard, whose invective was now turned against them.

Stephen's intervention in the troubled York election, with which Matilda was not concerned,[95] and his attempt to prevent the archbishop of Canterbury and all but three of the English bishops attending the 1148 council of Reims seriously damaged his cause.[96] His brother Henry of Winchester was never able to secure a renewal of his legateship after the death of Innocent II; and after his failure to attend the council of Reims himself he was suspended from office and compelled to visit Rome in person to obtain absolution. Eugenius suspected him of 'trailing his tail in the English sea', and disturbing the church even when he was out of the realm on his visit to Rome. Whether or not the accusation was unjust, as John of Salisbury who thought that 'the king took no advice from him or any wise man' alleged, the papal Curia remained relentlessly opposed both to Stephen's attempts to have his son Eustace crowned and to Bishop Henry's struggle to secure privileges for his see and recover his lost power.[97] Meanwhile Matilda, loyally seconded by her husband Geoffrey and increasingly favoured by influential churchmen, worked unremittingly to further the succession of her son Henry.

94 *Letters of Gilbert Foliot*, p. 98 (ep. 63), App. III, pp. 507–9. Since Nivard came to Margam in 1147 it is more likely that the monks of Cerne saw him as he crossed England than that they met him on their way back from the papal court, as the editors suggest.

95 For the York election see David Knowles, *The Historian and Character* (Cambridge, 1963), pp. 76–97; Gleber, *Papst Eugen III*, pp. 163–4; Barlow, *The English Church 1066–1154*, pp. 98–100.

96 *Historia Pontificalis*, pp. 6–7.

97 *Historia Pontificalis*, pp. 78–9.

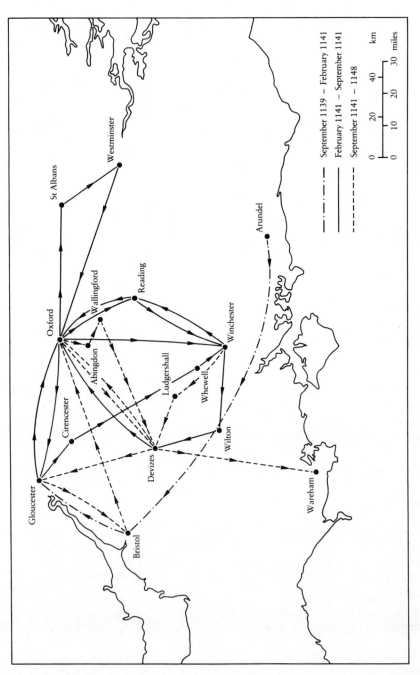

St Albans

Westminster

Wallingford

Reading

Oxford

Abingdon

Arundel

Ludgershall

Cirencester

Whewell

Winchester

Gloucester

Devizes

Wilton

Bristol

Wareham

km

0   10   20   40

0   10   20   30   miles

MAP 4   Itinerary of the empress

7

Greatest in her Offspring

The Rightful Heir

Henry Plantagenêt was first brought into English affairs in the heady days of July 1141, when his mother, repulsed at London but not yet assaulted in Winchester, was enlisting the dubious support of Geoffrey de Mandeville and Aubrey de Vere, and when his father had just completed a triumphant drive into Normandy, leading his armies right up to the Seine. There was still a chance that she might make good her claim to the throne, and in the hope of a victory she was prepared to promise the two earls lands in England that she did not yet control and lands and offices in half-conquered Normandy. These promises were intended to be lasting; the support of Count Geoffrey and of their heir was necessary. In these circumstances young Henry gave the same pledges as his mother to the earls. His charter to Aubrey de Vere began: 'Henry, son of the daughter of King Henry, rightful heir of England and Normandy, to his archbishops, bishops, abbots, earls, barons, justices, sheriffs, and all faithful men, French and English, of all England and Normandy, greeting.' It ended, 'I have given a pledge to keep this convention with my own hand in the hand of Hugh of Ing, as my mother the empress pledged in the hand of Earl Geoffrey.'[1] Hugh of Ing was one of the Essex vassals of Geoffrey de Mandeville, who had gone to Normandy to secure the consent of Henry and his father. We do not know if a similar charter was ever granted by Count Geoffrey. Some years were to pass before the young prince made so sweeping a claim to authority over the whole of England and Normandy, or even described himself as the rightful heir. Reality took over in the language of his charters, as it had in the conduct of his mother's campaign in England after the release of King Stephen.

1 *Regesta*, iii, no. 635. The charter for Aubrey de Vere, which follows Matilda's charter (ibid., no. 634) very closely, survives in a cartulary copy. It is to be presumed that Henry confirmed a similar charter for Geoffrey de Mandeville.

Henry may have spent some of his earliest years in Normandy in his mother's household. He witnessed one of her early charters for St Nicholas, Angers;[2] and he was with her at Carrouges when he and his youngest brother, William, who had been born two years earlier at Argentan, added their crosses to her charter for Saumur. Geoffrey, the middle brother, had remained at Saumur, where he in turn added his cross.[3] By the time Matilda left for England in 1139 Henry was well into his seventh year, an age at which he would almost certainly in any case have been ready to return to his father to begin his training as a knight. He set foot for the first time in the kingdom he hoped to rule when his uncle, Earl Robert, brought him across the Channel in the autumn of 1142.[4] His education continued in his uncle's household at Bristol. The literary side was not neglected. He was instructed by a certain Master Matthew, and had some contact with Adelard of Bath, who dedicated his treatise on the astrolabe to him.[5] Later he spoke of an early affection for the abbey of St Augustine's, Bristol, which he took under his protection; and probably some of his studies took place in the abbey.[6] However, his residence in England lasted only about fifteen months, and for the next five years his education continued intermittently in Anjou. William of Conches was received in the household of Count Geoffrey about this time, and probably taught his sons. In his *Dialogus de Substantiis* he praised the count for encouraging the boys from their earliest years in the study of letters rather than games of dice, so giving them a lasting love of learning.[7]

Simultaneously Henry was beginning to be drawn into the practical work of government. Before he left England after his first visit he received the homage of some vassals and began to issue charters jointly with his mother. At Devizes, early in 1144, in a charter for Humphrey de Bohun in which Henry called himself simply 'son of the count of Anjou', he and the empress confirmed Humphrey's lands and his office of steward in England and Normandy, in return for which Humphrey became their liege vassal against all men. He had been Matilda's steward for several years; the new element in this charter is his fealty to

2 *Regesta*, iii, no. 20.

3 Delisle/Berger, i, no. I*.

4 For the date of Henry's first visits to England and his early education see A. L. Poole, 'Henry Plantagenet's early visits to England', *EHR*, 47 (1932), pp. 447–51.

5 C. H. Haskins, 'Henry II as a patron of literature', *Essays in Medieval History presented to T. F. Tout* (Manchester, 1925), pp. 72–4.

6 *Regesta* iii, nos 126, 996; he refers to the church 'quam in initio juventutis mee beneficiis et protectione cepi juvare et fovere.'

7 R. L. Poole, *Illustrations in the History of Medieval Thought* (London, 1884), pp. 129–30, 347–8.

young Henry, who may have been brought in because of the Norman concessions.[8] A charter of the empress for Reading, possibly of the same date or a little later, is addressed somewhat unusually to Henry her son and all her faithful subjects.[9] In January 1144 Count Geoffrey captured the city of Rouen, and shortly afterwards he began to use the title 'duke of Normandy'.[10] This was probably the occasion for Henry's recall to his father's court to be prepared for taking over the government of the duchy in a few years time. Before the end of March he had recrossed the Channel and joined his father at Angers. There he added his cross to Geoffrey's charter settling the military obligations of the priory of Cunault, a daughter house of Tournus, and received a horse as a gift from Peter, abbot of Tournus.[11] From 1144 to 1150 Count Geoffrey's charters are difficult to date precisely; during these years, and quite possibly soon after his return from England, Henry was associated with his father in a few of them, and issued one or two charters in his own name as 'the son of the count of Anjou and duke of Normandy'.[12] His father made his intentions clear as early as April 1145, when he sent him notice of a judgement given in favour of the abbey of La Trinité, Vendôme. 'Since,' Geoffrey wrote, 'God willing, I believe that you will succeed me in the governance of my land, I ask you to protect the abbey of Vendôme by every means in your power... For our predecessors founded this house and have defended it vigorously up to now. I for my part have never failed to provide help and counsel when need arose. So I bid you, who by the grace of God will surpass me and all my predecessors in power and dignity, to take the monks of Vendôme into your protection, and see that they suffer no wrong.'[13] Although Geoffrey can never have foreseen what the extent of Henry's power was to be, he clearly anticipated that he would inherit the kingdom of England. He was already beginning to introduce him to the practical work of government in Normandy and Anjou.

Little is known of Henry's first attempt at personal intervention in England. The only chronicle account in the *Gesta Stephani*, which J. H. Round refused to accept, has been vindicated by A. L. Poole's redating of Henry's movements from the Angevin and Norman sources, and is

8 *Regesta*, iii, no. 111.

9 *Regesta*, iii, no. 702; Kemp, *Reading Cartularies*, no. 267.

10 Haskins, *Norman Institutions*, pp. 129–30.

11 Poole, *EHR* 47 (1932), p. 450; P. Juénin, *Nouvelle Histoire de l'Abbaye de Saint Filibert de Tournus* (Dijon, 1733), Preuves, p. 159; Chartrou, *L'Anjou* p. 294, no. 149.

12 *Regesta*, iii, nos 18, 78, 79, 304, 729, 735, 780; Haskins, *Norman Institutions*, pp. 131–2.

13 *Chartes de Saint-Julien de Tours (1002–1227)*, ed. L'Abbé L. J. Denis (Société des Archives historiques du Maine 12, Le Mans, 1912), no. 87, pp. 113/14.

probably substantially true.[14] By the end of 1146, when Stephen imprisoned R: ulf earl of Chester and forced him to surrender Lincoln castle,
the fortunes of the Angevins were at a very low ebb. Henry was nearly
fourteen, ambitious and impulsive; he raised a small force of knights
and crossed the Channel in late 1146 or early 1147. At first the news of
his arrival caused alarm among Stephen's supporters; but his band of
knights was too small to be effective and after failing to storm the
castles of Cricklade and Purton he had to apply to his mother in
Devizes for help even to pay his men. She herself had no money to
spare; but she took advantage of his presence to assert his rights
together with her own. A charter in favour of Geoffrey Ridel, issued
jointly with him, belongs to this visit.[15] It was dated at Devizes and
granted Geoffrey Ridel, the son of Richard Basset, all his inheritance in
England and Normandy; the witnesses included Robert earl of Gloucester and Geoffrey de Mandeville the younger, earl of Essex.[16] Earl
Robert, like Matilda, failed when asked to provide Henry with money
to pay his men. The *Gesta Stephani* accused him, perhaps unjustly, of
hoarding his money bags like a miser, adding more convincingly that he
preferred to keep them for his own needs. Earl Robert was at all times a
realist; it was to his just appreciation of how to match ambition with
available resources that Matilda probably owed the preservation of a
substantial region of England for her adherents. Although the author of
the *Gesta* qualified his statement that Henry's next step was to apply to
his kinsman Stephen for money by adding that this was hearsay, the
story is quite credible. Stephen was capable of magnanimous gestures,
and he would have seen that it was worth a small sum to send Henry
back to Normandy and not allow his knights to ravage royal lands to
supply their needs. The expedition was by no means a dead loss; the
young claimant was able to confer with his mother and his uncle for the
last time before Earl Robert's death the following autumn, and perhaps
to work out plans on how to rally his supporters and prepare to take
over the conduct of English affairs from his mother when the right time
came. By 29 May 1147, which was Ascension Day, he was back in
Normandy, and was ceremonially received by the whole convent of
Bec-Hellouin.[17]

14 *Gesta Stephani*, pp. xxi, 204–6.

15 *Regesta*, iii, no. 43; date corrected in Davis, *King Stephen*, p. 169.

16 Cf. *Regesta*, iii, no. 277 for the grant to the younger Geoffrey de Mandeville of his
father's tenures and inheritance. He witnessed one charter (*Regesta*, iii, no. 43) in 1146–7
as earl of Essex, and had evidently been recognized as earl not later than 1147, unless the
scribe copying the charter (BL Sloane Roll xxxi 4, no. 48) had anticipated his later title in
adding the witnesses.

17 Torigny, *Chronicle* (ed. Howlett, p. 154; ed. Delisle, i, p. 243).

One decision apparently taken at this time was to make another determined attempt to secure the support of the church for Henry's rights as heir. Stephen's son, Eustace, was knighted late in the year,[18] and Stephen was pressing for his coronation by the archbishop of Canterbury. Moreover the preaching of the crusade had added further ecclesiastical sanctions to attacks on the property of crusaders. Chroniclers cynically commented that the departure of crusaders made no difference,[19] but although local struggles continued there was a lull in the main fighting at about this time, accompanied by a flurry of diplomacy. The council of Reims in Lent, 1148, was an opportunity to raise once more questions of legitimacy. Stephen worsened his cause in the eyes of Eugenius III by attempting unsuccessfully to prevent Archbishop Theobald from attending the council.[20] Theobald evaded the king's officers, found a small fishing boat to take him across the Channel, and arrived in time to heap coals of fire by interceding with Eugenius and saving the king from excommunication. Stephen could not, however, save his reputation at Rome. He could reply firmly to Miles, bishop of Térouanne, sent by Count Geoffrey to charge him with usurpation, that he held both England and Normandy by his own right and with papal sanction;[21] but he could not induce Eugenius to consent to the coronation of his son Eustace.

The empress and her party meanwhile carefully avoided any provocative action. During the proceedings at Reims, Robert bishop of Hereford died, and Gilbert Foliot was appointed by the pope on the advice of Archbishop Theobald, without the need for any election in England. He was blessed at St Omer by the archbishop and the bishops of Cambrai and Térouanne, after swearing to do fealty to Henry Plantagenêt and not to Stephen. By now evidently there was no question that Henry, and not his mother, was to restore the regalia to a new bishop. On his return to England, Gilbert went back on his promise and swore fealty to Stephen. This might have led to angry words, but Theobald succeeded in appeasing Henry and his father by insisting that Gilbert had no right to cause schism within the church.[22] The acceptance of Stephen did not, however, extend to the next generation. There are signs that the church in England no less than the church in Normandy was beginning to favour Henry as the rightful heir, even though refusing to undermine Stephen's position as long as he lived. If the

18 *Gesta Stephani*, pp. 208–9.
19 *Gesta Stephani*, pp. 192–3.
20 *Historia Pontificalis*, pp. 6–8.
21 *Historia Pontificalis*, p. 44.
22 *Historia Pontificalis*, pp. 47–8; Knowles, *Episcopal Colleagues*, p. 43.

author of the *Gesta Stephani* was not the bishop of Bath, he was almost certainly one of the bishop's circle, and by the end of 1148 he was veering round towards Henry's cause.[23] In the summer of 1149 Arnulf, bishop of Lisieux, wrote to Robert Chesney, who had just been elected bishop of Lincoln, urging him to support the cause of the young duke of Normandy, 'who ought to succeed to the kingdom of England by hereditary right.'[24] Arnulf had come a long way since he had attacked the legitimacy of Henry's hereditary claim in the papal court ten years previously.

The empress meanwhile treated papal mandates with great circumspection. By 1146 her position at Devizes was becoming untenable. The castle was vital to her whole strategy; but although her supporters had taken it from the king's men it had been one of Bishop Roger of Salisbury's castles before Stephen took it from the bishop. Now Jocelyn bishop of Salisbury was demanding its return. He obtained from Eugenius III a bull, dated 26 November 1146, demanding the restoration of the possessions violently taken from the bishop, and naming the castle of Devizes together with Potterne and Canning. Anyone unjustly withholding them was threatened with excommunication after being admonished three times.[25] Matilda had to face the problem created by this threat. She was too experienced to risk excommunication by intransigence, but she knew how to play for time, and first offered compensation by augmenting the prebend of Heytesbury.[26] The threat may have been one of many factors that persuaded her to leave England for good and hand over the struggle there to her son. Within eighteen months she had left the defence of Devizes to a loyal garrison and withdrawn to Normandy. At Falaise, on 10 June 1148, she made her peace with the bishop of Salisbury and Hugh, archbishop of Rouen. Confessing her sin in unjustly appropriating the possessions of the church, she restored Canning (where Devizes was situated) and Potterne to Bishop Jocelin and promised that neither she nor anyone else she could restrain would again molest or occupy them.[27] She subsequently sent a letter to her son Henry in England, telling him what she had done to obey

23 *Gesta Stephani*, p. xxi.

24 Barlow, *Letters of Arnulf* p. 7 (no. 4). Although Henry was not formally invested with the duchy until early in 1150 he was evidently regarded as duke for some time before he assumed the title in his own charters. For Arnulf's work as justice in Henry's curia see Haskins, *Norman Institutions*, p. 163.

25 *Charters and Documents illustrating the History of the Cathedral Church and Diocese of Salisbury in the Twelfth and Thirteenth Centuries*, ed. W. R. Jones and W. D. Macray (RS, 1891), pp. 12–13.

26 *Regesta*, iii, nos 792, 793. The dating limits of these two charters are wide (1141–7), but they probably mark an attempt at appeasement shortly before or after the receipt of the papal bull.

27 *Charters of Salisbury*, pp. 14–15.

the pope's mandate, and urging him to comply in order to avoid excommunication.[28]

Did Henry take his cue from his mother, or had he already himself mastered the art of prudent prevarication? When he next led an expedition to England and reached Devizes in April 1149 he restored the manor of Canning to the bishop, with the exception of the castle of Devizes which, he explained, he needed to keep in his own hand until God had so helped his cause that he had no more need of it.[29] Four years later, in April 1153, he came to an agreement with the bishop that he should hold the castle for three more years, unless he recovered his inheritance within that time; in that case, if the archbishop of Canterbury and the bishops of Winchester, Bath and Chichester so advised, he would restore it.[30] Once the peril was over and he was safely on the throne he was able to find reasons for deferring indefinitely the date when it should be restored.[31] Henry I's daughter may have felt that he had learned much, through her, from his grandfather.

Nevertheless when she left England early in 1148 young Henry's position was still precarious. Of the men who had upheld his cause during the past nine years Miles of Gloucester and Earl Robert were both dead and Brian fitz Count was no longer active. There are conflicting reports of his last years; by 1150 or at latest 1151 the wording of charters suggests that he was dead.[32] A later Abergavenny chronicle, not a very reliable source, stated that he had gone on crusade to Jerusalem.[33] A story that both he and his wife entered religion dates from the thirteenth century, but is much more probable.[34] Statements in some modern histories claiming that it was he who withstood Stephen's siege of Wallingford in 1153 are based on a misreading of Gervase of Canterbury, who wrote that the castle had been invested on several previous occasions while the empress was in England, but had never been captured then because of Brian's skilful defence.[35] By 1151 at

28 *Regesta*, iii, no. 794.

29 *Regesta*, iii, no. 795.

30 *Regesta*, iii, no. 796.

31 R. Allen Brown, 'A list of castles, 1154–1216', *EHR*, 74 (1959), p. 250; reprinted, *Castles, Conquest and Charters*: Collected Papers (Woodbridge and Wolfeboro, 1989), p. 91.

32 The date of Brian's death is discussed by P. Walne, 'A "double" charter of the Empress Matilda and Henry, duke of Normandy c.1154', *EHR*, 252 (1961), pp. 651–2. He points out that the earliest reference to his taking religious vows is in the *Book of Fees*, and there is no reference to this in the Oxfordshire inquest of 1183 to 1184 (BL MS Cott. Vitell. E xv, fo. 22).

33 Dugdale, *Monasticon*, iv, p. 615.

34 *Book of Fees*, i, p. 116.

35 Gervase of Canterbury: *The Historical Works of Gervase of Canterbury*, ed. William Stubbs (2 vols, RS, 1879–80), i, pp. 153–4.

latest the constable of Wallingford was his kinsman William Boterel.[36] Apart from Reginald, earl of Cornwall, the men who emerged to keep up resistance in England had never been in Matilda's inner circle of trusted counsellors. Ranulf, earl of Chester, torn between his own divided interests, only very rarely witnessed her charters; family ties through his wife, the daughter of Robert of Gloucester, could not quite outweigh his territorial interests until he learnt through imprisonment and forfeiture that Stephen was not to be trusted. He began to emerge as the focal point for Angevin resistance in the Midlands and north of England very soon after the death of Earl Robert of Gloucester; and he joined young Henry when he returned to England in 1149.[37] One of Henry's main objectives was to reach Carlisle, where he was invested with the belt of knighthood by his uncle King David.[38] This was an important step, as the granting of arms was generally regarded as a necessary preliminary to the recognition of a ruler.[39] It fitted him to take over authority in Normandy no less than in England when conditions should become favourable. Ranulf, who accompanied him, received the honour of Lancaster from the king at the same time. Probably he did homage to Henry, whom he subsequently called his lord, on this occasion. The witnesses to his charters show that a number of leading magnates who supported the Angevins met in his court. His brother, William of Roumare, earl of Lincoln, was among them, together with Roger, the young earl of Hereford and William fitz Alan.[40] The occasional appearance of 'Kadwalader king of the Welsh' is a reminder that the Welsh allies who had brought such effective support at the battle of Lincoln were still a potential reserve in the background, even though they had not hesitated to overrun the province of Chester in September 1146, as soon as they heard of Ranulf's imprisonment by Stephen.[41]

With these men as a permanent body of Angevin supporters, the struggle for the kingdom entered a new phase. Henry, during his visits to England in 1149 and again in 1153–4, was their leader in the field, with his uncle Reginald of Cornwall frequently acting as his deputy, and the wealthy Robert fitz Harding of Bristol able to supply loans of cash.[42] The empress herself was no more than a distant influence,

---

36 *Regesta*, iii, no. 88.

37 Barraclough, *Chester Charters*, nos 85 note, 87 note.

38 *Gesta Stephani*, p. 216.

39 Flori, *L'Essor de la Chevalerie*, p. 58.

40 Barraclough, *Chester Charters*, no. 87.

41 *Annales Cestrenses*, ed. R. C. Christie, Record Society of Lancashire and Cheshire, 14, p. 20; cf. R. R. Davies, *Conquest, Coexistence and Change*, pp. 46–7.

42 Robert B. Patterson, 'Robert fitz Harding of Bristol: profile of an early Angevin burgess-baron and his family's urban involvement', *Haskins Society Journal*, 1 (1989), pp. 109–22.

adding her authority to grants of land to religious houses and offering advice on strategy. Her sphere of activity was now Normandy, to which she added her valuable experience of diplomacy in the wider world of European politics.

Last Years in Normandy

After Matilda's return to Normandy she is first heard of at Falaise.[43] Within a few months she had settled in Rouen, and all her later charters were dated either there or at Le Pré. Henry I had built a royal residence in his park at Quevilly, on the south side of the river Seine and adjacent to the priory of Notre-Dame-du-Pré in the parish of Saint-Sever. Stephen of Rouen, a monk of Bec who spent much of his life at the priory, described in his *Draco Normannicus* how he chose to stay there when he came to Rouen, near to the priory that he had endowed and enriched.[44] Something between a castle priory and a royal palace and monastery side by side as at Westminster, the complex at Saint-Sever gave Matilda a home similar, but on a smaller scale, to the home where her mother had passed most of her later years. She may have lived in the royal residence, but it is possible that she soon moved into guest quarters attached to the priory itself. A gift made by Geoffrey of Anjou on 27 March 1149 was probably intended to make provision for her. He gave three prebends in the church of St Stephen at Bures-en-Bray to Bec-Hellouin, to be taken over by the priory of Le Pré when the tenures of the three secular clerks holding the prebends came to an end.[45] This was a substantial endowment; in the next century Archbishop Eudes Rigaud of Rouen found that Le Pré received six hundred livres from Bures, at a time when its total Norman revenues were estimated at only a thousand livres.[46] Stephen of Rouen wrote that Matilda lived among the monks of Bec as if she had been one of them; the association was evidently as close as was possible for a lay woman.[47]

Although some treasure was still stored at Falaise and Caen, and financial business was frequently transacted when the ducal court met at Caen,[48] Rouen was emerging as the judicial, administrative and commercial nerve centre of Normandy. A little earlier Orderic Vitalis had described it in glowing terms:

43 *Regesta*, iii, no. 794.

44 *Draco Normannicus* (ed. Howlett, p. 713; ed. Omont, p. 121).

45 *Regesta*, iii, no. 77.

46 *Registrum visitationum archiepiscopi Rothomagensis*, ed. Th. Bonnin (Rouen, 1852), pp. 121, 267, 271, 326.

47 *Draco Normannicus* (ed. Howlett, p. 712; ed. Omont, p. 120).

48 Haskins, *Norman Institutions*, pp. 94–5, 106–7.

Rouen is a populous and wealthy city, thronged with merchants, a meeting-place of trade routes. A fair city set among murmuring streams and smiling meadows ... it stands surrounded by hills and woods, strongly encircled by walls and ramparts and battlements, and fair to behold with its dwellings, mansions and churches.[49]

From the great tower you could see to the south the wooded region where the dukes hunted; and, nearer, the river Seine with its fisheries 'laps the walls of Rouen and daily brings in ships laden with all kinds of merchandise.'[50] Orderic, who had not known Normandy in the days when Caen was the centre of ducal power, considered that Rouen had rightly been the chief city of Normandy from the earliest times, as well as the seat of the archbishop. When Matilda settled there it was undoubtedly a metropolitan city in the widest sense of the term. Wealth was accumulating from a thriving cloth manufacture as well as from trade; and citizens such as William Trentegeruns were able to provide substantial cash loans to the duke.[51] Matilda took an interest in the amenities and prosperity of the city. Her husband had restored the wooden bridge, damaged by fire and fighting, which rested on the Ile de la Roquette and connected the city with the suburb of Saint-Sever. She herself was almost certainly responsible for the construction of a stone bridge to replace it; when she died she left a large sum of money to complete the work she had begun, and her bridge, known as the 'Pont Mathilde' survived into the sixteenth century.[52]

The city was a centre of church life and culture. There was no great school, as at Laon or Chartres, but the cathedral clergy were for the most part well-educated men, making a career in ecclesiastical or secular administration: some of them served for part of their life in the royal household, some moved on to be bishops.[53] Two great Benedictine

49 Orderic, iii, pp. 36–7.

50 Orderic, iv, pp. 224–5.

51 Raymonde Foreville, 'Les origines normandes de la famille Becket', *Mélanges Pierre Andrieu Guitrancourt, L'Année Canonique* 17 (Paris, 1973), pp. 447–8; Lucien Musset, 'Notes relatives à de nouveaux documents sur l'industrie textile normande au Moyen Age', *BSAN*, 53 (1955–6), pp. 289–93.

52 Yves Fache, *Histoire des Ponts de Rouen et de sa Region* (Editions Bertout, 1985 reprint), pp. 22–8. Matilda's mother had financed the building and maintenance of the Bow and Chanelsea bridges over the river Lea to carry the main road from London into Essex, and save crossing a dangerous ford (*VCH Essex*, vi, p. 59).

53 For details see David S. Spear, 'Membership of the Norman cathedral chapters during the ducal period: some preliminary findings', *Medieval Prosopography*, 5 (1984), pp. 1–18; idem, 'Les doyens du chapitre cathédral de Rouen', *Annales de Normandie*, 33 (1983), pp. 91–119; idem, 'Les archidiacres de Rouen au cours de la période ducale', *Annales de Normandie*, 34 (1984), pp. 15–50; idem, 'Les dignitaires de la cathédral de Rouen pendant la période ducale', *Annales de Normandie*, 37 (1987), pp. 121–47.

abbeys for men were established there: Saint Ouen, in the city, and Sainte-Trinité-du-Mont on the hill just outside. There was a nunnery at Saint Amand, as well as several smaller houses. These included the hospital of St James on the Mont-aux-Malades, served by Augustinian canons, and the priory of Notre-Dame-du-Pré, where the monks of Bec provided Matilda with spiritual counsel, and probably also with intellectual companionship. By about 1157 hermit monks of Grandmont were established either in the forest of Rouvray or in the royal park at Rouen.[54]

In the autumn of 1148 Count Geoffrey was in Rouen with his wife and all three of his sons. An unusually worded charter for the abbey of Mortemer, issued on 11 October 1148, speaks explicitly of the consent of his wife Matilda and his sons Henry, Geoffrey and William in terms that imply their presence with him at the time the charter was granted.[55] This may have been the occasion when future plans were made for the residence of the empress in Normandy, and for Henry to renew his challenge in England and prepare to take over the governance of Normandy. His expedition to Carlisle to be knighted by King David and to receive the homage of the magnates who acknowledged his right was the first necessary step. From this time he seems to have been regarded informally as duke of Normandy. Arnulf of Lisieux called him 'our duke' in a letter to Robert, bishop of Lincoln, in the summer of 1149.[56] Henry did not, however, adopt the title in his own charters before formal investiture by his father. He also made an effort to obtain the consent of the king of France.

For recognition by Louis VII he would have to wait for the king to return from Jerusalem at the beginning of November 1149. Meanwhile

54 Carole A. Hutchison, *The Hermit Monks of Grandmont* (Kalamazoo, 1989), gives 1156 or 1157 as a possible date for the foundation of Notre Dame du Parc lès Rouen; Elizabeth Hallam, 'Henry II, Richard I and the Order of Grandmont', *Journal of Medieval History*, 1 (1975), pp. 165–86, esp. pp. 179–80, suggests that the monks may originally have been established in the forest of Rouvray, and moved from there to the park outside Rouen by Henry II soon after 1180, a date preferred by Léopold Delisle and Thomas Stapleton.

55 *Regesta*, iii, no. 599. Geoffrey's charter, known only from a copy, ends, 'Et hoc quidem concedentibus Mathilde uxore mea, filiisque meis Henrico, Gaufredo atque Willelmo ... Hec vero concessio facta est et hac carta data apud Rothomagum anno ab incarnatione domini M⁰C⁰XL⁰VII⁰ a Pasche, mense Octobris, V Idus ejusdem mensis, epacta xxviii.' This wording implies that Matilda and her sons were present in Rouen at the date given; but Matilda was in England in October 1147 and at Rouen a year later. The year of the incarnation and the epact do not agree, and there must be a scribal error. The epact would be correct for 1148, not for 1147, and it is therefore more likely that the scribe made a mistake in copying the year of the incarnation, and that 1148 should be accepted as the date.

56 Barlow, *Letters of Arnulf*, pp. 6–7, no. 4.

disturbances in Anjou forced Geoffrey to hurry there to begin the siege of Montreuil-Bellay, where Giraud Berlai was holding out against him.[57] Matilda, in Rouen, may have been needed to deal with ducal business during the absence of her son in England and her husband in another province. As soon as King Louis reached Paris, negotiations began to induce him to withdraw his support from Stephen's son Eustace and agree to Henry's succession. The help of both Arnulf, bishop of Lisieux, back in Normandy after his participation in the crusade, and Suger, abbot of Saint-Denis, was enlisted in this delicate business.[58] Arnulf wrote to Suger to ask for his support in putting their case. The abbot had known King Henry I from the time when, a young monk, he had been put in charge of the property of Saint-Denis in Normandy at Berneval; he retained a lifelong admiration for the old king, and recalled with gratitude the honour and good faith which he had shown in protecting the abbey's property during times of war and disorder. The two men had often discussed how best to procure peace, and Suger claimed that he had repeatedly done all in his power to restore and maintain peace between the kings of England and France. Now, remembering ancient friendship, he urged Geoffrey and Matilda to approach King Louis through intermediaries, and try to make peace with him before he could enter into any treaty with their enemies. At the same time he put in a word for the property of the abbey at Berneval.[59] Their enemies were already hard at work; King Stephen, supported by his brother Bishop Henry, was writing conciliatory letters to Suger, promising protection for these lands when he was in a position to provide it.[60] Whether remembered gratitude, present advantage or sound political judgement weighed more with Suger we do not know; but he used his influence to help the *de facto* duke of Normandy and the old king's daughter rather than the *de facto* king of England in seeking reconciliation with the king of France. St Bernard too added his voice to the peacemakers.[61] Louis, who at first had joined Stephen and Eustace in an attack on Normandy, was finally persuaded to agree to a truce and meet Count Geoffrey and his son.[62] The outcome was a meeting in Paris, where Henry did homage, though he was obliged to surrender the Norman Vexin to placate the king. There is no mention of Matilda in the sources briefly describing negotiations in Paris; although she was involved with her husband in the preliminary correspondence,

57 Chartrou, *L'Anjou*, ch. 4.
58 Barlow, *Letters of Arnulf*, pp. xxvii–xxviii, 9 (no. 6).
59 *RHF*, xv, pp. 520–1.
60 *RHF*, xv, p. 520.
61 Migne, *PL*, 185, col. 329.
62 Torigny, *Chronicle* (ed. Howlett, pp. 160–3; ed. Delisle, i, pp. 253–5).

there is no proof that she accompanied him to meet the king. By September 1151 Henry's position as duke of Normandy was fully recognized.[63]

Henry's homage to Louis VII in 1151 ended a first period of crisis, when the French king might have undermined the Angevins' still precarious conquest of Normandy. Then, almost immediately, the situation changed once more. Count Geoffrey, a man still in the prime of life, unexpectedly fell ill and died on 14 September 1151, leaving his patrimony of Anjou, at least for the time being, to his eldest son, Henry, and three or four castles to Geoffrey, his second son.[64] A story was later current that he had intended Henry to have Anjou only until he had recovered his maternal inheritance, and had wished it then to pass to Geoffrey; but this comes from the pen of William of Newburgh, writing some years later in the north of England, and it may have been put out by the dissatisfied younger brother. Henry's father most probably intended the family patrimony to pass to his eldest son, even if he succeeded in making good his claim to the kingdom of England.[65] He can have had no inkling of the extent of the domains that Henry would acquire within a year by his marriage.

The decision of Louis to separate from his wife, Eleanor of Aquitaine, was understandable, since in fifteen years of marriage she had borne him only two daughters and he had no wish for the kingdom to endure the difficulties involved in female succession. But when in March 1152 he finally secured the dissolution of his marriage, he did not foresee that within a few weeks the heiress of Aquitaine would, without seeking his permission, marry his already powerful vassal, Henry of Anjou. On 18 May Henry met Eleanor at Poitiers and married her in the cathedral there. Robert of Torigny was uncertain whether he acted on a sudden impulse or on a deep-laid plan; he had met her for the first time in Paris the previous summer.[66] Henry was nineteen years old, eleven years younger than Eleanor; the sources do not indicate whether Matilda

63 W. L. Warren, *Henry II* (London, 1973), p. 42.

64 Torigny, *Chronicle* (ed. Howlett, p. 163; ed. Delisle, i, p. 256).

65 Historians have been divided on whether or not to accept William of Newburgh's story. For recent discussions see Warren, *Henry II*, pp. 45–7; Hollister and Keefe, 'The making of the Angevin Empire', pp. 265–6; J. Le Patourel, *Feudal Empires Norman and Plantagenet* (London, 1984), ch. 9. Even if there are a few elements of truth in Newburgh's story about Count Geoffrey's wish to make some provision for his second son, Robert of Torigny's statement is more in line with Geoffrey's letter to Henry about the patronage of La Trinité Vendôme (above, p. 145) and with Angevin inheritance customs. John of Salisbury's letter to the bishop of Norwich in 1156 (*Letters of John of Salisbury*, i, pp. 21–2) implies, as Warren points out, that he was either ignorant of the story or did not believe it.

66 Warren, *Henry II*, pp. 42–5.

was consulted, or what she thought of the marriage. Louis was deeply offended, but Henry had at one stroke secured the southern frontiers of Anjou and acquired claims to dominions which stretched from the Mediterranean to the Atlantic and from the Pyrenees to the English Channel.

England was not yet won; the Angevin supporters were struggling desperately to resist a renewed offensive from King Stephen, and Henry's success had brought him turbulent vassals and jealous neighbours. He had to turn back from Barfleur in the summer of 1152, as he prepared to go to the help of his supporters in England, in order to fight off an attack by King Louis, Henry count of Champagne, and his own aggrieved brother Geoffrey. Campaigns in Normandy and Anjou occupied him until the end of the year; it was not until January, when his enemies must have expected that the bad weather would prevent him from risking a Channel crossing with his army, that he was able to confound them by landing in England, probably at Wareham, with a relatively small but seasoned army of paid troops, transported in thirty-six boats.[67]

This visit to England was a time when in many ways Henry established his position and raised the hopes of those who favoured his cause. He gave promise of advantages to come not only by demonstrating his ability as a leader, but by making grants to lay lords and churches both in the firmly Angevin provinces and in regions that had not yet definitely declared for him. His grant of the Leicester fees to the son of Robert II of Leicester was probably, as Edmund King has suggested, to secure the ultimate loyalty of the Beaumonts at a time when the earl of Leicester had not yet openly declared for the Angevins.[68] His concessions to the son of the loyal Robert fitz Harding were made for a different reason, probably to demonstrate that the grants to his father were intended to be hereditary.[69] Gifts to churches, such as those to Bermondsey and St Paul's, Bedford, were also made in anticipation of his gaining his just inheritance in England.[70] At the same time his activities in battle showed his will to make good his words.

---

67 The figures are Robert of Torigny's (*Chronicle*, ed. Howlett, p. 171; ed. Delisle, i, p. 270). For details of the campaign see Davis, *King Stephen*, pp. 114–19; Warren, *Henry II*, pp. 47–50.

68 Cited by Robert B. Patterson, 'The ducal and royal *acta* of Henry fitz Empress in Berkeley castle', forthcoming in the *Transactions of the Bristol and Glouc. Arch. Soc.*, n. 5; Henry subsequently confirmed Robert II's tenure of the fees (*Regesta*, iii, nos 438, 439).

69 *Regesta*, iii, no. 999. This grant was made about the same time as the grant to Robert fitz Harding himself (ibid., no. 310).

70 *Regesta*, iii, nos 81, 90.

Within a year of vigorous campaigning up and down the country he had induced Stephen to come to terms and make peace at Winchester on 6 November 1153.[71] The death of Stephen's eldest son Eustace in the previous August and the support of the church now openly given to Henry of Anjou had left Stephen ready to recognize that he could not hope to preserve the succession in his own line. He was ready to accept Henry as his heir, while himself retaining the crown for life. His son William was to be allowed to inherit the lands Stephen himself had held in the time of King Henry in both England and Normandy. From this date Henry's charters referred to Stephen as king.

The months of Henry's absence in England were probably the most perilous Matilda ever had to face after her return to Normandy. King Louis, offended by Henry's marriage, was ready to attack if the Normans showed any sign of weakening. Some of her vassals, who had been drawn to her side by strong interests in Normandy, could not be trusted to remain loyal if the Angevin position in Normandy were undermined. Ranulf of Chester and William of Roumare were with Henry in England and seemed committed to his cause, but Waleran of Meulan, who had important estates in France as well as Normandy, must have seemed to her a potential danger, and his conduct aroused her suspicions. She was acutely conscious of the difficulty of controlling some of the lesser barons, who were ready to take the law into their own hands and attack monastic property to which they thought they had a claim. This is probably the time when she sadly had to admit (perhaps for the only time in her life) that for the present she was powerless to prevent disorder.[72] The crisis passed when Henry returned with a firm promise of the English succession, as he was then able to devote his attention to his continental interests.

He had still to deal with troubles in Touraine, where Theobald of Blois had taken advantage of his absence to press claims against the lords of Amboise and occupy lands Henry regarded as his by right. His campaign, if the chronicle of the lords of Amboise is to be believed, was inglorious; his army was defeated and his brother Geoffrey captured.[73]

71 *Regesta*, iii, no. 272.

72 *Chronicon Valassense*, ed. F. Somménil (Rouen, 1868), p. 14. The Chronicle attributes this statement to her when she agreed to the return of the monks of Mortemer from property that was being ravaged: 'Piget me reditus hujus sed, quia non prevalemus hiis diebus, non est aliud facere modo.'

73 *Gesta Ambaziensium Dominorum* (ed. L. Halphen and R. Poupardin), pp. 127–31. J. Boussard, *Le Comté d'Anjou sous Henri Plantagenêt et ses fils (1151–1204)* (Paris, 1938), pp. 70–1, dates the campaign in late 1153, when Henry was in England; if this chronology is correct, Geoffrey, not Henry, intervened and was defeated. This is a possible alternative explanation.

To obtain the release of Geoffrey and other captives he had to secure the destruction of the castle of Chaumont-sur-Loire. Nevertheless peace was made with Theobald, so averting one threat to Henry's continental lands, and his position in England was never seriously undermined during the few remaining months of Stephen's life.[74] Most of the English barons were ready to support him; from the moment that Robert of Leicester, probably the most powerful and certainly the most astute of the magnates, came over to his side the outcome was virtually assured. The church which, led by Theobald, had supported Stephen mainly by virtue of his coronation, was ready to welcome Henry. No one can tell what might have happened had Stephen lived on for years; but he was already a broken man, shattered by the loss of both his wife and his eldest son. There can have been little surprise when he died on 25 October 1154 and Henry came into his inheritance.

During these years Matilda remained at Rouen, giving steady help and counsel that has too often been overlooked. Charters that she granted, sometimes jointly with her son, confirmed the possessions of English abbeys on the borders of the lands held by her party. Such grants were not empty words: if they could not protect these lands from enemy incursions they did at least ensure that any offence would lead to excommunication, and so acted to some extent as a deterrent. The establishment of Cistercian monks to replace hermits at Radmore dated from Matilda's first years in Normandy, as did the foundation at Loxwell that became Stanley Abbey.[75]

The Norman records are more scanty than the English and Matilda's activities appear only incidentally. But when Henry was not in the duchy she was the obvious person to leave as his deputy. On 27 May 1154 Robert of Torigny was elected abbot of Mont-Saint-Michel, and the election was confirmed by Hugh, archbishop of Rouen, and the empress while Duke Henry was in Aquitaine. On his return he added his own confirmation. These details are known only because the abbot-elect was the historian Robert of Torigny, who himself recorded them in his *Chronicle*.[76] Matilda may normally have confirmed elections of prelates and restored the temporalities on behalf of her son when he was not in Normandy. One writ probably of *c*.1152 in her name survived from the ducal period. Addressed to Osbert de Hosa, the

---

74 The arguments of Graeme J. White, 'The end of Stephen's reign', *History* 75 (1990), pp. 3–22, that Henry was more vulnerable in the last year of Stephen's reign than has generally been thought, are not entirely convincing.

75 See above, pp. 133–4.

76 Torigny, *Chronicle* (ed. Howlett, pp. 179–90; ed. Delisle, i, pp. 284–5).

constable of Cherbourg, it commanded him peremptorily to put the
abbot and canons of St Mary de Voto at Cherbourg in possession of
their land at Beaumont-Hague.[77]

Sometimes at first she acted jointly with her son in issuing Norman
no less than English charters. Together they confirmed a grant of
revenue to the hospital of Beaulieu de Chartres made by Henry I; both
charters relating to the payment begin, 'Mathildis imperatrix Henrici
regis filia et Henricus eius filius dux Normannorum.'[78] After leaving
England she dropped the title 'Lady of the English' in charters for
Normandy. Other surviving joint charters concerned lands in England,
where Henry was still joint claimant with her of her paternal
inheritance.[79] After Henry's expeditions to England in 1149 and 1153
he more frequently acted alone, and was beginning to confirm his
mother's earlier grants in his own charters.[80] Once Stephen had
accepted him as heir to the throne, he reciprocally recognized Stephen
as king for life. So he was prepared to confirm Stephen's earlier charters
instead of independently granting the same lands or privileges, as both
he and his mother had previously done.[81] After Henry's coronation in
1154 there was no doubt that the authority was his, though it might
be delegated to Matilda. He was very ready to delegate to her; her
activities continued and might exceptionally even extend to England.
Léopold Delisle considered that she frequently acted as viceregent in
Normandy, and was more deeply involved in administration than

77 *Regesta*, iii, no. 168; see Delisle, *Introduction*, p. 143. The writ was destroyed in
1944. The date must be later than December 1151, when Richard, bishop of Coutances,
was consecrated, as he had approved Matilda's proposal to re-found the house as an
abbey (cf. *CDF*, no. 933). The reference to Count Geoffrey's chaplain, Thomas, could
refer back to a decision taken in an earlier court, before the death of Count Geoffrey in
September 1151.

78 *Regesta*, iii, no. 71 (1150 – Sept. 1151); 72 (Sept. 1151 – Jan. 1153); the second
charter adds Henry's title of *comes Andegavorum*. See Delisle, *Introduction*, p. 140.

79 *Regesta*, iii, no. 80 (1150–1), a charter of Matilda of Wallingford confirming the
grant of the two Ogbournes to Bec was approved and confirmed by both Matilda and
Henry; *Regesta*, iii, no. 88 (1150–1) is an attempt to establish a house of canons regular
in Wallingford; no. 836 (1150–1) is a joint charter founding the abbey of Drownfront
(Stanley); cf. the earlier joint grant of land to Godstow (no. 372), when Henry was in
England in 1144, with a significantly different opening, 'M. imperatrix H. regis filia et
Anglorum domina et Henricus eius filius ...'

80 *Regesta*, iii, nos 840, 420, 379, 900. Some grants were anticipatory with a promise
of confirmation or augmentation when he became king (no. 90 for Bermondsey, no. 126
for St Augustine's, Bristol).

81 *Regesta* iii, no. 206; Henry confirmed King Stephen's grant to Cluny without
reference to a subsequent (lost) charter of Matilda (ibid., nos 204, 205).

Queen Eleanor, who (except in 1158) mostly authorized matters of only small importance.[82]

The one document clearly showing Matilda's intervention in England after 1153 is a writ, probably of 1159, addressed to Maurice, the sheriff of Herefordshire, ordering him, on her own authority and that of her son, to see that no court actions were brought against the monks of Reading about their chattels or lands, particularly in Broadward, which had been given to them when Henry left England for Normandy. It is an executive writ, ending with the conventional *nisi feceris* clause, 'Unless you do this, the justiciar of England is to see it done.'[83] Broadward was a recent endowment, given by Roger, earl of Hereford, in 1154x55, probably when he became a monk at Gloucester, in reparation for the damage done to the abbey's men and possessions by the earl and his men during the war.[84] Reading was a royal abbey, the burial place of Henry I, and perhaps for this reason Matilda's son specially turned to her for the protection of its most recently acquired property. His wife Eleanor had previously been acting on his behalf in England, as writs issued by her to the military tenants of Malmesbury and Reading, ordering them to render the service due to their abbeys, testify. She joined her husband in Normandy in December 1158.[85] Probably about then King Henry asked his mother to act on his behalf, at least in business of special interest to the royal family.

In Normandy Matilda's role was far more positive. Here she sometimes took the place of her son in his absence, sometimes heard cases jointly with him. An agreement about the descent of land in the honour of Bacton, between William de Bacton and his cousin, Robert de Valognes, was reached in the presence of King Henry and his mother at Rouen.[86] Waleran, count of Meulan, wrote asking her and all the king's justices in the Pays de Caux to protect twenty acres of land he had given

82 Delisle, *Introduction*, pp. 169–72. Eyton, on the other hand (*Court, Household and Itinerary of Henry II*, p. 16), considered that Queen Eleanor had been left in a position of considerable trust in 1156.

83 *Regesta*, iii, no. 711: Kemp, *Reading Cartularies*, i, pp. 265–6. The most likely date for this writ is June–September 1159, during Henry's expedition to Toulouse. In addition, in the charter she issued in December 1156, confirming the foundation of Bordesley Abbey, she addressed 'omnibus fidelibus suis, Anglis et Normannis'; Henry issued a similar charter at the same time (*Cal. Charter Rolls*, ii, pp. 63–4). Bordesley Abbey was at all times a special case.

84 Kemp, *Reading Cartularies*, i, pp. 264–5; D. Walker, 'Charters of the Earldom of Hereford, 1075–1201' *Camden Miscellany*, xxii, Camden Fourth Series, i (1964), 1–75, at pp. 23–4.

85 Delisle, *Introduction*, p. 173; Eyton, *Itinerary of Henry II*, pp. 40–1.

86 Barbara Dodwell, 'Bacton charters', in *Medieval Miscellany*, p. 149; the charter is dated between 1156 and 1162.

to the abbey of Le Valasse. If it had been unjustly occupied by Richard *de Busebosco* or his sons, he begged her to restore the almsland to the abbey, since it was she who was responsible for the provision of justice in the country.[87] Henry's writs and charters sometimes made her position plain. In a mandate of 1155x58 sent from England and addressed to his justices and bailiffs of Normandy and to the count of Eu and Count Walter Giffard, he ordered them to put the church of Fécamp in possession of land surrendered by Nicholas de Criel. The mandate ended, 'Unless you do it, let my lady and mother the empress see that it is done.'[88] She had special rights in the dues of the vicomté of Argentan and the forest of Gouffern, which made up her dowry; but some of her charters, such as that for Foucarmont, were addressed more widely to all her faithful men of Normandy and England.[89] When, in 1155, she confirmed the gift that Oelard de Cleis had made to Foucarmont in her presence she was certainly acting on behalf of Henry, who was restoring order in England after his coronation; and the same is probably true of her confirmation of Roscelin fitz Clarembald's gift of Longchamp to St Georges-de-Boscherville.[90] Her steady presence in Rouen meant that the business of the duchy would normally run smoothly during Henry's absence, and made it easier for him to concentrate on the other parts of his vast dominions. As late as 1164 Louis VII wrote to her as the person exercising authority in Normandy when one of his men, possibly a merchant, became involved in a lawsuit in Rouen. Her clerk, Lawrence archdeacon of Rouen, replied on her behalf that she would see that he had full justice exactly as if he had been one of the richest and most important burgesses of the city; further, that the French king's men and merchants in Rouen would be able to witness that justice had indeed been done.[91]

One of King Henry's first tasks after his coronation was to restore order in England and settle conflicting claims to property on both sides of the Channel. According to Robert of Torigny, he had agreed with Stephen at Winchester that 'the possessions which had been seized by intruders should be restored to their former legitimate possessors, who had held them in the time of the first King Henry.'[92] This did no more

---

87 'Precor vos, qui patria iuste providetis, quatenus elemosinas suas memorate abbatie ex integro restituatis.' (Cartulary of Le Valasse, Archives de la Seine Maritime 18 H (non coté), fos 24v-25r). I owe this reference to Dr David Crouch.

88 Delisle, *Introduction,* pp. 169–70; Delisle/Berger, i, pp. 147–8: 'Et nisi feceris, domina et mater mea imperatrix faciat fieri'.

89 *Regesta,* iii, nos 334, 748.

90 *Regesta,* iii, nos 334, 116a.

91 *RHF,* xvi, p. 105.

92 Torigny, *Chronicle* (ed. Howlett, p. 177; ed. Delisle, i, p. 281).

than establish a useful general principle as a basis for litigation; no date in the long reign was fixed arbitrarily as the point of legal possession and, as W. L. Warren pointed out, owing to the ill-defined rules of succession that allowed considerable manipulation to the king, there had been bitter rivalry between the 'lawful possessors' of the beginning and those of the end of the reign, even before 1135.[93] At least it was clear that no grants made since 1135 could be assumed to be lawful; and though Henry did not attempt a blanket application of the rule, wise claimants often took steps to have rights confirmed, whether or not they were directly threatened. Henry himself confirmed some of the grants made by his mother during the years of anarchy. This was not, as has sometimes been suggested, out of disrespect for her authority, but because he could hardly approve a legal principle in general and disregard its application himself. Some of these confirmations are the only evidence we have of lost charters of the empress, or, when charters are not expressly mentioned, of gifts made orally.[94] Among Henry's charters for houses to which she had made gifts, or in which she had an interest, are a number which include her among the witnesses.[95] When his court was at Rouen she might be there, whatever the business. One case, possibly of late date, between the king's chamberlain, Ralph fitz Stephen, and the monks of Saint-Georges-de-Boscherville about their rights in the wood of *Rispevilla*, was settled at Le Pré in the presence of King Henry and the empress.[96]

   Henry relied on her judgement in some matters at the beginning of his reign; and her influence was not negligible up to the time of her death. Walter Map, a harsh critic, thought her a bad influence; but some of the practices that he criticized were sound enough pragmatically even if they were ruthless.[97] The king was widely believed to respect

93 Warren, *Henry II*, pp. 62–3.

94 Delisle/Berger, i, p. 314 (no. 181) for Silly (1156–61), confirms *Regesta*, iii, no. 826; Delisle/Berger, i, pp. 256–7 (no. 146) (1156–61).

95 Delisle/Berger, i, pp. 220–1 (no. 116) for Reading; pp. 241–2 (no. 134) for St André-en-Gouffern; p. 318 (no. 186) for Bec-Hellouin and St Neots; pp. 350–1 (no. 213) for Tiron; pp. 412–13 (no. 265) for Foucarmont.

96 Delisle/Berger, i, pp. 411–12 (no. 264). Delisle suggests *c*.1167 as the probable, but not certain, date. The document ends, 'Hec autem conventio recognita fuit et concessa coram rege Henrico secundo et coram domino imperatrice, apud Pratum.' The witnesses on behalf of Ralph fitz Stephen include Bernard Cumin, Robert fitz Clarembald, Godard de Vaux, John de Lunda, Ralph fitz Urseline and his son Stephen, all of whom occur elsewhere as witnesses of the charters of Matilda and Henry. The last four also witnessed a case heard in Count Geoffrey's court at Rouen in 1149 (*Regesta*, iii, no. 665); their appearance together may imply an earlier date than that suggested by Delisle. Robert fitz Clarembald may be an error for Roscelin fitz Clarembald, who was rewarded by Duke Henry in 1151 for his service (*Regesta*, iii, no. 306a; cf. ibid., nos 116a, 824, 825).

97 See above, pp. 62–3.

his mother's advice. The author of the *Deeds of the Lords of Amboise* believed that she had insisted on Henry agreeing to the destruction of the castle of Chaumont-sur-Loire when Theobald of Blois refused to release Henry's brother Geoffrey and the sons of Sulpice of Amboise on any other terms in 1154. Since Sulpice himself had died of ill-treatment in captivity, maternal anxiety may have been added to a shrewd perception that Henry's immediate need was to secure Theobald's friendship or at least his neutrality.[98] Her voice was heard again in 1155, when Henry discussed the possibility of attempting to conquer Ireland and give it to his brother William. According to Robert of Torigny the subject was discussed at a council at Winchester at Michaelmas 1155, but the enterprise was put off because the empress was known to be opposed to it.[99] He gave no clue to her motives; she may have believed that Henry had already undertaken as much as he could reasonably manage and that William would be better off with a more substantial lordship in England. Henry owed much of his early success to his courage and daring, but he sometimes needed to be restrained. In 1151, when King Louis invaded Normandy, the Norman barons 'who were older and wiser than him' had had to warn him not to attempt an attack on the king who was his natural lord, unless he received greater provocation.[100] By 1155 he may have been less in need of restraint; but the speed with which he had amassed a realm of unequalled magnitude may have tempted him to attempt the impossible. Even if Matilda acted more out of consideration for the welfare of her youngest son, she acted wisely. William fitz Empress was far better off with the English lands given him within the next few years than he would have been with a titular but precarious lordship of unconquered Ireland. Thomas Keefe has shown that he became one of the wealthiest magnates in England, with estates in fifteen counties probably worth between £1,000 and £1,700 a year; he also held the vicomté of Dieppe in Normandy.[101] Richly endowed, he provided, until his early death in 1164, loyal

98 See above, pp. 157–8.

99 Torigny, *Chronicle* (ed. Howlett, p. 186; ed. Delisle, i, p. 296). Eyton, *Itinerary of Henry II*, p. 12, wrongly assumed that the empress was present at the council, but the text does not warrant this interpretation, and there is no evidence that she ever returned to England after 1148.

100 Torigny, *Chronicle* (ed. Howlett, p. 161; ed. Delisle, i, pp. 253–4): 'Principes exercitus ejus, qui maturiores eo erant et consilio et aetate, non permiserunt ut cum rege domino suo congrederetur, nisi amplius illum in aliquo quam antea fecerat opprimeret.'

101 Thomas K. Keefe, 'Place–date distribution of royal charters and the historical geography of patronage strategies at the court of King Henry II Plantagenet', forthcoming in *The Haskins Society Journal* 2 (1991). I am very grateful to Professor Keefe for allowing me to read this paper before publication.

support for his brother, particularly in Kent, Essex and East Anglia, where his greatest wealth lay.

Matilda's strength as a counsellor lay partly in her knowledge of European and papal politics, acquired during her years in Germany and through the contacts she had formed with the papal court. No chronicler suggested that she played any part in the negotiations with the Emperor Frederick Barbarossa, yet as he was a kinsman of her first husband and coveted the relic she had brought with her from Germany she must have been consulted, and the tone of the early correspondence suggests that it was inspired by someone very familiar with imperial etiquette and susceptibilities.[102] She may in any case have helped to keep alive contacts with the imperial court, at least after the election in 1137 of Frederick's uncle Conrad III, who was her first husband's nephew. A letter from Conrad written early in 1142 to John Comnenus in Constantinople stressed with some rhetorical exaggeration the strength of the support he could command. Regular embassies, he claimed, from France, Spain, England and Denmark expressed their willingness to carry out his 'imperial mandates'.[103] King Stephen, with his interests in Boulogne, might have sent embassies at an earlier date; but it is even more likely that Matilda, when her fortunes reached their highest point in 1141, decided to open communications with her kinsman. Much earlier, too, she had been involved in negotiations between the Emperor Henry V and her father; and she was well aware of the permanent interests of the Rhineland cities in trade with London. Her son Henry had learnt, both from his father in Rouen and from her, the importance of mercantile wealth to pay his armies; and his interests in good relations with Germany, like hers, were both mercantile and diplomatic.

When, however, Barbarossa sent envoys to King Henry with a request, it was on a matter involving prestige rather than trade. Among the treasures brought back to England by Matilda were at least two gold crowns and a precious relic, the hand of St James. The identification of the crowns has been a matter of much debate, but since Otto of Freising complained that Archbishop Adalbert had persuaded her to relinquish the imperial regalia left in her charge by her husband, they belonged most probably to the German rather than the imperial

102 This episode has been reconstructed by Karl Leyser, 'Frederick Barbarossa, Henry II and the hand of St James', *Medieval Germany and its Neighbours 900–1250*, pp. 191–214.

103 *Die Urkunden der deutschen Könige und Kaiser; die Urkunden Konrads III*, ed. Friedrich Hausmann, (MGH, Vienna, Cologne and Graz, 1969), pp. 122–3 no. 69. The letter is dated 12 February 1142.

ceremonial.[104] Frederick did not ask for them; but he regarded the hand of St James, which had been appropriated by Henry IV from the treasury of the archbishop of Hamburg-Bremen in 1072, as part of the regalia of the imperial chapel, particularly important to his own line. He wanted it to be returned. Matilda had given it to her father for the abbey of Reading; and though Henry of Blois had somehow carried it off into his private treasury early in Stephen's reign, Henry II had insisted on its return to Reading. It was providing a centre for a growing cult which attracted many pilgrims, and was the most prized relic in the abbey's possession. Henry and Matilda had no intention of returning it. If, as the Disibodenberg annalist suggested, the loss of the relic was thought in Germany to have done irreparable damage to the realm and caused the feuds and internal wars that followed,[105] Matilda may have felt equally that her troubles began when Henry of Blois took it away from the royal abbey of Reading. Henry II answered Barbarossa in fulsome terms, paying lip-service to his imperial dignity and authority and sending magnificent gifts, but instructing his envoy to refuse the request. Whoever drafted the letter (Thomas Becket, the chancellor, has been suggested), it was certainly not Matilda. Her education, though good, did not extend to Latin rhetoric; but she may have indicated the approach best calculated to sugar the pill, and she probably suggested the most magnificent of the gifts sent with the refusal. It was a tent made of the richest materials, so large that it had to be raised mechanically, large enough for a coronation ceremony or an archiepiscopal mass. Memories of her own travels in Italy forty years earlier must have suggested to the empress that no visible manifestation of imperial pomp could be more welcome to an emperor about to leave for campaigns in Lombardy. It attracted widespread admiration.

In the years after 1159 Matilda's relations with her German kinsfolk became less cordial. After the death of Pope Adrian IV a double election took place, and Frederick Barbarossa, backed by most of the princes of the empire, gave his support to Victor IV, while the kings of England and France, after some hesitation, recognized Alexander III.[106] Henry II was prepared to receive embassies from Barbarossa even when the struggle grew more bitter; Matilda refused to take any action that might compromise her. In April 1165 the archbishop of Cologne and other

104 See below, p. 189, P. Schramm, *Herrschaftszeichen und Staatssymbolik* (Schriften des MGH 13/III, Stuttgart, 1956), pp. 760–2, pointed out that hardly any English or Norman chronicler knew how to distinguish between king and emperor; the terms were used very loosely by Robert of Torigny and Roger Howden.

105 *Annales Sancti Disibodi, MGH SS,* xvii, 23.

106 See *Councils and Synods,* i, pp. 835–42 for the English documents.

ambassadors from the schismatic emperor met Henry in Rouen, to discuss business that included a projected marriage between Henry's eldest daughter, Matilda, and Henry duke of Saxony. Matilda refused to receive them.[107] When Archbishop Rotrou of Rouen informed Cardinal Henry of Pisa of her refusal, he was sufficiently sure of her to add, 'Do not imagine for a moment that she will vacillate in any way.'[108]

By this time, as her health declined, her interests were turning more and more to works of piety, and her influence over her son grew less. His practical experience had become much wider than hers, and he was well served by ministers thoroughly versed in the customs and administration of his kingdom. He had learnt to work with Archbishop Theobald who, while insisting that church law must be respected, was always ready to find ways of avoiding a challenge to customary royal rights. Theobald proved himself an archbishop faithfully schooled in the traditions of Bec. Like Lanfranc, he was prepared to work with King Henry for the peace of the church and the realm; like Anselm, he had chosen to risk exile and expropriation rather than disobey the pope, when Stephen tried to prevent him from attending the 1148 council of Reims. Henry never pressed him against his conscience. Their mutual understanding appeared when Henry had to decide which pope to support after the divided election. Theobald insisted that the church must be consulted but was no less insistent that it could only advise, not decide. Henry, his prerogatives safeguarded, was careful to accept the advice of the church and give his support to Alexander. Theobald's household, a community of learned clerks, provided some of the men for the royal administration, not least an able young clerk, Thomas Becket, whom Henry appointed his chancellor very soon after his coronation.[109] Thomas rapidly rose to become one of the closest of the king's advisers, entrusted with judicial work, given the custody of castles and bishoprics, and sent on embassies and even military expeditions.

Matilda must have met Becket on several occasions when he accompanied the king to Rouen; and certainly she had seen his splendid style of living, and knew that he was a wealthy pluralist, being simultaneously an absentee archdeacon of Canterbury, provost of Beverley, dean of Hastings and more besides, though he later insisted that none of his benefices involved cure of souls.[110] Since she later showed her

---

107 Eyton, *Itinerary of Henry II*, p. 78; Torigny, *Chronicle* (ed. Howlett, p. 224; ed. Delisle, i, pp. 355–6). The earl of Leicester also was unwilling to receive the envoys when they went on to England.

108 *Materials for the History of Thomas Becket*, v, pp. 194–5.

109 Frank Barlow, *Thomas Becket* (London, 1986), p. 42.

110 Barlow, *Becket*, pp. 36–8, 51–4.

disapproval of pluralism she must have found that side of his life objectionable, but there is no suggestion that she ever questioned his ability. Her opposition began only when, after the death of Archbishop Theobald, her son decided that the man best fitted to work with him at the head of the English church was his chancellor Thomas, Theobald's former clerk, trained and admired by the archbishop. She advised against the appointment, and was overruled.[111]

What was behind her opposition? She may have felt that Thomas was too worldly to deserve an archbishopric. But she may have remembered the experience of her first husband half a century before. Henry V had rewarded his chancellor Adalbert with the archbishopric of Mainz, and Adalbert, up to then the staunchest of his supporters in upholding imperial customs against papal opposition, had become the leader of the reforming party in the German church, and an active inciter of rebellion. By the time she left Germany Adalbert seems to have won Matilda's respect for his personal qualities and also, perhaps, for his political acumen; she had agreed to surrender the imperial regalia to him, and although Otto of Freising complained bitterly of his deceit she appears not to have felt deceived.[112] Nevertheless, the experience of the empire in the years after 1112 was a warning of what church preferment might do to the loyalties of an able royal servant. Whatever her motives, her failure to prevent the election of Thomas marks the beginning of a decline in her influence over her son. He still consulted her on some matters, and was ready to listen; and she was widely respected not merely in Normandy but also by the king of France and the pope as a fair and sometimes effective mediator. She could do nothing, however, to heal the breach between King Henry and his archbishop when the clash of wills came. Moreover she knew that he kept from her matters on which he suspected that their priorities differed.[113]

In the short time before the quarrel broke out Thomas Becket did nothing to ingratiate himself with her. After the death of Stephen's son, William of Blois, in 1159, Matilda's son William asked for the hand of his widow, Isabella of Warenne. In 1163 Thomas banned the marriage on the grounds of consanguinity. His decision was canonically correct: the two were distant cousins. King Henry made no objection, and was

111 Some of the bishops mentioned her objection in a letter to Thomas (*Materials*, v, p. 410). He replied (ibid., v, pp. 516–17) that if this was true her objections had not been made public.
112 See above, pp. 42–3. Orderic Vitalis (vi, pp. 360–5) described Adalbert as outstanding for his authority and energy, and thought that he had providently prevented a schism by his control of the election procedure; his most likely informant was someone from Matilda's court in Normandy.
113 See below, p. 169.

able to arrange a marriage for her with an illegitimate son of Geoffrey of Anjou, so keeping her fortune in the family while avoiding the charge of consanguinity.[114] When William died shortly afterwards many of his friends believed that the disappointment had helped to cause his death. Richard le Bret, one of Becket's murderers, was said to have delivered the *coup de grâce* with the words, 'Take this, for the love of my lord William, the King's brother!'[115] Matilda's feelings are not recorded; she was believed to have a special affection for her youngest son. However great her respect for canon law, she knew that she and Geoffrey of Anjou had married in spite of being more closely related than William and Isabella, and that dispensations could be procured with the help of political pressure and special pleading. Nevertheless, if she bore Becket a grudge at the time it did not influence her actions later when she interceded on his behalf.

The clash between king and archbishop came through Henry's determination to preserve intact the traditional royal rights in all his relations with the church, at a time when canon law was redefining ecclesiastical privilege and immunity. Investiture was no longer a burning issue, and free elections had been conceded, though there were still differences of interpretation over what made an election free. But as the activity of both secular and ecclesiastical courts increased, and appeals to Rome, already beginning to be protected by the court of Canterbury, became more frequent, clashes were inevitable. Henry insisted on his right to give or withhold permission for pleas to be taken outside the realm, and demanded special immunities for his royal servants. The procedure that ought to govern the punishment of criminous clerks was hotly contested.[116] Becket was equally intransigent. When Henry had a set of constitutions drafted to define essential royal customs in the disputed areas, and demanded at the council of Clarendon that the bishops should all swear to observe them, Thomas openly resisted. After a second council at Northampton in October 1164, where Thomas was subjected to further harassment, he decided to go in person, without permission, to the papal court and fled into exile. For six years all negotiations to reconcile the opposing parties ended in failure. Becket did not return until 1170, and then the reconciliation was so hollow that it was followed almost immediately by his murder.

The empress did not live to see the tragic outcome. She was closely

---

114 *Early Yorkshire Charters*, ed. C. T. Clay, 8 (1949), pp. 13–14; *Draco Normannicus* (ed. Howlett, p. 676; ed. Omont, pp. 84–5).

115 Barlow, *Becket*, p. 247; *Materials*, iii, p. 142.

116 For documents in the quarrel see *Councils and Synods*, i, pp. 852–914; for events, Barlow, *Becket*, ch. 6 and works there cited.

involved in the early stages of the dispute, from 1164 to 1167. Becket's friends and supporters believed that she might be able to intercede on his behalf, if she could be persuaded that his opposition was justified. It is interesting to note that she was considered a friend to church reform, and was believed to be able to influence her son. King Henry, for his part, wished to be sure of her support; before the end of the year John of Oxford arrived in Rouen to explain the cause of the dispute and present his case favourably. John was part of a royal delegation which had been sent to seek the favour of Pope Alexander, then holding court at Sens after being driven out of Rome by the armies of Barbarossa. What he said to the empress is known only from a hostile letter of Nicholas of Mont-Saint-Jacques.[117]

Nicholas, prior of the hospital just outside Rouen, had become a personal friend of Thomas Becket some years earlier when the chancellor was seriously ill in the nearby church of Saint-Gervais. He undertook to take letters from Thomas to the empress and persuade her of the justice of his cause. At first she refused to read the letters. John of Oxford had arrived three days before on his way back from the papal Curia. He had done his best to blacken Thomas's reputation, saying that he acted entirely out of pride and ambition, and that his professed defence of the liberty of the church was really a defence of the bishops' rights to extort money. At first the empress would not receive Nicholas, but he persisted. At his third attempt she agreed to receive the letters he had brought privately, so that her clerks would know nothing of it. After hearing them read, she expressed regret for the hard things she had said, and also for what she had already written to the king. She justified herself by insisting that her son concealed his relations with the church from her, because he knew that she rated the freedom of the church more highly than the royal will. Her next action was to send letters to her son through one of her clerks, asking him to let her know in writing what his intentions were towards the church and the archbishop. 'And if,' she concluded, 'when I know his wishes I consider that any efforts of mine can accomplish anything, I will do all in my power to bring about peace between him and the church.'

Matilda had no reason not to tell Nicholas at least a fair measure of the truth, though she was sufficiently schooled in diplomacy to avoid giving an opinion until she could be sure of her facts. It seems clear that she already knew the limits of her power to influence her son; also that she could not trust even her own household clerks not to misrepresent her if she was known to have received letters from the archbishop.

117 For details of Nicholas's attempts to see the empress and his interviews with her at Christmas 1164, see *Materials*, v, pp. 144–51.

Perhaps she exaggerated in claiming to rate the liberty of the church more highly than the royal will; her later words and letters show her determination to justify her son's actions as far as possible, and to insist on preserving legitimate royal customs intact. When Nicholas returned to her, after a visit to Arnulf of Lisieux, he went into more detail about the Constitutions of Clarendon. He told her their substance only, as his copy had been mislaid; he added that some of them were contrary to the Christian faith and almost all to the liberty of the church, so that she and her son ought to fear for their spiritual as well as their temporal welfare. If he thought this would satisfy the empress he had under-estimated her; she asked him to send to the king for a copy. This proved not to be necessary, as Nicholas succeeded in finding his own copy that evening, and he was back next day.

Matilda received him in her private room, after once again sending away the members of her household, and ordered him to read the constitutions to her in Latin and explain them in French. 'She is a woman of the stock of tyrants,' Nicholas wrote,

> She approved some, such as the one about not excommunicating the justices and ministers of the king without his consent. Others she con-demned; above all, she thought it wrong that they had been reduced to writing, and the bishops forced to promise to observe them; such a thing had never been done by their predecessors. After much discussion, when I urgently pressed her to suggest what might be a basis for peace, I made this proposal, and she agreed: that an attempt should be made to induce the king to submit to the advice of his mother and other reasonable persons, who might find a compromise so that, setting aside the written document and the promises, the ancient customs of the realm might be observed, with the proviso that the liberty of the church should neither be diminished by the secular justices nor abused by the bishops.
>
> You should know that the lady empress is very adroit in the defence of her son, excusing him by pointing out sometimes his zeal for justice, sometimes the malice of the bishops, sometimes his reasonable and shrewd perception of the origin of trouble in the church. She said some things which I found sound and praiseworthy. Bishops ordain clerks irresponsibly without a title to any church, and large numbers of ordained clerks turn to crime through poverty and idleness. They do not fear either losing their benefice, because they have none, or suffering any penalty, because the church defends them. They do not fear the prison of the bishop, who would rather allow them to go unpunished than have the trouble of feeding and guarding them. Yet one clerk might hold anything from four to seven churches or prebends, though the canons of the church everywhere forbade clerks to hold even two.

Since these were the kind of abuses that caused the trouble in the church it was remarkable that the axe of episcopal justice was not laid vigorously to the root of the tree, but only to the branches. 'Therefore,' he told Becket, 'if you love the freedom of the church ... show by your words and deeds that you disapprove of these things. If you send letters to the lady empress, make your disapproval clear.' Nicholas concluded, 'I could not possibly have sent word to you more quickly, for I prepared these letters while I was reading the constitutions with the empress.' This suggests that he was writing almost at her dictation; certainly in his account of the interview we seem to hear her speaking – as almost nowhere else – clearly and unmistakably with her own voice. The sting at the end was probably meant as a rebuke to Becket; he had held four – perhaps as many as seven – church benefices himself, and, though his change to an austere way of life was known to his close friends, the world at large, and possibly the empress herself, still thought of him as he had been. She was shrewd in assessing the failure of the bishops to correct evils which they themselves helped to foster. She valued practical reforms, but was more concerned with how to prevent clerks committing crimes than with the legal principles that ought to determine their appearance before secular or church courts if they were guilty of felonies. She was ready to defend the liberties of the church provided they did not conflict with any ancient and accepted royal customs. And she preferred unwritten customs that could be moulded gently as conditions changed to written constitutions that seemed to invite conflicts by their rigidity. Time was to show that written statutes could be modified by judicial interpretation, helped perhaps by deliberate ambiguity in the drafting; but she could not have anticipated this. In her attitude to the process of reform she still thought along the same lines as her Norman ancestors. William the Conqueror's canons of Lillebonne had been a record of agreed customs allowing for variation, not a written series of demands imposed on an unwilling episcopate.[118] In the political and legal climate of 1164 something more precise was needed to satisfy both parties in the dispute.

Although she told Nicholas that she was prepared to go further than her son in pressing the claims of the church, she never openly allowed any diminution of the royal dignity. Even to Nicholas she insisted that the king's servants were not to be excommunicated without reference to him. In a letter to Thomas Becket she censured Becket severely and justified her son.[119] She wrote, she explained, at the request of the pope to attempt to reconcile him with the king; but the king and his barons and counsellors took it hard that, after being raised to the highest dignity, he had attempted to subvert the realm and even disinherit the

118 Haskins, *Norman Institutions*, pp. 30–8; Orderic, iii, pp. 25–35.
119 *RHF*, xvi, p. 235; *Materials*, vi, pp. 128–9.

king. So she was sending her faithful clerk, Archdeacon Lawrence, to find out what his real intentions were, and how far he would be able to comply if she undertook to present his case. She warned him that only by showing great humility and unmistakable moderation could he hope to recover the king's favour.

Her letter would not have been out of place if written by the Emperor Henry V to Archbishop Adalbert. The emperor's manifesto of December 1112, explaining the reasons for the arrest of Adalbert, had been couched, at greater length, in much the same terms.[120] The accusations were more appropriate in Adalbert's case; whatever Henry may have feared, Thomas had not been fomenting active rebellion against him. To some extent the empress was judging from past experience and cherishing ancient dignity. Nevertheless her admission to Nicholas that her son no longer took her into his confidence was probably a recognition of diminished power. The pope, the king of France and Becket's friends all firmly believed from past experience that she was worth winning for their cause, and that as a mediator she might be valuable. She showed some sympathy with the archbishop and was prepared to give discreet help to some of his exiled and impoverished friends.[121] When King Henry, enraged at the attempt of Becket to have his supporters excommunicated, seized one of Becket's messengers and had the unfortunate man tortured and imprisoned in order to find out who had sent him, Matilda wrote demanding his release.[122] She treated sentences of excommunication with circumspection. No disrespect was implied by the way she received (in 1166) letters from Becket pronouncing the excommunication of some of the bishops supporting the king. Nicholas of Mont-Saint-Jacques told Becket that when she heard their names she did not take it very seriously, saying that they were excommunicate already. This was not because she belittled the sentences, but because she knew that the bishops had been part of a delegation to Frederick Barbarossa at Wurzburg, and had already incurred papal excommunication: as far as she was concerned Becket could add nothing further. When she was greeted on behalf of Richard of Ilchester she made no reply. He was one of the excommunicates, and she would have no dealings with him.[123]

---

120 *Mainzer Urkundenbuch*, pp. 358–9 (no. 451).

121 Barlow, *Becket*, p. 127.

122 Eyton, *Itinerary of Henry II*, p. 100. It is not certain if she succeeded.

123 *Materials*, v, p. 421, 'Domina imperatrix, audiens in quos sententiam dederatis, quasi ludo id accipiens, eos pridem excommunicatos esse respondit. Post haec, cum ex parte Ricardi de Ivelcestria salutaretur, nihil respondit.'

Personally Matilda was true to her convictions; politically she could do nothing to influence events. John of Salisbury felt let down by her, but this was scarcely reasonable. Although she had seemed sanguine in the first months of the struggle, she had always indicated that some conditions had to be met if her son were to agree to accept the pope's proposals.[124] Even if she had lived another three or four years it is doubtful if she could have applied any restraint to avert the final tragedy. In less contentious matters, where passions were not inflamed, she retained some influence as a mediator. Relations between King Henry and his overlord, Louis VII, were always uneasy, and in the summer of 1167 war was smouldering on the Vexin frontier.[125] There was in addition a minor quarrel about the collection of money for the Holy Land; Henry wished to send the contributions from his lands, which had been collected at Tours, through his own messengers; Louis insisted that Tours was in his kingdom and the money should be transmitted through him.[126] Matilda wrote urgently to Louis asking to know more about the issues between him and her son, in the hope that she could do something to check hostilities, so that the people of Jerusalem would not be kept waiting for badly needed subsidies.[127] Stephen of Rouen has a rather unlikely story that she had told Henry that Louis should be allowed to save his face after some defeats, and so should be permitted to ravage Andely.[128] Possibly she persuaded him that Louis ought to be left some way of honourable retreat; that she condoned ravaging is very unlikely. At all events a truce was success-fully arranged in August, and Henry immediately invaded Brittany to assert his claims there. If Matilda felt this new campaign was unjus-tified, she had no chance to raise objections. She died on 10 September, active in the affairs of government to the last. Stephen of Rouen himself went to Brittany to announce her death to Henry, and the news brought him back to Normandy.[129]

124 *Letters of John of Salisbury*, ii, pp. 30–1, refers to a hopeful reply she had given to an approach made to her by the pope; a year later he wrote more bitterly (ibid., ii, pp. 66–7).

125 For the background see Warren, *Henry II*, pp. 105–6.

126 Torigny, *Chronicle* (ed. Howlett, p. 230; ed. Delisle, i, pp. 363–4).

127 Her envoy on this occasion was Reginald of Gerponville.

128 *Draco Normannicus* (ed. Howlett, p. 688; ed. Omont, p. 97). The text of the poem at this point is lost and the content known only from a summary in the rubric.

129 *Draco Normannicus* (ed. Howlett, p. 596; ed. Omont, pp. 6, 117); Warren, *Henry II*, pp. 106, 108. Peter Johannek has suggested that the poem, written in Matilda's circle just after her death, implied a criticism of some aspects of her son's behaviour at that time (P. Johannek, 'König Arthur und die Plantagenets', *Frühmittelalterlichen Studien*, ed. Karl Hauck, 21 (1987), pp. 384–7.

Matilda's Household

The witnesses to Matilda's charters give some indication of the membership of her household at different times, and also of the kind of authority she was exercising through all the changes in her status. The handful of acts surviving from before 1125 show that, while she had her own clerks and chaplains, whatever she did was underwritten by the imperial chancellor.[130] After her marriage to Geoffrey of Anjou, an Angevin element appears in her household; some Angevins such as Alexander de Bohun accompanied her to England and remained with her at least until the end of 1141. For a few years witness lists indicate the presence of a semi-royal court no less than a personal household. In 1141 and for a few years afterwards former royal officers acted for her. Robert de Courcy and Humphrey de Bohun, her stewards, appear as witnesses in her charters.[131] She granted stewardships to Geoffrey de Mandeville and Aubrey de Vere in July 1141, but as both men returned to Stephen shortly afterwards the offices can have been little more than titular. Her chamberlains included William de Pont de l'Arche, who witnessed from 1141 to 1144, and William Mauduit, to whom as chamberlain she made a grant in 1141,[132] though he witnessed none of her charters. Drogo 'of Polwheile' also acted as her chamberlain, possibly from as early as 1140.[133] Her constables, known from her charters, were Miles of Gloucester, Robert d'Oilli at Oxford from 1141 until his death in September 1142, William de Beauchamp at Worcester in 1141 while she had authority in Worcester, and William Peverel at Dover in 1144.[134] Humphrey fitz Odo, to whom she gave land in Westbury, was called constable from 1144; the charters he witnessed were, however, always joint charters with her son Henry.[135] John fitz Gilbert, her loyal marshal, with his castle at Marlborough, was within easy reach of Devizes. His brother William fitz Gilbert was her chancellor; he was

130 See above, pp. 34, 38.

131 For her household see *Regesta*, iii, pp. xxx-xxxii, and above, p. 125. Humphrey de Bohun witnessed as steward from February or March 1141 (*Regesta*, iii, nos 697, 698); Robert de Courcy probably joined her at the same time as Robert of Gloucester, and first witnessed one of her charters before 1139 (*Regesta*, iii, no. 805); he witnessed as steward in 1141 (*Regesta*, iii, nos 275, 634, 651).

132 For William de Pont de l'Arche see *Regesta*, iii, nos 698, 116, 277; for Mauduit, *Regesta*, iii, no. 581. In a charter given in June 1153 (*Regesta*, iii, no. 582) Duke Henry stated that he had restored the chamberlainship to William Mauduit.

133 See above, p. 91.

134 *Regesta*, iii, pp. xxxi-xxxii.

135 See above, p. 125, and *Regesta*, iii, p. xxxvii.

still with her in Rouen in 1150–1.[136] Brian fitz Count, constable of Wallingford, was never described by her as constable; he was in any case one of her inner circle of counsellors, along with her brothers Robert of Gloucester and Reginald of Cornwall. During these years the names of a few household knights, like Hugh of Plucknet and William Defuble, are known from her charters; and Robert fitz Hildebrand, the mercenary captain who betrayed her, was for a time in her court.[137]

After her return to Normandy the public element was diminished and her household became more local. Her son Henry had built up his own household, taking over some of his father's servants in Normandy and his mother's in England, and introducing some new men like Manasser Bisset.[138] When he was with her in Rouen his court, first ducal and then royal, merged with her own little court in their joint acts. Reginald de St Valéry, steward, and Simon, butler, may have been Henry's officers, not hers.[139] When she acted officially the names of ducal officials such as Osbert de Hosa appear in her writs.[140] In her more private charters the circle was smaller; the archbishop of Rouen and Arnulf of Lisieux witnessed a few of her charters, other bishops only one or two. Magnates were present only if their own interests were directly involved, as were those of Waleran of Meulan in the foundation of Le Valasse. Among her clerks some who had served her earlier were promoted to bishoprics: Richard de Bohun, the nephew of Engelger and Alexander, became bishop of Coutances in 1151;[141] Herbert, who served as a chaplain or clerk of both Matilda and Henry from before 1139 to 1153, was probably the Herbert who became bishop of Avranches in that year.[142] Some belonged to the cathedral clergy of Rouen. Although it is unlikely that Roger le Norman, canon of Rouen from about 1165 to 1199, was Matilda's Roger *capellanus*,[143] there can be no doubt about Archdeacon Lawrence, her 'faithful clerk'. He acted as intermediary in negotiations with Becket and Louis VII, and frequently entertained monks from the abbey of Mortemer (a royal foundation) when they

---

136 *Regesta*, iii, no. 88.
137 See above, p. 120. Of the ladies in her service we hear of only one humble domestic dependant: Osa, her laundress, whom she settled (presumably at retirement) on a substantial holding of 23 acres arable and 7 acres meadow in Somerton (Somerset), which her descendants held for the next fifty years (*Book of Fees*, ii, 1384).
138 *Regesta*, iii, pp. xxxvi-xxxviii.
139 *Regesta*, iii, nos 71, 72, 88; these are all joint charters of Matilda and Henry.
140 *Regesta*, iii, no. 168.
141 *Regesta*, iii, no. 72.
142 *Regesta*, iii, pp. xxx, xxxiv, nos 20, 372, 839, 748.
143 *Regesta*, iii, no. 748; David Spear, *Annales de Normandie* (1983), p. 105.

visited Rouen.[144] Nothing further is known of Clarembald, except that
he was given land in Gloucestershire, unless he is the Clarembald who
had been a pupil of Thierry of Chartres.[145] Two of her last charters for
Le Valasse and La Noë were witnessed by a number of lesser persons,
who probably had territorial interests in the villages where the land
given by her to the abbey was situated.[146] The public element in her
circle declined in her last years, though it was never wholly absent even
when her charters show that she was turning her attention more and
more to pious benefactions as a principal interest of her old age.

144 *Regesta,* iii, nos 824, 825; David Spear, *Annales de Normandie* (1984), p. 25;
RHF, xvi, p. 235; *Chron. Valassense,* p. 21. The abbot of Le Valasse, Richard de Blosseville, also acted as her emissary on at least one occasion during the Becket dispute (*Letters
of John of Salisbury,* ii. pp. 30–1).
145 *Regesta,* iii, nos 168, 262a, 365a, 452; K. S. B. Keats-Rohan, 'John of Salisbury
and education in twelfth-century Paris', *History of Universities,* 6 (1987), pp. 1–45, at
p. 10.
146 *Regesta,* iii, nos 607, 910.

8

Personal Patronage

Matilda's personal wealth consisted largely of the jewels and relics she brought back from Germany, the dowry provided for her second marriage, which included revenues from the vicomté of Argentan and the forest of Gouffern, and any widow's dower she may have received after the death of her second husband. In the absence of any records from the Norman exchequer before 1172 and of any household rolls, the resources for the maintenance of her personal household remain unknown. Apart from what Robert of Torigny tells us about the disposal of her jewels, only her charters reveal her personal as well as her public gifts; almost all of these after 1154 were in favour of monastic houses in Normandy. They have at least left a record of the pattern of her personal almsgiving.

Up to a point her pious motives were those normal in any royal lady at the time. Just as she was prepared to intercede on behalf of petitioners seeking the favour of king or emperor, she herself made gifts to the saints who might intercede for her in a higher court.[1] Much of her almsgiving was of the conventional kind expected of the rich and powerful; but she had positive views on how some at least of her gifts were to be used. The praise of the monks of Bec goes beyond the normal gratitude due to a benefactor. When she lay ill at Rouen in 1134 and insisted, against her father's wishes, that she should be buried at Bec and not in the cathedral of Rouen, Robert of Torigny praised her for rejecting temporal glory. 'She knew', he wrote, 'that it was more salutary for the souls of the departed if their bodies might lie in the place where prayers for them were offered most frequently and devoutly to God.'[2] Stephen of Rouen, the younger monk of Bec who knew her at Le Pré, was fulsome in his praise. He wrote that as the wife of the

---

1 See for example Stephen D. White, *Custom, Kinship and Gifts to Saints* (Chapel Hill and London, 1988), pp. 161–3.
2 Torigny, *Interpolations*, pp. 304–5.

emperor she had been loved by the poor as a pious mother, by the nobles as their lady. In her later years she heaped gifts on the monks of Bec; she loved them as if they had been her children and lived among them like one of them. When she died the flower of the meadow withered and a star fell. Great as was her distinction as empress, daughter and mother of kings, it was a greater thing that she was wise and pious, merciful to the poor, generous to monks, the refuge of the wretched, and a lover of peace.[3] Some of this was conventional exaggeration; a little, at least, was true. The Cistercians of Le Valasse remembered her not just as one who gave generously to many pious causes, but as a woman of intelligence and sense, devoted at heart to the Lord.[4]

Among the older Benedictine houses Cluny, after Bec, stood high in her regard. Cluny did not take sides in the struggle for the English crown; Henry I's munificence was remembered with gratitude, but Henry of Blois, bishop of Winchester and King Stephen's brother, was also respected as a Cluniac monk who had helped Peter the Venerable to restore the finances of the abbey.[5] There was probably no political undertone in her devotion to Cluny; more than any other house, it provided conspicuous commemoration for its benefactors in its continual intercession and magnificent liturgy. Matilda followed her father in wishing to be commemorated in all its houses. She had personally ratified her father's gift of annual revenues from the farms of London and Lincoln when it was made.[6] She also made other gifts to the monks.[7] Peter the Venerable wrote to her gratefully of the outstanding generosity of her father to Cluny, and the lavish donations that had enabled the new church to be completed. Matilda herself, he added, was the living image of her father, in that she loved the church of Cluny as he had done.[8] Shortly before he died she persuaded him to visit her in Rouen, and at her request he agreed that after her death her obit should be celebrated throughout the order, with masses and prayers and alms

3 *Draco Normannicus* (ed. Howlett, pp. 596–601, 712–14; ed. Omont, pp. 6–9, 120–2).

4 *Chron. Valassense*, pp. 18–19: 'Que cum esset una de sensatis in terra mulieribus, bene etiam interius in Dominum affecta, plurima plurimis in pias causas erogabat.'

5 *Letters of Peter the Venerable*, ii, pp. 130–1; Lena Voss, *Heinrich von Blois, Bischof von Winchester 1129–1171* (Berlin, 1932), pp. 108–21.

6 See above, p. 59.

7 A charter of Geoffrey of Anjou (*Regesta*, iii, no. 205) refers to a lost charter of Matilda for Cluny.

8 *Recueil des Chartes de l'abbaye de Cluny*, ed. Auguste Bernard and Alexander Bruel (Paris, 1876–1903), v, pp. 532–3, no. 4183.

to the poor. The calendars of various Cluniac houses show that this was done.[9]

She distributed her personal alms more widely. Her wealth was considerable; she had brought back a treasure in jewels and church ornaments from Germany, most of which she gave to religious houses. Her second dowry included the castle of Argentan, together with the dues of the vicomté collected there, and the revenues from the forest of Gouffern which had once been enjoyed by Robert of Bellême. She must have received a widow's dower when Geoffrey of Anjou died in September 1151. This may have been made up largely of revenues, for many of her gifts were of cash or lands that she had purchased. Some, however, were of demesne lands and rights in the forests of Roumare, Lillebonne and Fécamp, and these may have come from dower. Much went to houses of the newer orders. She shared the keen interest of her parents in the orders of Augustinian canons. Her mother had actively furthered the foundation of Merton Priory and had encouraged her son William to love the house. Queen Matilda must also have taken an interest in Llanthony Prima, where her chaplain, Ernisius, became the first prior; perhaps Matilda remembered from her childhood the origins of that house through the conversion to religion of a former knight, when in 1122 she made her early gifts to a similar semi-eremitical community of converted knights at Oostbroek.[10] Nostell Priory had been established with the help of her father's chaplain, Adelulf, who later became the first bishop of Carlisle when Henry I founded the see in 1133 with a chapter of Augustinian canons.[11] Her uncle King David had been a generous benefactor of the same order.[12]

Matilda's own wealth went more frequently to the newer orders of Augustinian canons. Using her own personal resources, she re-founded the house of secular canons (Notre-Dame-du-Voeu) established at Cherbourg by her grandfather and, with the permission of Richard, bishop

9 She appears in the necrology of S. Bénigne de Dijon as *Matildis imperatrix* (Dijon, Bibl. mun., MS 634, f. 15r); and in the necrologies of S. Martin-des-Champs and Moissac, also as *Matildis* (or *Mathildis*) *imperatrix*. *Synopse der cluniacensischen Necrologien*, unter Mitwirkung von W.-D. Heim, J. Mehne, F. Neiske u. D. Poeck, ed. J. Wollasch (Münstersche Mittelalter-Schriften 39/2), Munich, 1982, pp. 507, 509. I owe these references to Dr Maria Hillebrandt.

10 M. L. Colker, 'Latin texts concerning Gilbert, founder of Merton Priory', *Studia Monastica*, 12 (1970), p. 252, describes a visit to the priory by the queen with her son William in 1118 (J. C. Dickinson, *The Origin of the Austin Canons and their Introduction into England* (London, 1950), p. 117; and see above, p. 50.

11 Martin Brett, *The English Church under Henry I* (Oxford, 1975), pp. 25–6.

12 Barrow, *Kingdom of the Scots*, pp. 178–84.

of Coutances, placed there canons from the reformed house of Saint-Victor in Paris.[13] Both she and her son were generous to the abbey, which was well placed to provide hospitality on journeys to and from England by way of Cherbourg and Wareham, and which gave them a Parisian contact with a learned and thriving community enjoying papal favour. In 1155 Henry II promoted Achard, the abbot of Saint-Victor, to be bishop of Avranches.[14] Matilda's interest in the Victorines may have been encouraged by her son, after his visit to Paris to do homage for Normandy. Her attachment to the Premonstratensians, however, went back to her early days in Germany. After her return Drogo, one of her knights, decided to become a canon of Prémontré, partly through friendship with its founder, St Norbert. The date of his decision is not known. According to a manuscript account of the abbey of Notre-Dame de Silly, at one time in the Boze collection in the Bibliothèque Nationale, the first steps to found an abbey were taken in or soon after 1136.[15] The story told there is that the empress, after the birth of her third son William at Argentan in 1136, 'in order to obtain a happy enterprise against the usurper Stephen, and at the same time to fulfil her good intentions in times past', and out of affection to St Norbert whom she had seen at the court of the emperor her husband, determined to found an abbey in honour of Our Lady. Drogo, on her advice, went to Prémontré to consult Abbot Hugh, who had succeeded Norbert. Hugh, who had been a chaplain in the suite of Burchard, bishop of Cambrai, in 1109, when envoys went to England to arrange the marriage between the emperor and Matilda, already knew both Drogo and the empress herself; he agreed to send some canons to help to establish the new house. So a small community may have existed there before or soon after Matilda went to England, though her two earliest charters date from after her return in 1148, most probably c.1157 or 1158.[16] In the first, she made a grant of the lands of St Leonard of Gouffern, which she had purchased for ten livres of Anjou from the abbot of Saint-Pierre-sur-Dives, and a house in the new bourg of Argentan; it was ratified by her son Henry and witnessed by his brothers Geoffrey and William. The second charter confirmed this and added £10 from her

13 *Regesta*, iii, 168; *Gallia Christiana*, xi, Instr. 229; *CDF*, nos 933–8. Her son's confirmation, Delisle/Berger, i, pp. 399–400 (no. 259), states that she had founded the house 'proprio censu'.

14 Dietrich Lohrmann, *Papsturkunden in Frankreich*, neue folge 8 (Abhandlungen der Academie der Wissenschaften in Göttingen, 1988), pp. 48–9.

15 Stapleton, *Magni Rotuli Scaccarii*, i, pp. lxix-lxx, lxxxix-xc. For her patronage of reform before she left Germany see above, p. 50.

16 *Regesta*, iii, nos 824, 825. So many of the witnesses are the same in the two charters that they appear to have been issued within a few weeks of each other.

rent from Argentan and £10 from the tithe of the forest of Gouffern, as well as rights of pasture in the forest and the right to take wood both for burning and for building their houses. Her gifts also included a little demesne land of her own. Both charters were addressed to Drogo, the founder of the house, and all the brethren there, and they imply that the community had been in existence for some time.

If any clear theme runs through Matilda's almsgiving, it is special devotion to the Virgin Mary. The cult gained in strength during the early twelfth century. The earliest known carving in England representing the Coronation of the Virgin comes from Henry I's abbey at Reading. Although the surviving capital with the carving is unfinished and may have been used as building material in the cloister, it is possible that there was also a tympanum showing the Coronation of the Virgin at the abbey.[17] The feast was celebrated in Germany at that time, and Matilda may have helped to encourage the devotion shown by her family in England. Of the religious houses that received her patronage, both Bec-Hellouin and its priory of Notre-Dame-du-Pré were dedicated in honour of the Virgin, as was Drogo's Premonstratensian abbey at Silly; the abbey of Oostbroek had a double dedication, to the Virgin Mary and St Lawrence. All Cistercian houses were dedicated in honour of the Virgin, and the Cistercians became increasingly the order that Matilda favoured most. Besides endowing Bordesley, Radmore (Stoneleigh) and Loxwell (Stanley) in England, she played a part in encouraging the spread of the order in Normandy.

There is nothing surprising in this. Devotion to the austere Cistercian monks took the aristocracy of England by storm after the conversion of St Bernard. When Ailred of Rievaulx, as a young man serving in the household of King David of Scotland, happened to be near York on business, he 'heard tell', Walter Daniel relates, 'from a close friend of his, how, two years or more before, certain monks had come to England from across the sea, wonderful men, famous adepts in the religious life, white monks by name and white by vesture.' They were said to venerate poverty, 'not the penury of the idle and negligent, but a poverty directed by a necessity of will and sustained by the thoroughness of faith, and approved by divine love.'[18] A single visit, according to Walter Daniel, convinced him that his vocation lay there; he entered Rievaulx in 1134, to become in time its abbot and a great spiritual leader in an order of which even monks in older Benedictine houses

17 G. Zarnecki, 'English Romanesque Art 1066–1200' (*Catalogue of the Exhibition of Romanesque Art at the Hayward Gallery*, London, 1984), p. 159. See Plate 8.

18 *The Life of Ailred of Rievaulx by Walter Daniel*, ed. F. M. Powicke (NMT, 1950; OMT, 1978), pp. 10–11.

could speak with admiration. Orderic Vitalis, writing at the same time in Saint-Evroult, described the impression made by the best of the first Cistercians:

> They have built monasteries with their own hands in remote, wooded places, and by a wise providence have given them holy names, such as Maison-Dieu, Clairvaux, Bonmont and L'Aumône and others of like kind, so that the sweet sound of the name alone invites all who hear to hasten and discover for themselves how great the blessedness must be which is described by so rare a name.[19]

King David was one among many who may have spoken to Matilda about the white monks, and conditions during the Anarchy encouraged monastic foundations everywhere. Monastic lands were plundered and ravaged during the fighting; monasteries were sometimes occupied by troops, desecrated and burnt. Leaders on both sides were equally guilty, along with some lesser lords out for their own advantage. Some new foundations were explicitly said to be made as reparation for damage caused in the wars.[20] Moreover vows were often made in moments of danger, and new foundations might be thanks offerings for safe preservation. The undercurrent of political motive encouraging the establishment of holy men in lands held insecurely was always present. New religious foundations were exceptionally numerous at this time, and the Cistercians in particular benefited from both the pious and the worldly motives of the magnates.

When Matilda first granted charters to Cistercian houses the choice was not entirely hers. One of her earliest English charters confirmed William de Berkeley's gift of Kingswood to Tintern Abbey.[21] A more difficult problem arose in the summer of 1141, when she was faced with the need to legalize, as she saw it, the position of the Cistercian abbey of Bordesley, founded by Waleran of Meulan out of royal demesne in Worcestershire given him by King Stephen. To expel the community was unthinkable; to accept that Waleran had any right to found it was equally unacceptable to her. She therefore took it over as a royal foundation and issued charters in her own name.[22] Before long she had a new, strong motive to attempt a personal foundation of her own. According to the chronicle of Le Valasse, when she was besieged in Oxford in the late autumn of 1142, she took a vow that if she escaped

19 Orderic, iv, pp. 326–7.
20 See Thomas Callahan Jnr, 'Ecclesiastical reparations and the soldiers of the "Anarchy"', *Albion*, 10 (1978), pp. 300–18.
21 *Regesta*, iii, no. 419.
22 See above, pp. 134–5.

safely she would found an abbey.[23] There is nothing improbable in this story and her actions support it; even before she left England she did her best to encourage new foundations, however modest, and it was already clear that her favour was going to the Cistercians. Increasingly good relations with St Bernard must have added to her preference. When Robert of Gloucester founded the Cistercian abbey of Margam, shortly before his death, St Bernard's brother Nivard crossed the sea to be present at the foundation ceremony in October 1147.[24] He may have visited Matilda as he travelled through England; he was certainly in communication with her. Both at Radmore and at Loxwell, Matilda and her son took the initiative in establishing Cistercian monks, though political insecurity and lack of resources made it impossible for them to add more than the minimum endowments to gifts from their vassals.

When she returned to Normandy in 1148 Matilda's vow was still unfulfilled, and she found new reasons for choosing the Cistercians. In 1134 her father had established a community of monks of Savigny at Mortemer; three years later they applied successfully for admission to the Cistercian order. When King Stephen paid his only visit to Normandy in 1137 they looked to him for confirmation of their privileges. This was readily granted, and the queen gave money for the building of a new church.[25] For the Angevins in 1148 Stephen's grants were of questionable validity; the abbey was a royal house and its protection part of their cherished rights of inheritance. In October 1148 Count Geoffrey, his wife and his three sons granted lands in the valley of Mortemer to the house; some three years later Henry, as duke of Normandy, was to issue a general charter of confirmation.[26] Mortemer was gathered once more into the royal patronage; after Henry became king he took over the building of the church, barely begun by Stephen's queen, and, according to the abbey's chronicle, gave more than a thousand livres to complete it in three years in a magnificent style. The empress herself gave two large guest houses, designed so that separate lodgings could be provided for the poor, for stipendiary knights, for rich persons and for religious.[27]

23 *Chron. Valassense*, p. 12. The writer of the Mortemer Chronicle (J. Bouvet, 'Le récit de la fondation de Mortemer', *Collectanea Ordinis Cisterciensium reformatorum*, 22 (1960), pp. 149–168, at p. 159), thought that she had taken the vow when in danger of shipwreck, probably through confusing her vow and Waleran's.

24 Chibnall, 'The Empress Matilda and church reform', pp. 122–3; *Letters of Gilbert Foliot*, p. 98 (no. 63), App. III, pp. 507–9.

25 Bouvet, pp. 149–58.

26 *Regesta*, nos 599, 600.

27 Bouvet, p. 158. For the architecture of Mortemer see Lindy Grant, 'The architecture of the early Savigniacs and Cistercians in Normandy', *Anglo-Norman Studies*, 10 (1988), pp. 113–24.

It is clear that from the earliest days of her residence in Normandy Matilda had marked out Mortemer as the house to which she would turn for monks when the time came to make a new foundation. Her hand was forced a little prematurely by Waleran of Meulan. On his way home from the crusade in 1149 he narrowly escaped death in a shipwreck and was persuaded, the chronicler of Le Valasse asserts, by his companion Reginald de Gerponville to vow to found a Cistercian abbey. The chronicler had the story from Reginald himself, and it is plausible.[28] His motives were probably sincere; but when he decided to make the foundation very near to Lillebonne, in property that was a part of his wife's dowry just across a stream from ducal demesne lands, and to invite the abbot of Bordesley to provide the first monks, Matilda's suspicions were aroused.

The early months of 1150 were a critical time for her; young Henry's expedition to England in 1149 had put heart into his supporters but had not succeeded in breaking Stephen's power, and delicate negotiations were in progress to try to persuade Louis VII to receive his homage for Normandy. Waleran's action must have looked political; he had done homage to the empress only under duress, because his wealth and power lay in Normandy and France, and he seems to have retained some vestiges of power in Worcestershire until 1153. He was quite capable of changing sides again if King Louis could be persuaded to give military support against Henry to Stephen and his son Eustace. The monks of Bordesley, settling almost on ducal demesne at the gateway up the Seine to Rouen, must have seemed to her the equivalent of later fifth columnists. Any Cistercian abbey in such a place must be her abbey, peopled by her monks from Mortemer. Haimo, abbot of Bordesley, was initially reluctant to undertake responsibility for a daughter house so far away, and the archbishop of Rouen was asked to settle the dispute. He observed, sensibly enough, that since two vows were involved and the resources of both parties had been so overstrained by war that they were scarcely enough to provide proper endowments for two separate houses, it would be wise to combine the vows and found one abbey jointly, as a daughter house of Mortemer. Count Waleran bought out claims that the monks of Bernay had on the site, and the archbishop confirmed both his gifts and those of the empress.[29]

The question of affiliation, however, caused further difficulties. At an uncertain date monks of Mortemer were sent there by Abbot Adam. They were beset by dangers. Local lords had conflicting claims to some

---

28 *Chron. Valassense*, pp. 8–9.
29 *Chron. Valassense*, pp. 12–13, 59–60; the archbishop's charter is dated 1152.

of the lands of the endowment. William of Mortain, a man, said the chronicler, famous only for his cruelty, invaded the lands with his brothers, burnt the crops and barns and hamstrung the oxen. Matilda's fortunes reached a low point; King Louis was attacking Normandy, and loyal supporters in England were desperately asking for help against Stephen's fresh onslaught. Probably it was in 1153 that she agreed reluctantly that the monks must return to Mortemer because she was powerless to protect them.[30] This was apparently the only time in her life she came near to despair, but she refused to give up.

Matilda's actions during the later disputes are not easily understood unless the background of political and monastic change is remembered. One change occurred in the abbey of Mortemer, when a new abbot, Stephen, succeeded Adam; an old man reluctant to send out colonies of his beloved monks was replaced by a younger, more outward-looking abbot. Politically the Angevin cause triumphed; during the English expedition of 1153 Henry was able to establish his power in the Midlands and confiscate Waleran's honour of Worcester,[31] so that Bordesley Abbey, already claimed by Matilda, firmly and finally joined Mortemer under the royal patronage. Monks of Bordesley no longer appeared a threat in Normandy, and the difficulties of communication with England ceased to be an obstacle once Henry had become king in 1154. There was one further attempt to establish monks of Bordesley in Le Valasse. Matilda raised no objection, perhaps because Bordesley was once again a royal abbey; and Abbot Haimo was willing to renounce his position there to become abbot of the new house. To this, however, the abbot and chapter of Cîteaux would not consent, and by this time conditions in the infant community left much to be desired. But for Matilda's determination and forcefulness negotiations might have dragged on for years. She heard a disquieting account of conditions in the half-founded cell from her former doctor, Gerard, who had taken religious vows, and she put an end to further debates among the senior Cistercian abbots about the affiliation of the house by declaring that she would give the place to a different religious order unless monks from Mortemer were allowed to settle there.[32]

30 Chron. Valassense, p. 14. The Chronicle of Mortemer (Bouvet, p. 168) has a different and less convincing story: that the abbot, Adam, loved his monks so much he could not bear to part with them, and gave Le Valasse to Bordesley Abbey.
31 The account of the foundation of Le Valasse given by Crouch, Beaumont Twins, pp. 75–6, compresses the events of seven years into two, and so distorts the motives of the participants.
32 Chron. Valassense, pp. 15–20. Grant, 'Early Savigniacs and Cistercians', p. 124, described the dispute as 'lengthy, bitter and of Byzantine complexity'.

In this she was actively encouraged by another Matilda, the abbess of Montivilliers, who was her half-sister.[33] Montivilliers naturally had a keen interest in the fortunes of such a near neighbour, and both Matildas wished to extend the influence of a house founded by their father. The chronicle of Le Valasse describes the scene, and gives one of the few glimpses we have of the empress going about her business.[34] On Monday 10 June 1157, a group of monks chosen to form the new community left Mortemer for Rouen, followed by the abbots of Ourscamp, Lannoy and Mortemer. At Rouen they were received by Archdeacon Lawrence, who was accustomed to entertain the monks of Mortemer when they were in Rouen. After dining, the monks embarked on the Seine, ready to travel downstream to Le Valasse, while the abbots crossed the bridge over the river.[35] All were met in the meadow on the opposite bank by the two Matildas. The abbess commended the monks to her sister the empress and urged her to aid and protect them. The boats were then provisioned, and the monks sent on their way, while the abbots remained in Rouen to bless Richard de Blosseville, the abbot-elect of the new community. They then followed for the formal inception of the abbey which, concluded the chronicler, was rightly named 'of the vows' (*Votum*). Waleran at first was outraged that the monks of Bordesley had withdrawn and been replaced by monks of Mortemer and tried to take back some of the gifts he had made from his French lands. Within a year, won over by his wife, he restored the lands and wrote graciously to the empress asking her to support their abbey of Le Valasse and protect its endowments.[36]

Matilda's foundation charter for Le Valasse belongs to the period after her son became king and was probably not earlier than 1157. In it she stated that the abbey of 'Sancta Maria de Voto' had been founded by her and her son King Henry; she confirmed Count Waleran's gifts, but did not treat him as a co-founder, and by referring to 'the Vow' in

33 Matilda was one of Henry I's numerous illegitimate daughters; her mother was thought by Dom Jouvelin to have been Elizabeth, the sister of Waleran of Meulan (*Chron. Valassense*, pp. 19–22, 105–8); but this is not accepted in the *Complete Peerage*, xi, pp. 117–19.

34 *Chron. Valassense*, pp. 20–1. The scribe transcribing the chronicle gave the date as 1151; but Somménil has shown (ibid., p. 116) that this must be a slip for 1157. See also *Letters of John of Salisbury*, ii, p. 30 n. 1.

35 *Chron. Valassense*, Introduction, and p. 111, Somménil thought that this implied that Matilda's stone bridge had been completed by 1157, but they could have crossed by the wooden bridge repaired by her husband. She left money in her will for the completion of the bridge.

36 *Chron. Valassense*, p. 119; the date of the letter must have been 1158, if it was written about a year after the foundation.

the singular apparently deleted any reference to his vow.[37] Later, after the death of her son William in 1164, she purchased land for forty Angevin livres and gave it to the abbey.[38] Among the witnesses to her charter is Reginald de Gerponville, the former companion of Waleran on his crusade, who had encouraged him to take his vow. Political necessity sometimes played strange tricks with men's loyalties, especially when their territorial interests forced them to perform homage to more than one lord. Reginald, a minor tenant-in-chief in Normandy, had no difficulty in attaching himself to the Angevins, and bettering himself in the service of both Earl Walter Giffard and King Henry.[39] Count Waleran himself, with lands in Normandy, England and France, had vacillated at different times between King Henry and William Clito, between Stephen and the empress, and finally between Henry II of England and Louis VII of France. However good his intentions, his political judgement was not very sound and his loyalty was uncertain. No wonder the empress did not trust him, for all his charm and talents. Mostly she treated him as a vassal of uncertain allegiance; but if any element of personal antagonism ever crept into her conduct it was over the patronage of Le Valasse. She never forgave him for breaking faith when he went over to Stephen and accepted the earldom of Worcester, even though Henry I had forgiven him his earlier treason and released him from prison and restored him to favour. Yet in addition to this, his harassment of the monks of Mortemer must have been enough to convince her that he had forfeited all right to be considered the abbey's patron.

She began the foundation of one more Cistercian abbey at the end of her life, by purchasing land worth £40 to provide a site. Here, in the diocese of Evreux, the abbey of La Noë was founded as a daughter house of Jouy. The date of the foundation has often been given as 1144, through a misdating of the charter, which cannot be earlier than 1166 since the lords consenting to the purchase of land for the foundation included Robert, count of Meulan, who succeeded his father Waleran in 1166.[40] Perhaps she feared that her vow was not quite fulfilled by the litigious foundation of Le Valasse. Certainly her devotion to the Cistercian monks lasted until her death.

Her interest in the abbeys she founded was not confined to giving endowments. All through the chronicle of Le Valasse the themes of her

---

37 *Regesta*, iii, no. 909.
38 *Regesta*, iii, no. 910.
39 Crouch, *Beaumont Twins*, p. 67.
40 *Regesta*, iii, no. 607; *Gallia Christiana*, xi, App. 133 prints a version of the charter which includes Rotrou, who became archbishop of Rouen in 1165, among the witnesses.

determination and insistence on the project being brought to completion without endless delays are dominant. The nave of the abbey church
at Mortemer has been described as 'every inch a royal building'.[41]
Matilda's interest in providing that abbey with guest houses large
enough to accommodate pilgrims in four different categories shows that
she planned on a grand scale and had, perhaps in the course of her own
travels, decided that it was desirable to keep rich and poor, monks and
knights, apart. One can only conjecture how far her intervention in the
choice of architect or of decoration may have gone. The priory of Le
Pré and the adjacent royal residence have been completely destroyed,
and an industrial suburb of Rouen covers the meadows where she and
her sister, the abbess of Montivilliers, met the monks from Mortemer
and sent them on to found Le Valasse. All that remains is the chapel of
St Julian at Petit Quevilly, built by Henry II about 1160. The beautiful
paintings on the vaults of choir and apse, which depict scenes from the
life of the Virgin, could well have been chosen by her.[42] The dedication
to St Julian was a natural choice for either her or her son; he had been
born at Le Mans and baptized in the cathedral church of St Julian.[43]

Matilda made other gifts, possibly connected with her major foundations. Lannoy Abbey received sixty acres of land in the forest of Lillebonne from her, and Abbot William of Lannoy later surrendered it to
her for 120 livres of Beauvais so that she could give it to Le Valasse.[44]
Abbot William was well disposed to Le Valasse, and was one of the
three abbots present at its foundation; the ultimate transfer may have
been intended from the start, and delayed by controversies over the site
and filiation of the new house. Most of the land which was in Matilda's
gift lay in one or other of the ducal forests; elsewhere she had to
purchase land out of her ample revenues. Cash gifts to churches are
difficult to trace, since many were made without charter.[45] After re-
covering from a serious illness in 1161 she gave her silk mattress to be
sold for the leper hospital of St James at Rouen.[46] Chronicles from

41 Grant, 'Early Savigniacs and Cistercians', p. 122.

42 L. Musset, *La Normandie Romane* (2 vols, La Pierre-qui-Vire, Yonne, 1974), ii,
pp. 30–1. Part of the original, mid-twelfth-century structure survives; the paintings are
now thought to be contemporary with the building. I owe this information to Dr Lindy
Grant. The chapel was incorporated in a leper hospital for women in 1183. See Plates
9–11.

43 D. H. Farmer, *The Oxford Dictionary of Saints* (Oxford, 1978), p. 226. See above,
pp. 60–1.

44 *Regesta*, iii, no. 432.

45 Some charters granted annual revenues; she gave 100s. from the rent of Argentan to
the Hospitallers (*Regesta*, iii, no. 409).

46 P. Langlois, *Histoire du Prieuré du Mont-aux-Malades-lès-Rouen* (Rouen, 1851),
p. 12.

Bec-Hellouin and Mortemer refer to her generous almsgiving to many religious houses, as well as to widows, orphans and the poor.

Her rich jewels, precious vestments and relics were showered upon the abbeys she favoured. Some treasures went to Saint-Denis; Abbot Suger mentioned a gift of gold flowers from the decoration of one of her crowns.[47] Others went to the austere monk hermits of Grandmont. Gifts to the brethren of Grandmont are particularly hard to trace, since they refused title deeds and other documents in their early days, and even the dates of foundation of their cells are not easy to determine. They were certainly established near to Rouen, and possibly already in the royal park at Petit Quevilly in Matilda's lifetime.[48] According to a fifteenth-century inventory of the abbey of Grandmont, a dalmatic of reddish gold silk still preserved in the parish church of Ambazac was given by her to Stephen Muret. Since Stephen died in 1124, another prior, Stephen Liciac (1139–63), who may well have met Matilda in Rouen, is more likely to have been the recipient.[49] Many other gifts she made have not been traced; Reading received the hand of St James.[50] Apart from the dalmatic at Ambazac only one of her many treasures survives: a beautiful gemstone and gold filigree reliquary cross, said to have been given by her to Le Valasse.[51]

The bulk of her richest treasures went to Bec-Hellouin, and an impressive list of them was preserved in the abbey.[52] They included two crowns worn by the emperor. One, of solid gold decorated with gems, was also worn by Henry II at his coronation. It was so heavy that it was supported by two silver rods when used for the coronation of king or emperor; in front was a jewel of great size and value, and a cross of solid gold was superimposed. The smaller golden crown was used by the emperor on great feast days. There was a golden cross decorated with precious stones, and the foot of another cross; two gospel books

47 *Abbot Suger, On the Abbey Church of St Denis and its Art Teasures,* ed. and trans. Erwin Panofsky (Princeton, 1946), pp. 76, 203–4, 'cum quibusdam floribus coronae imperatricis ... '

48 See above, ch. 7, n. 54.

49 Hutchison, *Grandmont,* pp. 32, 57, 63; Judy Martin and L. E. M. Walker, 'At the feet of St Stephen Muret: Henry II and the order of Grandmont *redivivus*', *Journal of Medieval History,* 16 (1990), pp. 1–12; p. 6 for illustration.

50 See above, pp. 164–5.

51 It is now in the Musée Départementale at Rouen. See *The Plantagenet Chronicles,* ed. Elizabeth Hallam (London, 1986), p. 47 for illustration. That Le Valasse was the recipient has been questioned because of the richness of the reliquary, which might have been thought unsuitable for a Cistercian house, but Matilda clearly believed that even ascetic and poor orders might have rich treasures for their churches, as the silk dalmatic she gave to the Grandmontines shows.

52 Porée, *Histoire de l'abbaye du Bec* (Evreux, 1902), i. pp. 650–1.

bound in gold studded with gems; two censers of silver gilt; a silver
incense-box and spoon; a gold dish and a gold pyx for the Eucharist;
three silver flasks, a ewer for holy water and a silver basin. There were
two portable altars of marble mounted in silver, and an ebony chest full
of relics. The vestments were sumptuous: chasubles, dalmatics, copes,
and an imperial cloak of her own besprinkled with gold, which was
used to make albs. All these were given in her lifetime. After her death
the abbey received the ornaments used by her in her private chapel:
service books, a gold chalice and spoon, four chasubles, two tunics, two
dalmatics, six copes, two of which were interwoven with silver, two
silver censers, and two boxes described as eggs of griffins, whose legs
and claws gripping the egg were silver.[53] The final list shows that in
her later private worship she preferred a more austere ritual. Only the
chalice, receptacle of the host, was of gold, and most of the vestments
were plain. The griffin's egg boxes alone add a more fanciful touch,
suggestive of her courtly interest in sibylline legends and popular
bestiaries.

It is arguable that her benefactions simply represented the pious
almsgiving of any royal lady, with perhaps the added urgency of one
who had survived many hazards in an adventurous life. If anything, her
piety is more nearly modelled on that of her father than that of her
mother and grandmother; none of the monks who praised her virtues
suggested that she washed the feet of beggars in person. There is,
however, a hint of sincerity that is more than conventional, especially in
the language of the Le Valasse chronicler who knew her in her old age,
and wrote that her devotion to the Lord came from the heart. Her
determination to be buried at Bec, so much praised by Robert of
Torigny, shows respect for an abbey famous for its religious observance, and perhaps gratitude to its saintly second abbot, Anselm. It was
not simply the wish of any wealthy benefactor to be buried in a family
monastery, for Bec, in spite of its many royal connections, was not one
of the many houses founded by Norman kings. For all her shrewd
perception of worldly motive and her pragmatic approach to the business of government, her piety was deep and sincere. Possibly her son's
devotion to the austere monk hermits of Grandmont owed something to
her.

When Matilda died on 10 September 1167 she was buried in the
abbey church of Bec-Hellouin, before the high altar dedicated in honour
of the Virgin Mary, in accordance with her wishes and with the prior
consent of her son Henry.[54] Geoffrey of Vigeois called her a nun of

53 Porée, Bec, i, p. 653.
54 Porée, Chronique du Bec (Rouen, 1883), p. 19.

Fontevraud, and added that she gave thirty thousand shillings to the Grandmontines and her son added an equal sum for her.[55] Geoffrey wrote a little later in La Marche, where he would have known of her benefactions to Grandmont; but there is no other evidence that she was a nun of Fontevraud and he probably confused her with her sister-in-law, another Matilda. If his statement is true she took the habit on her deathbed; but Stephen of Rouen, in his very full account of her death and the funeral he himself attended, says nothing of her ever having been a nun.[56] Rotrou, who had succeeded her friend Hugh as archbishop of Rouen, conducted the funeral service, in the presence of Arnulf of Lisieux and a great company of monks and clergy. Stephen of Rouen described the scene, with the tomb lit by a great seven-branched candlestick and a crown of lighted lamps. Of the epitaph inscribed on her tomb two lines became especially famous:

> Great by birth, greater by marriage, greatest in her offspring,
> Here lies the daughter, wife and mother of Henry.[57]

She was commemorated in similar but more verbose terms by Arnulf of Lisieux, who wrote two epitaphs praising her royal lineage and imperial marriage, but adding that her virtues were greater than her noble blood and that, though a woman, she was without feminine weakness.[58] Arnulf had come to appreciate her during her years in Normandy. Pragmatic, but not unprincipled, they had much in common in their belief in moderate church reform and their appreciation of the realities of everyday relationships between clergy and magnates, as opposed to the more idealized confrontations of church and state. The monks of Bec, whose respect for her had never wavered, described her in their chronicle, with some exaggeration, as 'the most noble lady Matilda, empress of the Romans, daughter of the first Henry king of the English, wife first of Henry the emperor of the Romans and then countess of Anjou, queen of England and mother of Henry II, king of the English.'[59] Strictly speaking she was never queen of England, and possibly she was never so described in the inscription on her tomb. The

---

55 *RHF*, xii, p. 441. Monsieur Bienvenu, who is editing the Cartulary of Fontevraud, kindly informed me that he has found no reference there to Matilda being a nun, and that Geoffrey of Vigeois must have confused her with her sister-in-law, another Matilda.

56 *Draco Normannicus* (ed. Howlett, ii, pp. 711–16; ed. Omont, pp. 119–24).

57 Porée, *Bec,* ii, p. 615: 'Ortu magna, viro major, sed maxima partu, / Hic jacet Henrici filia, sponsa, parens.' The wording was copied with minor variations in several medieval chronicles.

58 Migne, *PL,* 101, col. 199; one epitaph includes the lines: 'Virtutum titulis humani culmen honoris / Excessit mulier, nil mulieris habens.'

59 Porée, *Chronique du Bec,* p. 19.

original monument was destroyed by the English during the wars of 1421; when, over two centuries later, it was restored by the Maurists, the new inscription was composed by none other than the eminent historian, Jean Mabillon, who was accurate about her status.[60]

Matilda's bones were fated to suffer almost as many vicissitudes after her death as during her lifetime. The tomb was buried in rubble when the church was seriously damaged by fire in 1263. During the restoration carried out in 1282 her body was found sown into an ox-skin, which was a common method of burial in the twelfth century.[61] In 1421 the church was pillaged by the English and the tombs destroyed; only in 1684 were measures taken to restore it. The Maurists then found some bones with a few rags of silk and fragments of an inscription, which enabled them to be identified as Matilda's. They were then wrapped in a cloth of green silk embroidered with gold, and placed in a double coffin of wood and lead, with an inscription stating that they were the bones of the Empress Matilda, found under the high altar on 2 March 1684, and reburied the same month. A solemn Mass, preceded on the vigil by the Vespers for the dead, was celebrated. Her remains were then left in peace until the abbey church was destroyed by Napoleon; not until 1846 were they rediscovered under the debris. Fortunately this was a time when Normandy was rich in scholars and archaeologists, including Auguste Le Prévost, and these men prevailed upon King Louis-Philippe not to bury the bones in Saint-Denis with the kings of France, where the empress would surely have turned in her troubled grave, but to reinter them in the cathedral of Rouen.[62] In the absence of monks at Bec no more suitable place could have been found, though in the end the empress was to lie in the place chosen not by her but by her father Henry I in 1134.

Matilda's descendants more than justified the claim of her epitaph. Quite apart from the royal line in England, her three granddaughters married into the royal families of Europe, and proved, through all the troubles they had to endure, to be remarkable women, courageous, cultured, and, above all, adaptable.[63] Matilda, the eldest, was married to Henry the Lion, duke of Saxony, in 1168 when she was twelve years old. A violent quarrel between Henry, the head of the house of Welf, and the Hohenstauffen emperor, Frederick Barbarossa, later forced her and her husband into exile, and she was installed by her father in the

---

60 Porée, *Bec*, ii, pp. 415–16, 615; *Chronique du Bec*, pp. 90–1, 129.
61 Porée, *Bec*, ii, p. 4.
62 Porée, *Bec*, ii, p. 416 and n. 1.
63 For their careers see Edmond-René Labande, 'Les filles d'Aliénor d'Aquitaine: étude comparative', *Cahiers de Civilisation Médiévale*, 29 (1986), pp. 105–12.

castle of Argentan. During her stay in the Angevin dominions she evidently became the centre of a cultured court. The troubadour, Bertran de Born, was introduced into her circle by her brother Richard, and wrote two 'passionate but no doubt conventional' songs to her.[64] She lived only four years after her return with her husband to Saxony in 1185 and was never a queen herself, but her son became emperor as Otto IV.

Joan, the most unfortunate, was married first to William II, king of Sicily, known as 'the Good'. She must have known the splendour and beauty of the Palazzo dei Normanni in Palermo and the cathedral of Monreale, but they were not to last for her. Like her grandmother, after only twelve years as a royal consort, she was widowed in 1189 at the age of twenty-four, without having borne a child to her husband. Her brother Richard, on his way to the crusade, rescued her from a dangerous situation where she was practically a hostage in her own palace, and took her with him in the company of his wife Berengaria. After the perils and vicissitudes of the return from the Holy Land, she was married again, at a humbler level, to Count Raymond VI of Toulouse and became the mother of the future Count Raymond VII. War was raging in Toulouse; she was in constant danger, and after only three years she died in childbirth at Rouen, where she had taken refuge with her mother.

Eleanor had the happiest life and the most distinguished descendants. Brought up with her sister Joan at Fontevraud, she was betrothed to Alfonso VIII of Castile in 1168, when she was seven, and was taken to Tarazona two years later to wait, like her grandmother, until she was old enough for the marriage to be consummated. Although her husband suffered some defeats in his wars against the Almohades, she lived to see his final triumph at Las Navas de Tolosa. Of her ten children six survived and four of her five daughters became queens: Berengaria of León, Urraca of Portugal, Eleanor of Aragon, and Blanche of France. When Blanche's husband, Louis VIII, died leaving a young son, she proved to be a wise regent until he came of age and succeeded to the throne as Louis IX. So it happened that the empress was the great-great-grandmother of both Edward I of England and St Louis of France. The Capetian line ended in 1792; the descendants of the Angevins are still on the throne of England.

When Ralph of Diss described the family of Henry II in his *Ymagines Historiarum,* his eulogy showed that even thirty years after the death of the empress she was remembered and admired. He wrote of the king's

64 Bertran de Born, *Oeuvres*, ed. A. Thomas (Toulouse, 1888), p. xxiv; the songs are 'Ges de disnar' and 'Chazutz sui de mal en pena'.

three daughters that they had married into royal stock, and their husbands had governed the Saxons, Spaniards and Sicilians with firmness. The king's daughters were obliged to spend their lives among peoples far from England, differing in diet, dress and customs. 'They might', he declared, 'have lived in continual terror from the cold barbarism of the Saxons, the uncertain wars against the Saracens, and the fierce tyranny of the Sicilians, had not the nobility of their grandmother the empress, and her masculine courage in a female body, shown her granddaughters an example of fortitude and patience.'[65] Her epitaph, which dwelt on her conventional roles as daughter, wife and mother, omitted any comment on her true character and her personal achievement through all the changes of fortune. Ralph of Diss showed how she was remembered, and worthily completed the picture.

65 *Radulfi de Diceto Decani Lundoniensis Opera Historica*, ed. W. Stubbs (2 vols, RS, 1876), ii. pp. 15–18.

9

The Empress in History

The triumph of the Angevins gradually silenced the criticisms of Stephen's partisans. Robert of Torigny, devoted to Henry II, set the pattern for the mainstream of historical writing for the next two hundred years.[1] The dominant theme was legitimacy: to the legitimacy of William I's conquest of England, which had been hammered home by Norman historians from William of Poitiers onwards, was now added the legitimacy of Henry II's claim by hereditary right. This was the favoured motif; but for a generation after Matilda's death historians continued to add information and rumour about the events of her lifetime to the earlier Anglo-Norman chronicles. Two or three decades later William of Newburgh, aware of conditions in the north, dwelt sadly on the divisions of England in 1149; part of the country obeyed the empress, part the king, but neither leader could control his or her own followers and prevent them looting the districts round their castles; there were as many kings, or rather tyrants, as lords of castles. This may have been the experience of Yorkshire, where lords like William of Albemarle worked in their own interests even when giving nominal support to one of the rivals; Newburgh noticed a contrast north of Tees, where King David was in control and kept the peace.[2] Had he been more familiar with the south he might have found some regions where both Stephen and Matilda had maintained authority as effective as David's for at least some of the time. His contemporary, Gervase of Canterbury, looked back with greater detachment; still able to draw on some oral memory as well as the written sources, he produced a more balanced narrative. He took a kindlier view of the motives of Geoffrey of Anjou than Malmesbury, writing before the outcome could be

1 See R. Foreville, 'Robert de Torigni et Clio', *Millénaire Monastique du Mont Saint-Michel* (4 vols, Paris, 1967), vol. ii, ed. R. Foreville, pp. 141–54.
2 William of Newburgh, *Historia rerum Anglicarum, Chronicles of the Reigns of Stephen, Henry II and Richard I*, ed. R. Howlett (4 vols, RS, 1884–70), i, pp. 69–70.

known, was prepared to do. He recognized that Geoffrey's refusal to send forces to England in 1142 was due to the still unsettled state of Normandy and Anjou, and believed that Robert of Gloucester accepted this, and was content to take back to England just a small contingent of seasoned Angevin knights and his nephew Henry; he added that the empress, in spite of having lost Oxford, forgot her troubles in the delight of welcoming her son.[3] Gervase, with hindsight, was quietly placing the emphasis on the long-term strategies of the empress and her party that had ended in the Angevin triumph. In the process a few dates were telescoped and facts blurred. He did not write a panegyric, but although in common with Henry of Huntingdon and the *Gesta Stephani* he believed that Matilda's refusal to grant concessions had lost her the support of the Londoners, he did not paint an exaggerated picture of her conduct at the time. His interest was in the successful outcome for her son.

Matilda herself was sometimes remembered in the reflected glory of her royal and imperial status. A note of early date in one manuscript of the *Defloratio Plinii* of Robert of Cricklade, dedicated to Henry II, seems to echo her epitaph, but may have been independent of it. In glossing Pliny's statement that only one woman could be found in the whole of history (the Spartan Lampido) who was daughter, wife and mother of a king, the writer added, 'In our age there is one woman, Matilda, daughter and wife of a king, who has seen her son become a most powerful king and – what is even more wonderful – each of them has the name of Henry.'[4] In both Germany and England her place in the German imperial hierarchy was a source of pride. A miniature, executed between 1173 and 1180 on the order of Henry the Lion, duke of Saxony, to portray his own coronation with his second wife Matilda, daughter of Henry II, shows the Empress Matilda among the kinsfolk who emphasized the almost imperial dignity of the ducal pair.[5] When in 1235 Isabella, the sister of King Henry III, was betrothed to Frederick II, the St Albans chroniclers drew up a genealogy to demonstrate that she was worthy to marry an emperor, and Matilda as empress added a little extra lustre to an already impressive list.[6]

From the late twelfth century onwards, chroniclers in England pre-

3 *Gervase of Canterbury*, i, pp. 123, 125.

4 C. H. Haskins, 'Henry II as a patron of literature', *Essays in Medieval History presented to Thomas Frederick Tout*, ed. A. G. Little and F. M. Powicke (Manchester, 1925), p. 75.

5 Haverkamp, *Medieval Germany*, p. 266.

6 *Chronica Majora*, RS, iii, pp. 325–6. It is interesting to note that as soon as a ring was placed on Isabella's finger during the proxy betrothal she was greeted as empress, though not yet crowned, with shouts of *Vivat imperatrix vivat* (ibid., pp. 318–19).

sented a pastiche of extracts from the more familiar historians, notably William of Malmesbury, Henry of Huntingdon, some continuations of the Durham and Worcester chronicles, William of Newburgh, Gervase of Canterbury and his contemporaries, especially Roger of Howden and Ralph of Diss. Orderic Vitalis was little read until the sixteenth century; but Robert of Torigny's work spread, partly through the vernacular history of Benoît of Sainte-Maure, who helped to make known the details of Matilda's education in Germany.[7] Fortunately, perhaps, for Matilda's reputation, the hostile *Gesta Stephani* had a limited circulation in the period of Plantagenêt ascendancy. At first the elements were variously mixed by personal selection, as in the chronicle of Walter of Guisborough, who relied heavily on Newburgh and a Durham chronicle indebted to Henry of Huntingdon.[8] From the fourteenth century, borrowing tended to be at second hand. The *Polychronicon* of Ranulf Higden provided a kind of historical anthology made up of sizeable extracts from the most popular authors, and many later historians copied directly from it.[9] In all these potted histories of the kings of England Matilda's part was a minor one; the emphasis was on Stephen's perjury and the legitimacy of Henry's ultimate succession. Some of the most abbreviated, such as the long fifteenth-century scroll, *Considerans*, which traced the descent of Henry VI from Adam, were content to reduce her biography to the epitaph which proclaimed the importance of the three Henrys in her life.[10]

Legends almost invariably gathered round rulers after their death, and various rumours attempted to provide a posthumous history for the emperor Henry V. Walter Map had heard that he had repented his numerous sins of extortion and injustice, feigned death, and wandered abroad to do penance. He was, however, scrupulous enough to add that the various pretenders, including a monk at Cluny, who claimed to be the emperor, had all been proved to be imposters. Gerald of Wales, on the other hand, in an exceptionally bitter passage in which he made much of the legendary diabolic origin of the Angevins and accused Henry II and his whole family of every kind of vice, repeated the story with embellishments. He claimed that the ex-emperor had lived for some years as a hermit, so that Matilda's second marriage was bigamous and her son illegitimate. When Ranulf Higden found the story in

7 Benoît, ed. Fahlin, vv. 43255–63.

8 *The Chronicle of Walter of Guisburgh*, ed. H. Rothwell (Camden 3rd ser., 89, 1956), pp. xxv-xxvi; Gransden, *Historical Writing*, ii, pp. 225–6, 471.

9 Gransden, *Historical Writing*, ii, ch. 2.

10 Magdalen College, Oxford, MS 248. The forty-foot-long scroll is thought to be the work of Roger Alban, a London Carmelite. I owe this reference to Mr Michael Moynihan.

Gerald's works he omitted the scandalous allegations, and simply gave a version of the legend in which Henry V spent his last years in a cell near Chester, expiating his sins as a humble and penitent hermit called Godescalc; he avoided casting any doubts on the validity of Matilda's marriage.[11] The most bizarre legend to circulate concerned Matilda herself. It appears early in the thirteenth century, in an interpretation of the prophecies of Merlin, recorded in the St Albans Chronicle, and relates that when, in 1153, the armies of Stephen and Henry were ready to join battle, Matilda herself, dishevelled and distracted, had pleaded with the opponents not to fight, telling Stephen and Henry in turn that they were father and son, and that Henry had been conceived when Stephen was escorting her to Normandy to marry Geoffrey of Anjou.[12] The origin no doubt lay in Stephen's decision to adopt Henry as his heir when peace was made between them at Winchester; but for a historian of the calibre of Roger Wendover to present this tale without comment must have involved a suspension of his critical faculties, not least since Henry's birth occurred almost five years after the marriage.

The story, with its popular element of the father and son who unwittingly meet in battle, was a very old one, and shows how romance and popular legend had been at work on the bare bones of history.[13] The vernacular verse histories were naturally prone to imaginative embellishments. They added personal touches: Benoît of Sainte-Maure wrote that when Matilda was betrothed she was very well-mannered, courageous and beautiful.[14] Pierre de Langtoft called her 'the greatest beauty ever seen.'[15] Speculation about her personal life was usually restrained. Robert of Gloucester referred to Matilda's breach with her husband as 'some little strife', and placed it just before Henry I's death.[16] One German chronicler, who called her 'die gute Methilt', accused her husband of ill-treating her, but this was no more than a common literary topos.[17] Apart from the interpretation of Merlin's

11 Walter Map, *De Nugis Curialium*, pp. 478–83; *Giraldi Cambrensis Opera*, viii (*Liber de Principis Instructione*), pp. 298–300; *Polychronicon Ranulfi Higden*, ed. J. W. Lumby (9 vols, RS, 1865–6), vii, pp. 466–8.

12 *Matthaei Parisiensis monachi Sancti Albani Chronica Majora*, ed. H. R. Luard (7 vols, RS, 1872–83), ii, pp. 294–5, interpreting the passage in the prophecies of Merlin, 'Nocebit possidenti ex impiis pietas, donec sese genitae induerit.' This part of the St Albans Chronicle was the work of Roger Wendover.

13 For this topos see Shulamith Shahar, *Childhood in the Middle Ages* (London and New York, 1990), pp. 256–8.

14 'Qui mult fu sage e prex e belle' (Benoît, ed. Fahlin, v. 43198).

15 *The Chronicle of Pierre de Langtoft*, ed. Thomas Wright (2 vols, RS, 1866–8), i, p. 462.

16 *The Metrical Chronicle of Robert of Gloucester*, ed. W. A. Wright (2 vols, RS, 1887), ii p. 650.

17 Epkonis de Repkau, *Breve Chronicon Magdeburgense: Scriptores Rerum Germanicarum*, ed. I. B. Menckenius, vol. 3 (Leipzig, 1730), col. 356.

prophecy that turned Henry into Stephen's son, there was no hint during the Middle Ages that she ever took a lover. When her reputation is compared with that of Queen Urraca, Queen Melisende, and her own daughter-in-law, Eleanor of Aquitaine, this is very remarkable. Any such story had to wait until the twentieth century, when Nesta Pain tried to discover passion in her relations with Brian fitz Count. Brian was her vassal; brought up at her father's court, he was almost a foster brother and possibly a distant kinsman. Two charters issued by Matilda and her son Henry for Reading Abbey expressed gratitude for the loyal service and *amor* they had received from Brian, and the words should be interpreted in their contemporary meaning.[18] *Amor* was the term used very commonly to describe the benevolence of a sovereign to his vassal and the faithful service of a vassal to his lord or lady.[19] The author of the *Gesta Stephani* wrote with admiration of the mutual devotion of Matilda and Brian which endured through all adversity, but his language implied the strong bonds of honourable kinship and fealty at its best. Whether or not he was the bishop of Bath, he was certainly a churchman and a hostile critic of the empress; if he had suspected a liaison he would have denounced her as a harlot and Brian as an adulterer.[20] As far as the sources go, many historians must have shared James Tyrell's feelings when, at the close of the seventeenth century, he attempted to give a character sketch of the empress: 'This Character we may gather from her Actions, for I do not find any given of her by the Historians of that Age.'[21]

Because the sources do indeed force readers to judge her chiefly by her actions, interpretations of her life and conduct have varied, partly with the legal and constitutional assumptions of historians and partly

18 *Regesta,* iii, nos 703, 704.

19 H. B. Teunis, 'Benoît of St Maure and William the Conqueror's *amor*', Anglo-Norman Studies, 12 (1990), pp. 199–209, shows how Benoît in the later twelfth century used the term exclusively of feudal relationships, whereas a century earlier William of Poitiers had used it to describe both feudal and family bonds.

20 See *Gesta Stephani,* pp. 134–5 for the escape from Winchester, 'Andegavensis comitissa, femineam semper excedens mollitiem ... ante omnes, Brieno tantum cum paucis comite, ad Divisas confugit, immensum per hoc, ipsa et Brienus, nacti praeconii titulum, ut sicut sese antea mutuo et indivise dilexerunt, ita nec in adversis, plurimo impediente periculo, aliquatenus separarentur.' It is presumably to this that Nesta Pain (*Empress Matilda,* p. 113) referred when she wrote of the comment of an unnamed 'contemporary', 'Is he suggesting that Brian and the Empress were lovers? There must have been some gossip about them or he would hardly have written in this way.' On the contrary, if there had been any gossip, he would have written very differently, as Orderic Vitalis wrote of Bertrade of Montfort, whom he pitied for her forced marriage to the reprehensible Fulk of Anjou, but condemned roundly after she absconded with the king of France (Chibnall, *World of Orderic,* pp. 128–9).

21 James Tyrrell, *The General History of England both Ecclesiastical and Civil,* vol. ii (London, 1700), pp. 339–40.

with the sources available to them. Although the full texts of chroniclers such as Orderic Vitalis and even the *Gesta Stephani* became more readily accessible from the sixteenth century onwards, historians continued for some time to depend almost exclusively on older narratives. The changes came first in their assumptions about the conditions governing female succession. Even before the accession of Mary Tudor and Elizabeth I, lawyers accepted the possibility of rule by an English queen with full rights. Holinshed, putting the succession problem faced by Henry I in the context of the sixteenth century, believed that the king called a parliament, and by its authority caused his daughter 'to be established as his lawful heir and successor, with an article of intaile upon her issue.'[22] Reading backwards, historians with a legal outlook usually assumed that any rights of a woman who succeeded in default of a male heir would be identical with those of a man. This led to speculation on whether, and when, Matilda had 'renounced her rights' in favour of her son. Stephen was still regarded as a usurper. Sir Richard Baker, at the end of a long, muddled and somewhat credulous account of the reign, expressed his bewilderment at Matilda's apparent relinquishment of her rights when Henry was acknowledged at Stephen's heir and successor:

> But what became of Maud the Empress at this time? . . . To say that she consented to the agreement without any provision made for herself, is to make her too much a woman, a very weak vessel; and to say there might be provision made, though it be not Recorded, is to make all Writers defective in great excess. And besides, being so stirring a woman as she was, that upon a sudden she should be so quiet as not to deserve to have one word spoken of her in all the long time she lived after . . . is as strange as the rest. And if she placed her contentment wholly in her Son, that in regard of him she regarded not herself at all, it deserves at least the *Encomium* of such motherly love as is very unusual and not always safe. Whatsoever it was, I must be fain to leave it as a Gordian Knot which no Writer helps me to unty.[23]

George Harbin, in a more cogently reasoned examination of the question of hereditary right, argued that when Geoffrey of Anjou resigned the duchy of Normandy that he held in right of his wife to his son, Matilda must have given her consent, and that presumably she also resigned her right in the kingdom. He suggested further that there is some evidence that 'she never intended to sit longer on the Throne than

22 *Holinshed's Chronicles of England, Scotland and Ireland* (6 vols, London, 1807, 1965 reprint), ii, p. 72.
23 Sir Richard Baker, *A Chronicle of the Kings of England* (London, 1674), p. 49.

until her Son became capable of Government, since she never took the Title of Queen.'[24]

Not until the eighteenth century was the succession question attacked with a keener appreciation of the realities of law and custom in the twelfth century. David Hume compared the changes in the feudal law of succession to fiefs with the rights of succession in the kingdom. He believed that as long as estates were transmitted only to such as could give the military service and perform the other obligations involved in person, female succession to fiefs could not be admitted; but once hereditary succession for some generations in one family had 'obliterated the primitive idea', females were gradually admitted to the possession of feudal property. Although the same changes might be expected to occur in succession to the crown, this could not be guaranteed; history showed him that 'the irregular manner in which Henry I had acquired the crown might have instructed him that neither his Norman nor his English subjects were as yet capable of adhering to a strict rule of government.'[25] If Hume had not yet fully mastered the complex customs governing succession to fiefs at that time, he was at least looking at the question in the right way.

The other change leading gradually to a different assessment of Matilda's life was the discovery of new sources, through exploration both of the public records and of the charters accumulated in private archives. In this work the antiquaries and local historians unobtrusively played their part. Charters showed that Matilda was not inactive during the years between 1142 and 1148 when the chroniclers had very little to say about her. R. Polwhele, in his History of Cornwall, noted the activities of the earl of Cornwall and his Cornish troops, and wrote of the empress that 'Her various adventures, as related by William of Malmesbury, have all the air of romance. In military spirit, she seems to have equalled her antagonist, and in gratitude to her adherents, to have far outshone him.' He added as evidence of this gratitude that after she made Stephen her prisoner she began to reward the fidelity of her friends with grants of land and the distribution of honours, and cited a local Cornish charter as one example.[26] W. L. Bowles, investigating the early history of Stanley Abbey, related its foundations to the activities of the empress at a slightly later date. 'In my opinion,' he wrote,

24 George Harbin, The Hereditary Right of the Crown of England asserted by a Gentleman (London, 1713), pp. 56–8.

25 David Hume, The History of England from the Invasion of Julius Caesar to the Revolution of 1688 (Reprint of 1786 edn, London), pp. 191–3. The realities of succession by women in the twelfth century are nicely balanced by Jane Martindale, 'Succession and politics', pp. 19–41.

26 Polwhele, History of Cornwall, ii, pp. 22–3.

the abbey was removed from Lockswell to Stanley in consequence of a religious vow on the part of Matilda on her son's accession to the throne of England, for in that year it was removed. She had nobly, aided by her half brother the brave earl of Gloucester, contended, with various fortunes, with ardent courage, and romantic adventures, for the crown of her father.[27]

These and numerous other local studies were producing a new body of evidence, but the best part of a century was to pass before the charter evidence began to be incorporated in general histories of the period. Mrs M. A. E. Green, in her *Lives of the Princesses of England*, Kate Norgate and Sir James Ramsay, did painstaking research for their general histories, but still relied for the most part on the chronicles. Mrs Green, needing to give personal touches, made some use, not uncritically, of the vernacular chronicles.[28] The particular merit of Kate Norgate's work was that she was familiar with Norman and Angevin material, and could deal at length with the activities of Geoffrey of Anjou in the struggle for the inheritance. She acknowledged briefly that Matilda had a role to play in Normandy in the last two decades of her life, and some of her comments on her character were shrewd and perceptive. Of her marriage to Geoffrey she wrote: 'Fortunately for the ill-matched couple they were both of that cold-blooded temperament to which intense personal affection is not a necessary of life. Henceforth they were content to work together as partners in political enterprise, and to find in a community of worldly interests a sufficient bond of union.' Her final assessment was just and convincing, at least in part:

> Matilda had been a harsh, violent, impracticable woman; but there was in her character an element of moral and intellectual grandeur that even in her worst days had won and kept for her the devotion of men like Miles of Hereford and Brian Fitz-Count, and which in her later years had fairly gained the mastery over her less admirable qualities. She had inherited a considerable share of her father's talents for government.[29]

Ramsay, on the other hand, who relied heavily on the *Gesta Stephani* and was not much concerned with Normandy, was particularly unsympathetic to Matilda.[30]

One new dimension was added by the semi-biography of Oskar

---

27 Bowles, *The Parochial History of Bremhill*, pp. 112–13.

28 M. A. E. Green, *The Lives of the Princesses of England* (6 vols, London, 1869–75), i, pp. 82–90.

29 Kate Norgate, *England under the Angevin Kings* (2 vols, London and New York, 1887), pp. 268, 442–3.

30 James A. Ramsay, *The Foundations of England* (2 vols, London, 1898), ii, pp. 403–7.

Rössler, in his *Kaiserin Mathilde und der Zeitalter der Anarchie in England*. A pupil of Scheffer-Boichorst, he was thoroughly schooled in documentary study, and used charters to give some body to Matilda's years in Germany, and to underline her practical experience as the wife of the emperor. For England he relied mostly on the chronicles, though both he and Ramsay looked at a few charters to discuss the possible implications of the title *domina Anglorum*. They both had the advantage of the work of J. H. Round, but did not exploit it very fully. Rössler, though he made as much as the sources allowed of Matilda's early experience, had almost nothing to say about her after she left England in 1148.

The book that in many ways marked a new stage in the study of Stephen's reign was J. H. Round's *Geoffrey de Mandeville*.[31] It was a pioneering work that succeeded in bringing the study of charters out of the private libraries of local antiquaries into the mainstream of historical writing. Although Round both misdated and misinterpreted some of the key charters in the reign, he began the systematic ordering of the charter evidence, and brought into historical discussion the lesser men who were witnesses to and recipients of charters. He also noted entries in the early Pipe Rolls of Henry II recording gifts of royal demesne, and so began to show the activities of Matilda and her son in the territories they controlled. The work of the twentieth-century historians, aided by the researches of the numismatists, was to build on this foundation, and show that the 'Anarchy' implied rather a breakdown of central royal authority and an increase in provincial autonomy than a total collapse of government. In the regions most securely held by either party the revenues were collected more or less efficiently, coins were struck, and judicial business was done.

Systematic publication of the royal charters began in France, with the great work of Léopold Delisle on the acts of Henry II relating to his French provinces, which was completed after his death by Elie Berger.[32] Delisle's introduction to the collection underlined the importance of the work that Matilda, together with Geoffrey, had done in preparing the way for the accession of her son. He emphasized her courage and determination, and showed how even after Henry's accession, the young king relied on her for a kind of regency in Normandy during his absences in England or Anjou. This, together with the evidence of the English records for her activities in Oxford and Devizes from 1141 to 1148, added some positive qualities to the often negative accounts of

---

31 J. H. Round, *Geoffrey de Mandeville* (London, 1892).
32 L. Delisle, *Recueil des actes de Henri II*; the *Introduction* by Delisle appeared in 1909, and was followed by two volumes of charters, completed by E. Berger.

the chroniclers. With the appearance of the third and fourth volumes of the *Regesta Regum Anglo-Normannorum* in 1968 and 1970, a much deeper appreciation of Matilda's share in holding on to her hereditary right became possible, though the material has still not been fully used in some of the more general histories. Indeed the most recent attempt at a 'biography' of Matilda by Nesta Pain, though fluent and readable, is based very largely on narrative chronicles and a few letters, giving no indication of which sources (early or late) are used for any allegation, and seasoned with a generous dash of imagination.[33] The earlier popular biography by the Earl of Onslow, though published before the appearance of the *Regesta* and, like Nesta Pain's book, totally lacking in footnote references, has at least a firmer grasp of political reality.[34] Good, critical work on different aspects of her struggle for the English crown has come from the pen of Karl Schnith; his papers, written in German, focus principally on her activities in England and bring out the limitations to the possibility of female succession in the second quarter of the twelfth century.[35]

There will never be a definitive and final assessment of the character and motives of the empress, but at least it is now becoming more possible to see her career in the round. There is general agreement that she was either proud or at least keenly conscious of the high status of an empress, and that she could behave autocratically. She was, said Nicholas of Mont St Jacques, who met her in her more mellow old age, 'of the stock of tyrants', and evidently it showed. The same could have been said about both her father and her eldest son; in Matilda the quality aroused more hostility because it was contrasted with the 'feminine softness' she lacked. The role she was obliged to play brought out all her masculine qualities; when they revealed themselves in courage and fortitude, as they frequently did, they were praised even by her enemies. It is time now to recognize more positively the 'element of moral and intellectual grandeur' in her character.

While she must take responsibility for the errors of judgement during the crucial summer of 1141, the evidence of the charters indicates that she did not act arbitrarily and alone; she had the leaders of her party, including Robert earl of Gloucester and King David with her during the months of crisis. In the disastrous attempt to intrude William Cumin into the see of Durham it is more likely that she was overpersuaded by King David (who continued to support Cumin's brutal attempts to take over the see long afterwards) than that she did not listen to him. When in late July the decision to march on Winchester and confront Bishop

33 Nesta Pain, *Empress Matilda*.
34 Onslow, *The Empress Maud*.
35 See below, Bibliography, under Schnith.

Henry was taken, Robert of Gloucester was with her and cannot have been ignorant of her intentions, as the continuator of the Worcester chronicle alleged.[36] Chroniclers writing in the first shock of Stephen's defeat at Lincoln could not assess how far the country had genuinely been won over to her cause. Perhaps historians eight centuries later are no better judges of the odds against her; yet it now seems clear from the evidence that the opposition remained unbeaten and was gathering strength. The queen, backed by William of Ypres and his mercenaries, was a focus of loyalty for all whose family and territorial interests lay in the restoration of Stephen's rule. The church that had crowned him would not give him up; papal approval helped to determine the actions of Henry of Blois. Matilda could not have given way to the queen's request that she should free Stephen if he renounced the throne and was allowed to keep the honours he had held in Henry I's lifetime; Stephen's conduct in 1135 had shown how little his word was to be trusted. If Matilda had showered favours on the Londoners she would have lost the help of Geoffrey de Mandeville; perhaps she totally misjudged the situation, since in the end she lost both.

Yet when all things are considered, it remains clear that the real difficulty preventing her final triumph was that in twelfth-century England there was virtually no place for female succession of the kind that could be made acceptable in the sixteenth, and still more in the nineteenth, century. This was due not to blind prejudice, but to the realities of feudal life, even though custom was still flexible. Hume grasped an important point when he wrote that the circumstances in which Henry I himself gained the crown showed that the customs becoming more fixed for the descent of private estates still did not apply to the inheritance of the kingdom. Henry may have imagined that because he still had the power to manipulate inheritance within a vassal family through carefully chosen marriages, he could settle the kingdom in the same way. Matilda's experience showed that he had taken too much for granted and left too many questions unanswered. Even without the complication of Normandy, it was uncertain whether a woman could rule England in her own right alone, or whether a minor would be acceptable. The second question was settled in 1216, when Henry III became king at the age of nine; the first not until 1553. In the early twelfth century rules of inheritance to any crown were still being worked out pragmatically; events in each kingdom were to show what was and was not acceptable within the limits of customs which were only in the process of crystallization. The experience of Queen Urraca in Castilla-León and Queen Melisende in Jerusalem showed that, to

36 Florence of Worcester, ii, p. 133; this part of the chronicle was probably written at Gloucester, and tended to exaggerate the importance of Miles of Gloucester.

fight off rivals, it was essential to bring in either a husband or a son as a nominal co-ruler at the earliest possible moment.

In England this was not done. Robert of Gloucester may have wished to stress the claims of the infant Henry from the outset, but Matilda's thoughts seem to have turned initially towards ruling directly herself. Count Geoffrey of Anjou, as far as can be judged from his actions, decided against taking part in the English fighting, preferring to concentrate on Normandy with a view to handing it over when his son came of age.[37] The year 1141 may still have been a time of doubt and hesitation. When Geoffrey and Earl Robert met in Normandy the following summer they appear to have agreed on the future strategy to be pursued. Robert brought his young nephew back to England with him, while Geoffrey remained in Normandy and consolidated his hold on the continental dominions. From that time Henry was associated occasionally in his mother's grants to vassals. Whatever her earlier hopes and ambitions may have been, Matilda had evidently accepted that she would never wear the crown herself, and must work for him. For the remaining twenty-five years of her life she made this her aim, and avoided repeating the mistakes of the previous year. Her task was to demonstrate that a daughter could at least transmit the right of succession when sons failed. Moreover she did nothing that excluded the possibility of female succession to the crown of England when social conditions should have changed.

How well she succeeded appears in the comments of her near-contemporary, Ralph of Diss, who wrote when partisan passions had subsided on the qualities of patience and fortitude she bequeathed to her granddaughters, and in the judgement of Delisle, based on a scholarly assessment of the charter evidence. Once she had accepted what was possible for a woman claimant to the throne of England, in a feudal society where even rules of private inheritance were still flexible and where the success of a putative heir might depend on quick action and armed force, she proved herself able (in spite of many difficulties and a few stumbles) to establish the succession in the line intended by her father. The fact that she was a strong-willed woman and no passive cipher led at first to problems that cost her dear; but in the end her determined character, and her ability to make use of the wide experience gained in an eventful life, enabled her to succeed where a woman of greater 'feminine softness' might have been swept aside.

---

37 This view, put forward by Haskins (*Norman Institutions*, pp. 130–2), has been questioned by John Le Patourel (*Feudal Empires*, ch. 9, pp. 13–15), who thought it possible that Geoffrey aimed at association rather than substitution when he invested Henry with the duchy of Normandy, and possibly did not give up the ducal title, though he rarely used it.

Bibliography of Abbreviated Titles

This bibliography includes only works that are cited more than once. Where a reference has been greatly abbreviated and might not be easily recognizable, the shortened form is given before the full reference. Abbreviated references to series and journals are included.

Actus pontificum cenomannis in urbe degentium, ed. G. Busson and A. Ledru, Société des Archives historiques du Maine, 2, 1902.

Anglo-Norman Studies: Proceedings of the Battle Conference on Anglo-Norman Studies, 1–11, 1979–89, ed. R. Allen Brown; 12, 1990, ed. Marjorie Chibnall; continued from 1983 as *Anglo-Norman Studies*.

Annales Monastici, ed. H. R. Luard, 4 vols, RS, 1864–9.

Annales Patherbrunnenses, ed. Paul Scheffer-Boichorst, Innsbruck, 1870.

Anonymi Chronica Imperatorum, *see* Schmale.

Anselm, *Opera Omnia*: *S. Anselmi Opera Omnia*, ed. F. S. Schmitt, 6 vols, Edinburgh, 1938–61.

A-SC: The Anglo-Saxon Chronicle (citations are by year).

Baker, Derek (ed.), *Medieval Women*, Studies in Church History, Subsidia 1, Oxford, 1978.

Barlow, Frank *Edward the Confessor*, 2nd edn London, 1979.

—— *The English Church 1066–1154*, London and New York, 1979.

—— *Thomas Becket*, London, 1986.

—— *William Rufus*, London, 1983.

—— (ed.), *The Letters of Arnulf of Lisieux*, Camden Society, 61, 1939.

Barraclough, *Chester Charters*: ed. Geoffrey Barraclough, *The Charters of the Anglo-Norman Earls of Chester c. 1071–1233*, Record Society of Lancashire and Cheshire, 126, 1988.

Barrow, G. W. S., *The Kingdom of the Scots*, London, 1973.

Beeler, J., *Warfare in England 1066–1189*, Ithaca and New York, 1966.

Benoît: Fahlin, Carin (ed.), *Chronique des ducs de Normandie par Benoît*, 2 vols, Lund, 1951–67.

Benson, R. L., *The Bishop Elect*, Princeton, 1968.

Bernard, St, *S. Bernardi Opera*, ed. J. Leclercq, C. H. Talbot and H. M. Rochais, 8 vols in 9, Rome, 1957–77.

Biddle, Martin, 'Seasonal festivals and residence: Winchester, Westminster and

Gloucester in the tenth to twelfth centuries', *Anglo-Norman Studies*, 8, 1986 for 1985, pp. 51–72.

Birch, W. de G., 'Collections of the Cistercian abbey of Stanley', *Wiltshire Archaeological and Natural History Magazine*, 15 (1875).

Bishop, T. A. M., *Scriptores Regis*, Oxford, 1961.

Bishop, T. A. M., and Chaplais, P., *Facsimiles of English Royal Writs to A.D. 1100*, Oxford, 1957.

BL: British Library.

Blumenthal, Uta-Renate, *The Investiture Controversy*, Philadelphia, 1988.

Böhmer, H., *Kirche und Staat in England und in der Normandie im xi und xii Jahrhundert*, Leipzig, 1899.

Book of Fees, HMSO, London, 1920–31.

Boon, George C., *Coins of the Anarchy 1135–54*, National Museum of Wales, Cardiff, 1988.

Bouvet, J., 'Le récit de la fondation de Mortemer', *Collectanea Ordinis Cisterciensium reformatorum*, 22 (1960), pp. 149–68.

Bowles, W. L., *Parochial History of Bremhill in the County of Wiltshire*, London, 1828.

Brett, Martin, *The English Church under Henry I*, Oxford, 1975.

Brooke, Christopher, assisted by Gillian Keir, *London 800–1216: The Shaping of a City*, London, 1975.

Brown, R. Allen, *Castles, Conquest and Charters*: Collected Papers, Wood-bridge and Wolfeboro, 1989.

—— *Castles from the Air*, Cambridge, 1989.

BSAN: Bulletin de la Société des Antiquaires de Normandie.

Büttner, Heinrich, 'Die Bischofsstädte Basel bis Mainz in der Zeit des Investitur-streits', in *Investiturstreit und Reichsverfassung*, pp. 351–61.

—— 'Erzbischof Adalbert von Mainz, die Kurie und das Reich in den Jahren 1118 bis 1122', in *Investiturstreit und Reichsverfassung*, pp. 396–410.

Calendar of the Charter Rolls preserved in the Public Record Office, 6 vols, London, 1903–27.

CDF: Calendar of Documents preserved in France, 1, ed. J. H. Round, London, 1899.

Charters of Salisbury: ed. W. R. Jones, and W. D. Macray, *Charters and Documents illustrating the History of the Cathedral City and Diocese of Salisbury in the Twelfth and Thirteenth Centuries*, RS, 1891.

Chartrou, J., *L'Anjou de 1109 à 1151*, Paris, 1928.

Chibnall, Marjorie, *Anglo-Norman England 1066–1166*, Oxford, 1986.

—— 'The Empress Matilda and Bec-Hellouin', *Anglo-Norman Studies*, 10 (1988 for 1987), pp. 35–48.

—— 'The Empress Matilda and Church reform', *TRHS*, 5th ser., 38 (1988), pp. 107–33.

—— *The World of Orderic Vitalis*, Oxford, 1984.

Chronica Majora: Luard, H. R. (ed.), *Matthaei Parisiensis monachi Sancti Albani Chronica Majora*, 7 vols, RS, 1872–83.

Chronicae Sancti Albini Andegavensis, in *Chroniques des Eglises d'Anjou*, ed. P. Marchegay and E. Mabille, Paris, 1869.

Chronicles of the Reigns of Stephen, Henry II and Richard I, ed. Richard Howlett, 4 vols, RS, 1884–9.

Chron. Valassense: F. Sommènil (ed.), *Chronicon Valassense*, Rouen, 1868.

Classen, P., and Scheibert, P. (eds), *Festschrift Peter Ernst Schramm*, Wiesbaden, 1964.

CNRS: Centre National de la Recherche Scientifique.

Complete Peerage: *The Complete Peerage of England, Scotland, Ireland*, by G. E. C[okayne], new edn, 13 vols in 14, London, 1910–59.

Councils and Synods: *Councils and Synods with other documents relating to the English Church*, 1, ed. D. Whitelock, M. Brett and C. N. L. Brooke, Oxford, 1981.

Cronne, H. A., 'Ranulf de Gernons, earl of Chester, 1129–1153', *TRHS* 4th ser., 20 (1937), pp. 103–34.

Crouch, David, *The Beaumont Twins*, Cambridge, 1987.

Daniel, Samuel, *The Collection of the History of England*, revised edn, London, 1634.

Davies, R. R., *Conquest, Coexistence and Change in Wales 1063–1415*, Oxford, 1987.

Davis, H. W. C., 'Henry of Blois and Brian fitz Count', *EHR*, 25 (1910), pp. 297–303.

—— 'Some documents of the Anarchy', in *Essays in History presented to Reginald Lane Poole*, ed. H. W. C. Davis, Oxford, 1927, pp. 168–89.

Davis, R. H. C., 'Geoffrey de Mandeville reconsidered', *EHR*, 79 (1964), pp. 299–307.

—— *King Stephen*, 3rd edn, London and New York, 1990.

—— reply to J. O. Prestwich, 'The treason of Geoffrey de Mandeville', *EHR*, 103 (1988), pp. 313–17, 967–8.

—— 'Treaty between William Earl of Gloucester and Roger Earl of Hereford', in *Medieval Miscellany*, pp. 139–46.

Delisle, L., *Introduction*: vol. 1 of Delisle/Berger.

Delisle/Berger: L. Delisle and E. Berger, (eds), *Recueil des actes de Henri II concernant les provinces françaises et les affaires de France*, 3 vols, Paris, 1909–27.

Dodwell, Barbara, 'Some charters relating to the honour of Bacton', in *Medieval Miscellany*, pp. 147–68.

Douglas, D. C., *William the Conqueror*, London, 1964.

Draco Normannicus: (ed. Howlett), *The 'Draco Normannicus' of Etienne de Rouen*, ed. Richard Howlett, in *Chronicles of the Reigns of Stephen, Henry II and Richard I* vol. 2; (ed. Omont), *Le Draco Normand*, ed. Henri Omont, Société de l'Histoire de Normandie, Rouen, 1884.

Dugdale, William, *Monasticon Anglicanum*, ed. J. Caley, H. Ellis and B. Bandinel, 6 vols, London, 1846.

Eadmer, *HN*: *Eadmeri Historia Novorum in Anglia*, ed. M. Rule, RS, 1884.

Early Yorkshire Charters, vols 1–3, ed. W. Farrer (Edinburgh); vols 4–12, ed. C. T. Clay, Yorkshire Archaeological Society, 1914–65.

EHR: *English Historical Review*.

Ekkehard, *Chronicon*, in *MGH SS*, 6, pp. 1–265; ed. Schmale, *see* Schmale.

Eyton, R. W., *The Antiquities of Shropshire*, 12 vols, London, 1856–60.

—— *Court, Household and Itinerary of Henry II*, London, 1878.

Farrer, William, *An Outline Itinerary of King Henry the First*, Oxford, 1919.

Fleckenstein, Joseph, 'Hofkapelle und Reichsepiskopat unter Heinrich IV', in *Investiturstreit und Reichsverfassung*, pp. 117–40.

Florence of Worcester, *Chronicon ex Chronicis*, ed. B. Thorpe, 2 vols, English Historical Society, London, 1848–9.

Flori, Jean, *L'Essor de la Chevalerie*, Geneva, 1986.

Fuhrmann, Horst, *Germany in the High Middle Ages c.1050–1200*, trans. Timothy Reuter, Cambridge, 1986.

Galbert of Bruges, *The Murder of Charles the Good*, trans. James Bruce Ross, New York, 1967.

Gallia Christiana in provincias ecclesiasticas distributa, xi. *Provincia Rotomagensis*, ed. Paul Piolin, 1874.

Geldner, Ferdinand, 'Kaiserin Mathilde, die deutsche Königswahl von 1125 und das Gegenkönigtum Konrads III', *Zeitschrift für bayersiche Landesgeschichte*, 40 (1977), pp. 3–22.

Gervase of Canterbury: *The Historical Works of Gervase of Canterbury*, ed. W. Stubbs, 2 vols, RS, 1879–80.

Gesta Ambaziensium Dominorum, in *Chroniques des comtes d'Anjou et des seigneurs d'Amboise*, ed. L. Halphen and R. Poupardin, Paris, 1913.

Gesta Stephani, ed. K. R. Potter, revised R. H. C. Davis, OMT, 1976.

Gesta Treverorum, ed. G. Waitz, in *MGH SS*, 8, pp. 111–260.

Gillingham, John, *The Angevin Empire*, London, 1984.

Giraldi Cambrensis Opera, ed. J. S. Brewer, J. F. Dimock and G. F. Warner, 7 vols, RS, 1861–91.

Gleber, Helmut, *Papst Eugen III*, Beiträge zur mittelalterlichen und neueren Geschichte, 6, Jena, 1936.

Gloucester Charters: Robert B. Patterson (ed.), *Earldom of Gloucester Charters: The Charters and Scribes of the Earls and Countesses of Gloucester to A.D. 1217*, Oxford, 1973.

Gransden, Antonia, *Historical Writing in England* (vol. 1) *c.550–c.1307*; (vol. 2) *c.1307 to the Early Sixteenth Century*, London, 1974, 1982.

Grant, Lindy, 'The architecture of the early Savigniacs and Cistercians in Normandy', *Anglo-Norman Studies*, 10 (1988), pp. 113–24.

Green, Judith A., *The Government of England under Henry I*, Cambridge, 1986.

Greenway, *Fasti*: John Le Neve, *Fasti Ecclesiae Anglicanae*, compiled by D. E. Greenway, 1–3, London, 1968–77.

Guillou, Olivier, *Le comte d'Anjou et son entourage au xie siècle*, 2 vols, Paris, 1972.

Halphen, L., and Poupardin, R. (eds), *Chroniques des comtes d'Anjou et des seigneurs d'Amboise*, Paris, 1913.

Hamilton, Bernard, 'Women in the crusader states: the queens of Jerusalem (1100–1190)', in *Medieval Women*, ed. Derek Baker.

Haskins, C. H., *Norman Institutions*, Harvard Historical Studies, 24, Cambridge, Mass., 1925.

Hausmann, Friedrich, *Reichskanzlei und Hofkapelle unter Heinrich V und Konrad III, Schriften der MGH* 14, Stuttgart, 1956.

Haverkamp, Alfred, *Medieval Germany 1056–1273*, trans. Helga Braun and Richard Mortimer, Oxford, 1988.

Henry of Huntingdon: *Henrici Archidiaconi Huntendunensis Historia Anglorum*, ed. Thomas Arnold, RS, 1879.

Hermann of Tournai, *Liber de restauratione monasterii S. Martini Tornacensis*, *MGH SS*, 14, pp. 274–327.

Historia Pontificalis, see John of Salisbury.

Hollister, C. Warren, 'The Anglo-Norman succession debate of 1126', *Journal of Medieval History*, 1 (1975), pp. 19–39; reprinted, *Monarchy, Magnates and Institutions*, pp. 145–69.

—— 'The misfortunes of the Mandevilles', *History*, 58 (1973), pp. 18–28; reprinted, *Monarchy, Magnates and Institutions*, pp. 117–28.

—— *Monarchy, Magnates and Institutions in the Anglo-Norman World*, London and Ronceverte, 1986.

—— and Baldwin, J. W., 'The rise of administrative kingship: Henry I and Philip Augustus', *American Historical Review*, 83 (1978), pp. 867–905; reprinted *Monarchy, Magnates and Institutions*, pp. 229–30.

—— and Keefe, T. K., 'The making of the Angevin Empire', *Journal of British Studies*, 12 (1973), pp. 1–25; reprinted, *Monarchy, Magnates and Institutions*, pp. 247–71.

Howden: *Chronica Rogeri de Hoveden*, ed. W. Stubbs, 4 vols, RS 1868–71.

Hull, P. L. (ed.), *The Cartulary of Launceston Priory*, Devon and Cornwall Record Society, new ser., 30 (1987).

Hutchison, Carole A., *The Hermit Monks of Grandmont*, Kalamazoo, 1989.

Investiturstreit und Reichsverfassung, ed. Joseph Fleckenstein, Sigmaringen, 1973.

JL: Philip Jaffé, *Regesta pontificum Romanorum*, ed. S. Löwenfeld, F. Kalterbrunner and P. Ewald, Leipzig, 1885–8.

John of Marmoutier, *Historia Gaufredi ducis Normannorum et comitis Andegavorum*, in *Chroniques des comtes d'Anjou et des seigneurs d'Amboise*, ed. L. Halphen and R. Poupardin, Paris, 1913.

John of Salisbury, *Historia Pontificalis*, ed. M. Chibnall, OMT, Oxford, 1986.

John of Worcester: *The Chronicle of John of Worcester 1118–1140*, ed. J. R. H. Weaver, Oxford, 1908.

Kealey, Edward J., *Roger of Salisbury*, Berkeley, Los Angeles and London, 1972.

Kemp, B. R. (ed.), *Reading Abbey Cartularies*, 2 vols, Camden 4th ser., 31, 33, London, 1985–6.

King, Edmund, 'The Anarchy of Stephen's reign', *TRHS*, 5th ser., 34 (1984), pp. 133–54.

Knowles, David, *The Episcopal Colleagues of Archbishop Thomas Becket*, Cambridge, 1951.

—— and R. Neville Hadcock, *Medieval Religious Houses: England and Wales*, London, 1971.

Könsgen, E., 'Zwei unbekannte Briefe zu den *Gesta Regum Anglorum* des Wilhelm von Malmesbury', *Deutsches Archiv*, 31 (1975), pp. 202–14.

Le Patourel, John, *Feudal Empires Norman and Plantagenet*, London, 1984.

—— *The Norman Empire*, Oxford, 1976.

Lees, Beatrice A. (ed.), *Records of the Templars in England in the Twelfth Century*, British Academy Records of Social and Economic History, 9, London, 1935.

Letters of Gilbert Foliot: The Letters and Charters of Gilbert Foliot, ed. Adrian Morey and C. N. L. Brooke, Cambridge, 1967.

Letters of John of Salisbury (The), vol. 1, ed. W. J. Millor and H. E. Butler, rev. C. N. L. Brooke, NMT, 1955; vol. 2, ed. W. J. Millor and C. N. L. Brooke, OMT, 1979.

Letters of Lanfranc (The), ed. H. Clover and M. Gibson, OMT, 1979.

Letters of Peter the Venerable, ed. Giles Constable, 2 vols, Harvard Historical Studies, Cambridge, Mass., 1967.

Leyser, Karl, 'The Anglo-Norman succession 1120–1125', *Anglo-Norman Studies*, 13 (1991 for 1990), pp. 233–9.

—— 'The crisis of medieval Germany', *Proceedings of the British Academy*, 69 (1983), pp. 409–43.

—— 'England and the empire in the early twelfth century', *TRHS* 5th ser., 10 (1960), pp. 61–83; reprinted, *Medieval Germany and its Neighbours*, pp. 191–213.

—— 'Frederick Barbarossa, Henry II and the hand of St James', *EHR* 90 (1975), pp. 481–506; reprinted, *Medieval Germany and its Neighbours*, pp. 215–40.

—— 'The German aristocracy from the ninth to the early twelfth century: a historical and cultural sketch', *Past and Present*, 41 (1968), pp. 25–53; reprinted *Medieval Germany and its Neighbours*, pp. 161–89.

—— *Medieval Germany and its Neighbours 900–1250*, London, 1982.

—— *Rule and Conflict in an Early Medieval Society*, London, 1979.

Liber Pontificalis, ed. L. Duchesne, 3 vols, Paris, 1886–1957.

Loyd, L. C., *The Origins of Some Anglo-Norman Families*, ed. C. T. Clay and D. C. Douglas, Publications of the Harleian Society 103, 1951.

Mainzer Urkundenbuch, ed. Manfred Stimmung, Arbeiten der Historischen Kommission für den Volkstaat Hessen, Darmstadt, 1932.

Malmesbury, *GP: Willelmi Malmesbiriensis de gestis pontificum Anglorum libri quinque*, ed. N. E. S. A. Hamilton, RS, 1870.

Malmesbury, *GR: Willelmi Malmesbiriensis de gestis regum Anglorum libri quinque*, ed. W. Stubbs, 2 vols, RS, 1887–9.

Malmesbury, *HN: The Historia Novella by William of Malmesbury*, ed. K. R. Potter, NMT, 1955.

Marchegay, P., and Mabille, E. (eds), *Chroniques des Eglises d'Anjou*, Paris, 1869.

Martindale, Jane, 'Succession and politics in the Romance-speaking world c.1000–1140', in *England and her Neighbours 1066–1453*, ed. Michael Jones and Malcolm Vale, London and Ronceverte, 1989, pp. 19–41.

Materials: J. C. Robertson (ed.), *Materials for the History of Thomas Becket*, 7 vols, RS, 1875–85.

Medieval Miscellany: A Medieval Miscellany for Doris Mary Stenton, ed. Patricia M. Barnes and C. F. Slade, PRS, London, 1962.

Meyer, Paul (ed.), *L'histoire de Guillaume le Maréchal*, 3 vols, Société de l'Histoire de France, Paris, 1891–4.

Meyer von Knonau, G., *Jahrbücher des deutschen Reiches unter Heinrich IV und Heinrich V*, vols 6, 7, Leipzig, 1890–1909.

MGH: *Monumenta Germaniae Historica. SS Scriptores.*

Migne, PL: *Patrologiae cursus completus series latina*, ed. J. P. Migne, 221 vols, Paris, 1844–64.

Morey, Adrian, and Brooke, C. N. L., *Gilbert Foliot and his Letters*, Cambridge, 1965.

Newburgh: William of Newburgh, *Historia rerum Anglicarum*, in *Chronicles of the reigns of Stephen, Henry II and Richard I*, ed. R. Howlett, vol. 1.

NMT: Nelson's Medieval Texts.

Norgate, Kate, *England under the Angevin Kings*, 2 vols, London and New York, 1887.

OMT: Oxford Medieval Texts.

Onslow, The Earl of, *The Empress Maud*, London, 1939.

Oorkondenboek van het Sticht Utrecht tot 1301, ed. S. Muller en A. C. Bouman, 5 vols, Utrecht, 1920–59.

Oppl, Ferdinand, *Stadt und Reich im 12 Jahrhundert (1125–1190)*, Vienna, Cologne and Graz, 1986.

Orderic: *The Ecclesiastical History of Orderic Vitalis*, ed. Marjorie Chibnall, 6 vols, OMT, 1969–80.

Origines Guelficae, ed. C. L. Scheid, 5 vols, Hanover, 1750.

Otto of Freising, *The Deeds of Frederick Barbarossa*, trans. C. C. Mierow, New York, 1953.

—— *The Two Cities*, trans. C. C. Mierow, New York, 1928.

Pain, Nesta, *Empress Matilda, Uncrowned Queen of England*, London, 1978.

Petke, Wolfgang, *Kanzlei Kapelle und Königliche Kurie unter Lothar III (1125–1137)*, Forschungen zur Kaiser und Papstgeschichte des Mittelalters, Beihäfte zu J. F. Böhmer, Regesta Imperii, 5, Cologne and Vienna, 1985.

Polwhele, R., *The History of Cornwall*, 2 vols and supplement, Falmouth, 1803.

Poole, A. L., *From Domesday Book to Magna Carta 1087–1216*, Oxford, 1951.

—— 'Henry Plantagenet's early visits to England', *EHR* 47 (1932), pp. 447–51.

Porée, A. A. (ed.), *Chronique du Bec*, Rouen, 1883.

—— *Histoire de l'abbaye du Bec*, 2 vols, Evreux, 1901.

Powicke, F. M. (ed.), *The Life of Ailred of Rievaulx by Walter Daniel*, OMT, 1978.

PR: Pipe Roll (cited by regnal years).

Prestwich, J. O., 'The treason of Geoffrey de Mandeville' *EHR*, 103 (1988), pp. 283–312, 960–7.

PRO: Public Record Office.

PRS: Pipe Roll Society.

Radulfi de Diceto Decani Lundoniensis Opera Historica, ed. W. Stubbs, 2 vols, RS, 1876.

Red Book of the Exchequer: Liber Rubeus de Scaccario, ed. Hubert Hall, 3 vols, RS, 1896.

Rees, Una (ed.), *The Cartulary of Haughmond Abbey,* Cardiff, 1985.

—— (ed.), *The Cartulary of Shrewsbury Abbey,* 2 vols, Aberystwyth, 1975.

Regesta: Regesta Regum Anglo-Normannorum, 1, ed. H. W. C. Davis; 2, ed. C. Johnson and H. A. Cronne; 3 and 4, ed. H. A. Cronne and R. H. C. Davis, Oxford, 1913–70.

Reilly, Bernard F., *The Kingdom of León-Castilla under Queen Urraca 1109–1126,* Princeton, 1982.

Renn, D. F., *Norman Castles in Britain,* 2nd edn, London, 1973.

RHF: Recueil des Historiens des Gaules et de la France, new edn, ed. L. Delisle, 16 vols, Paris, 1869–1904.

Richard of Hexham, *Historia de gestis regis Stephani et de bello de Standardo,* in Howlett, *Chronicles of the Reigns of Stephen, Henry II and Richard I,* vol. 3.

Richter, Michael (ed.), *Canterbury Professions,* Canterbury and York Society, 67, 1973.

Robert of Torigny, *see* Torigny.

Roger of Howden, *see* Howden.

Rössler, Oskar, *Kaiserin Mathilde und der Zeitalter der Anarchie in England,* Historische Studien, 7, Berlin, 1897.

Round, J. H., *Geoffrey de Mandeville. A Study of the Anarchy,* London, 1892.

RS: Rolls Series (Chronicles and Memorials of Great Britain and Ireland during the Middle Ages).

Salter, H. E. (ed.), *Facsimiles of Early Oxford Charters in Oxford Muniment Rooms,* Oxford, 1929.

Saltman, A., *Theobald Archbishop of Canterbury,* London, 1956.

Schmale, F. J., and Schmale-Ott, I. (eds), *Frutolfi et Ekkehardi Chronica necnon Anonymi Chronica Imperatorum,* Ausgewählte Quellen zur Deutschen Geschichte des Mittelalters, 15, Darmstadt, 1972.

Schmidt, Ulrich, *Königswahl und Thronfolge im 12 Jahrhundert,* Beihefte zu J. F. Böhmer Regesta Imperii, 7, Cologne, Vienna, 1987.

Schnith, Karl, 'Domina Anglorum, Zur Bedeutungstreite eines hochmittelalterlichen Herrscherinentitels', *Festschrift für Peter Acht,* Münchener Historische Studien, 15 (1972), pp. 101–11.

—— 'Regni et pacis inquietatrix: Zur Rolle der Kaiserin Mathilde in der "Anarchie"', *Journal of Medieval History,* 2 (1976), pp. 135–57.

—— 'Zur Problematik englischer Konzilien im Zeitalter der "Anarchie"', *Annuarium Historiae Conciliorum,* 8 (1976), pp. 103–15.

—— 'Zur Vorgeschichte der "Anarchie" in England, 1135–54', *Historisches Jahrbuch,* 95 (1975), pp. 68–87.

SD: Symeon of Durham, *Symeonis monachi opera omnia,* 2 vols, ed. T. Arnold, RS, 1882–5.

Southern, R. W., *St Anselm and his Biographer,* Cambridge, 1963.

Spear, David S., 'Les doyens du chapitre cathédral de Rouen', *Annales de Normandie,* 33 (1983), pp. 91–119.

—— 'Les archidiacres de Rouen au cours de la période ducale', *Annales de Normandie*, 34 (1984), pp. 15–50.

—— 'Les dignitaires de la cathédral de Rouen pendant la période ducale', *Annales de Normandie*, 37 (1987), pp. 121–47.

Speer, Lothar, *Kaiser Lothar III und Erzbishof Adalbert I von Mainz*, Cologne and Vienna, 1983.

Stapleton, Thomas, *Magni Rotuli Scaccarii Normanniae sub Regibus Angliae*, 2 vols, London, 1840.

Stenton, F. M., *The First Century of English Feudalism 1066–1166*, 2nd edn, Oxford, 1961.

Studies in Medieval History presented to R. Allen Brown, ed. Christopher Harper-Bill, Christopher Holdsworth and Janet L. Nelson, Woodbridge and Wolfeboro, 1989.

Suger, *Vita Ludovici grossi regis*, ed. H. Waquet, Les classiques de l'histoire de France au Moyen Age, 11, Paris, 1929.

Torigny, *Chronicle*: (ed. Howlett), in *Chronicles of the Reigns of Stephen, Henry II and Richard I*, vol. 4; (ed. Delisle), *Chronique de Robert de Torigny*, 2 vols, Société de l'Histoire de Normandie, Rouen/Paris, 1872–3.

—— *Interpolations*: Robert of Torigny's *Interpolations in the Gesta Normannorum ducum*, ed. Jean Marx, Société de l'Histoire de Normandie, Rouen/Paris, 1914.

TRHS: Transactions of the Royal Historical Society.

Ughelli, F. (ed.), *Italia Sacra*, Venice, 1717–22.

Van Engen, John, *Rupert of Deutz*, Berkeley, Los Angeles and London, 1983.

VCH: The Victoria History of the Counties of England.

Von Moos, P., *Hildebert von Lavardin*, Pariser historische Studien, 3, Stuttgart, 1965.

Voss, Lena, *Heinrich von Blois, Bischof von Winchester 1129–1171*, Berlin, 1932.

Wace: *Le Roman de Rou de Wace*, ed. A. J. Holden, Société des anciens textes français, 3 vols in 2, Paris, 1970–3.

Walker, David, 'The "honours" of the earls of Hereford in the twelfth century', *Transactions of the Bristol and Gloucester Archaeological Society*, 79 (1960), pp. 174–211.

—— 'Miles of Gloucester, Earl of Hereford', *Transactions of the Bristol and Gloucester Archaeological Society*, 77 (1959), pp. 64–84.

—— 'Ralph son of Pichard', *BIHR* 33 (1960), pp. 195–202.

Walter Map, *De Nugis Curialium*, ed. M. R. James, revised C. N. L. Brooke and Roger Mynors, OMT, 1983.

Warren, W. L., *Henry II*, London, 1973.

Waverley Annals: Annales Monasterii de Waverleia, in *Annales Monastici* RS, 2, pp. 127–411.

William of Malmesbury, *see* Malmesbury.

William of Newburgh, *see* Newburgh.

Yoshitake, Kenji, 'The arrest of the bishops in 1139 and its consequences', *Journal of Medieval History*, 14 (1988), pp. 97–114.

—— 'The exchequer in the reign of Stephen', *EHR* 103 (1988), pp. 950–9.

Index

Abbreviations used: abp, archbishop; bp, bishop; ct, count; d., duke kg, king. Place names have been located by historic county (before 1974) in England and department in France.

69, 70, 74, 81, 99, 100, 101, 107, 113
Bayeux (Calvados), 74; bp *see* Philip of Harcourt; castle, 74
Beaulieu de Chartres (Eure-et-Loir), hospital, 159
Beaumont twins *see* Robert, earl of Leicester; Waleran, count of Meulan
Bec-Hellouin (Eure), abbey, 96, 146, 166, 181, 189, 190–2; *and see* Matilda, empress
Benoît of Sainte-Maure, 25, 197, 198
Berkeley (Glos.), church, 131
Bernard (St), abbot of Clairvaux, 97, 138, 140, 141, 154, 181, 183
Bernard, bp of St Davids, 10, 98, 99
Berneval (Seine-Maritime), 154
Bishop's Stortford (Herts.), castle, 109
Blewbury (Berks.), 131
Bohun *see* Alexander; Engelger; Humphrey; Jocelin
Bologna, 30, 48
Bordesley (Worcs.), abbey, 134–5, 181, 182, 185; abbot *see* Haimo; monks, 184, 185
Boulogne (Pas-de-Calais), 17, 79, 164; counts *see* Eustace; Stephen; county, 54, 64, 106; honour, 12, 65, 88, 103, 132
Bourgthéroulde (Rougemontier, Eure), battle, 39, 51
Brecknock, honour, 82
Brenner Pass, 28, 30
Bretons, 74, 120, 123, 124
Brian fitz Count, 12–13, 53, 54, 56, 76, 77, 84, 85, 87, 90, 91, 92, 100, 101, 113, 114, 116, 117, 122, 131, 136, 149, 175, 199; his wife *see* Matilda of Wallingford
Brill (Bucks.), 124
Bristol (Glos.), 78, 81, 82, 83, 84, 88, 92, 115, 117, 144; castle, 95; mint, 121; St Augustine's abbey, 131n., 144
Brittany, 173
Bruno, abp of Trier, 21–2, 25, 27, 29, 35, 46, 47–8

Burchard, bp of Cambrai, 16, 49, 180

Caen (Calvados), 66, 67n., 74, 151; abbey of St Stephen, 58; castle, 74
Calixtus II, pope, formerly Guy, bp of Vienne, 28, 34–5, 36, 37, 51
Canning (Wilts.), 148, 149
Cannock (Staffs.), 134; forest, 133
Canossa, 28, 30
Canterbury (Kent), abp of *see* Anselm; Lanfranc; Ralph d'Escures; Theobald; Thomas Becket; William of Corbeil
Cardiff (Glam.), 53; mint, 121
Carlisle (Cumb.), 93, 150; castle, 77, 78; mint, 122n.
Carrouges (Orne), castle, 68, 71, 72, 74, 144
Castle Cary, 79
castles, 60, 61, 64, 66, 78, 79, 88, 89, 90, 104, 109, 115, 116, 127, 130; *and see* Abergavenny; Alençon; Ambrières; Argentan, Arundel; Asnebec; Bayeux; Bishop's Stortford; Caen; Carlisle; Carrouges; Châtillon-sur-Colmont; Cricklade; Devizes; Domfront; Dover; Exmes; Gorron; Harptree; Lincoln; London; Ludgershall; Ludlow; Maine; Malmesbury; Marlborough; Newark; Newbury; Oxford; Porchester; St Briavel; Salisbury; Sées; Sherborne; Sleaford; Trifels; Wallingford; Wareham; Winchester, Worcester
Castrocaro (Romagnola), 33, 48
Celestine II, pope, 76
Cerne (Dorset), monks, 141
Charles the Good, ct of Flanders, x, 38–9, 43, 54
Châtillon-sur-Colmont (Mayenne), castle, 66, 106
Cherbourg (Manche), abbey of St Mary de Voto, 159, 179

Treviso, 30
Trier, 25; abp *see* Bruno
Trifels, castle, 27, 41
Trowbridge (Wilts.), 89

Uffculme (Devon), 129
Ulger, bp of Angers, 68, 69, 75–6
Urraca, queen of Castile and León,
    1–2, 53, 199; her husband,
    Alfonso of Aragon, 1–2; her son,
    1, 2
Utrecht, 24, 39, 40, 48, 50;
    Godebold, bp of, 50n.

Vendôme, abbey of La Trinité, 145,
    155
Venice, 30
Vexin (Eure, Seine-et-Oise), 154, 173
Victor IV, schismatic pope, 165

Walchelin Maminot, 78
Walden (Essex), abbey, chronicle, 103
Waleran, ct of Meulan, 13, 51, 66,
    72, 73, 74, 78, 79, 81, 93, 106,
    107, 112, 113, 134–5, 157,
    160–1, 182, 184, 185, 186, 187
Wales, 77, 88–9; allies from, 95, 122,
    150; revolt in, 70
Wallingford (Berks.), 123; castle, 84,
    90, 117, 131, 149–50; constable,
    102, 150
Walter fitz Alan, 132, 133
Walter Giffard, 161, 187
Walter Map, 62, 162, 197
Walter de Pinkeney, 120, 121
Waltham (Essex), chronicle, 130
Wareham (Dorset), 116, 136, 156,
    180; castle, 117; mint, 121, 122
Warin fitz Gerold, 126
Welfesholz, battle, 28
Westbury (Wilts.), 125, 134, 174
Westminster, 10, 103, 151
Wherwell (Hants.), 97–8, 113, 114
White Ship, 37, 38, 43
William, duke of Aquitaine, 72, 73
William, earl of Gloucester, 125
William I, kg of England (1066–87),

duke of Normandy, ix, 5, 6, 53,
    58, 64, 68, 83, 171
William II (Rufus), kg of England
    (1087–1100), ix, 6, 7, 58, 64, 83
William (atheling), son of Henry I, ix,
    9, 14–15, 38, 43, 54; his wife
    Matilda, 38, 43, 191
William, son of Richard fitz Turold,
    89
William fitz Alan, 77, 78, 82, 89, 99,
    113, 123, 125, 127, 132, 133,
    150
William of Albemarle, 194
William of Albini, *pincerna*, earl of
    Arundel, 80, 93, 130
William de Beauchamp, sheriff of
    Worcester, 99, 101, 107, 112,
    174
William de Berkeley, 9, 129, 182
William of Blois, son of King Stephen,
    156, 167
William Clito, son of Robert
    Curthose, 38, 51, 53, 81, 93;
    count of Flanders, 54–5, 56
William of Conches, 144
William of Corbeil, abp of
    Canterbury, 52, 65, 69, 76
William Cumin, 100, 101, 104,
    138–9
William Defuble, 100, 125, 175
William fitz Empress, ix, 67, 68, 144,
    163–4, 167–8, 180
William fitz Gilbert, chancellor,
    174–5
William fitz John, 78
William of Malmesbury, 10, 46–7,
    52, 55, 57, 65, 73, 79, 81, 83,
    88, 90, 92, 98, 99, 105, 112,
    113, 114, 116–17, 197, 200
William Mauduit, 174
William de Mohun, earl of Dorset,
    107, 112, 113
William of Newburgh, 101, 155, 194,
    197
William Peverel of Dover, 174
William Pont de l'Arche, 99, 100,
    120, 174

William of Roumare, earl of Lincoln,
     73, 92, 93, 94, 99, 100, 105,
     111–12, 113, 150, 157
William of Salisbury, 114, 115
William Talvas, son of Robert of
     Bellême, 61, 64, 66, 72
William Trentegeruns, 152
William of Warenne, 66
William of Ypres, xi, 73, 74, 75, 102,
     113, 114, 115
Wilton (Wilts.), abbey, 10, 98; abbess
     see Christina
Winchester (Hants.), 58, 64, 65, 98,
     100, 101, 107, 111, 112, 157,
     161, 163, 198; bp *see* Henry of
     Blois; castle besieged, 97,

113–14; fair at, 99, 116; farm of,
     58, 127; rout, 114, 118, 123
Windsor (Berks.), 52, 94
Worcester, castle, 107; earldom, 78,
     107; honour, 185
Worms, 24, 26, 38, 39, 45; concordat
     of, 35–6, 38
Wurth (Wilts.), 125
Wurzburg, 35, 172

York, abp *see* Thurstan; disputed
     election, 141

Zähringer, dukes of, 49–50
Zelophehad, daughters of, 85